John Goldworth Alger

Glimpses of the French Revolution

Myths, Ideals, and Realities

John Goldworth Alger

Glimpses of the French Revolution
Myths, Ideals, and Realities

ISBN/EAN: 9783337032029

Printed in Europe, USA, Canada, Australia, Japan

Cover: Foto ©ninafisch / pixelio.de

More available books at **www.hansebooks.com**

GLIMPSES

OF

THE FRENCH REVOLUTION

MYTHS, IDEALS, AND REALITIES

BY

JOHN G. ALGER

AUTHOR OF 'ENGLISHMEN IN THE FRENCH REVOLUTION'

LONDON
SAMPSON LOW, MARSTON & COMPANY
(LIMITED)
St. Dunstan's House
FETTER LANE, FLEET STREET, E.C.
1894

PREFACE

THE French Revolution has been related in more
detail and from a greater variety of standpoints
than any other event in history. Carlyle has
depicted it in flashes of lightning, Louis Blanc has
described it as a Robespierrist, Michelet has viewed
it as a Girondin, Taine has dissected it with the
scalpel of a sceptic. The Royalist side alone is
unrepresented; for, though among contemporary
pamphleteers and philosophers it commanded an
overwhelming preponderance of ability—need I
mention Burke, De Maistre, and Mallet du Pan ?—
it has produced no historian worthy of the name.
Researches in public archives and the appearance
of fresh memoirs have of late years filled in or
corrected many details, but have not appreciably
altered the general effect. A Frenchman is necessarily a partisan, for the Revolution is still too
unfinished to be looked at by him in perspective,
and political parties are still mainly based on their
conceptions of it. Hence Michelet has insufficient

PREFACE

THE French Revolution has been related in more detail and from a greater variety of standpoints than any other event in history. Carlyle has depicted it in flashes of lightning, Louis Blanc has described it as a Robespierrist, Michelet has viewed it as a Girondin, Taine has dissected it with the scalpel of a sceptic. The Royalist side alone is unrepresented; for, though among contemporary pamphleteers and philosophers it commanded an overwhelming preponderance of ability—need I mention Burke, De Maistre, and Mallet du Pan ?—it has produced no historian worthy of the name. Researches in public archives and the appearance of fresh memoirs have of late years filled in or corrected many details, but have not appreciably altered the general effect. A Frenchman is necessarily a partisan, for the Revolution is still too unfinished to be looked at by him in perspective, and political parties are still mainly based on their conceptions of it. Hence Michelet has insufficient sympathy for the Royalists, Louis Blanc is too severe on the Girondins and on Danton, and Taine does not take due account of the temper and difficulties of the time. Carlyle alone combines commiseration for the victims with allowance for the murderers, perceiving with De Maistre that the actors were scarcely responsible, but were entangled in the grip of a machine which crushed them the moment they attempted to regulate its movements. If Carlyle occasionally errs in details, whether from carelessness or from non-access to sources of information since thrown open, he nevertheless remains for English readers the most acceptable of historians, and is not likely to be supplanted, though he should now be carefully edited and corrected.

But while no new history is called for, there is plenty of scope for treating particular episodes or aspects of the Revolution with greater fulness than was consistent with the dimensions of Carlyle's work or with the materials at his disposal. Having, therefore, in a previous book sketched the part played, or rather suffered, by Englishmen in this political cyclone, I now deal with some more general incidents or phases of the Revolution.

I commence with its myths, first because I might otherwise be supposed to ignore some of the apparently most striking episodes, and secondly because the rapid growth and the considerable number of these myths are one of the most curious features of the Revolution, while their persistent vitality is a standing warning for historical students. I claim to show that Cazotte's vision was invented by Laharpe, that Sombreuil's daughter did not purchase his liberty by quaffing blood, that the locksmith Gamain was not poisoned, that Labussière did not save hundreds of prisoners by destroying the documents incriminating them, that the Girondins had no last supper, that some famous ejaculations have been fabricated or distorted, that no attempt was made to save the last batch of victims, that the boys Barra and Viala were not heroes, that no leather was made of human skins, that no Englishmen plied the September assassins with drink, that the ' Vengeur ' crew did not perish rather than surrender, that the ice-bound Dutch fleet was not captured, that Robespierre's wound was not the work of Merda, but was self-inflicted, and that Thomas Paine had no miraculous escape. Dreams naturally following inventions, I next show how equality was the ruling passion of the Jacobins. They quoted and imitated the Greeks and Romans, and to a limited extent they copied England and America. They desired the abolition of negro slavery, the naturalisation of aliens, the fraternity of religions, the relaxation of the marriage tie, the improved status of natural children, the abolition of literary corporations, and humanity to animals. Above all, they sought to regulate wages and prices. But on almost all these points their efforts were premature or impracticable. Next comes Cloots's deputation, which throws a flood of light on the enthusiasm and restlessness of the eighteenth century, but which has never yet been related with any minuteness. We see how Cloots, a well-meaning but light-headed egotist, was guillotined for being more extreme than Robespierre; how Olavide, a fugitive from the Spanish Inquisition, could compare French with Peninsular jailers, and by a natural reaction reverted from scepticism to Catholicism; how General Miranda ended a life full of vicissitudes in a Cadiz prison; how Pigott, the enemy of hats, animal food, and bread, died just before the end of the Terror which had so cruelly belied his hopes. We also witness the American deputation, which had held aloof from Cloots. It included Paul Jones, who privately decried the Revolution and died with his head still full of schemes for injuring his native country but for enriching himself; Joel Barlow, versifier, speculator, and diplomatist, a future *quasi* victim to the retreat from Moscow; Vernon, whose courtly appearance was to be nearly fatal to him; and Swan, one of the Boston 'tea-party,' who was to spend one-third of his life in a Paris prison rather than satisfy a disputed claim.

Turning from legends and aspirations to realities, we behold the prominent part played by

women—how they initiated patriotic gifts to clear
off the deficit, how they brought the royal family,
virtual captives, from Versailles to Paris, how a
flower-girl kissed the King, and how Théroigne de
Méricourt, the 'Queen of Sheba' of the Revolution,
after honours and indignities, became a hopeless
maniac. We behold women joining in the rap-
tures of the Federation, levying blackmail on the
'coming' but intercepting 'parting guests,' coer-
cing or ousting the Convention, pillaging shops and
market carts, and sharing in the last desperate on-
sets of a moribund Jacobinism. Next come children.
We see how theorists would have had the State
supersede the parent, how schools were closed or
disorganised, how boys presented gifts or addresses
and girls figured in processions, how toy guillotines
amused but demoralised childhood. We also notice
how the revolutionary leaders mostly left no issue,
how the exceptions had descendants marked sometimes by insanity, but usually by mediocrity, and
how the Revolution led to intellectual sterility and
physical debility. The working of the Revolutionary Tribunal is then illustrated by the acquittal
of Sir William Codrington, the conviction of General
Dillon, and the summary execution of Arthur. We
see how the judges were sanguinary fanatics, the
jurors barbarous or callous, the spectators apathe-
tic or brutal, how commiseration was occasionally
displayed, not always without danger, and how the

stoicism of the victims .helped to deaden the
sensibility of the lookers-on, the infliction of death
thus becoming as in China a mere amusement.
Depicting women under the guillotine, we see how
their numbers went on steadily increasing, how
they sometimes threw away their lives rather than
survive husbands or brothers, how the witness-box
might suddenly be exchanged for the dock, how
similarity of names might lead to fatal mistakes,
but how timely hysterics might ensure deliverance.
A full account is given of the women of Verdun,
guillotined for offering sweetmeats to the King of
Prussia in order to save their town from pillage,
and of the Carmelite nuns of Compiègne, who,
executed for possessing royalist papers, chanted
piously all the way to the scaffold. Four women,
it is shown, were guillotined in the ensuing two
years, but the ' equality of the sexes ' in political
prosecutions virtually ceased with Robespierre.

Lastly, we inspect the prisons with their 300,000
inmates, the majority of them republicans and of
humble rank, yet incarcerated for heedless talk, for
infringing the maximum, or out of private malice.
We see the difficulty of accommodating the prisoners,
the remarkable absence of resistance or escapes, the
varied tempers of keepers and turnkeys, the high
charges made for the smallest comforts, the stu-
diousness of a few inmates, the frivolity of the
rest, the sham guillotining and other pastimes, the

manifestation occasionally of religion but generally of stoicism. The English so-called hostages and the Girondin deputies are shown to have experienced comparative lenity. The pictures of Chantilly and Lyons give an idea of imprisonment in the provinces, and whatever Robespierre's intentions may have been, his fall is shown to have been the signal for relaxed rigour and for gradual liberations.

Enthusiasm and despair, heroism and savagery, fanaticism and frivolity—such are the main elements of a Revolution 'prepared,' as Tocqueville says, 'by the most civilised classes of the nation, and carried out by the rudest and most uncultivated.' 'The French nation,' he adds, 'is always better or worse than had been expected—now below the general level of mankind, now much above it . . . more capable of heroism than of virtue, of genius than of common sense, fitter to conceive immense designs than to accomplish great enterprises, the most brilliant and the most dangerous of European nations, and the one most calculated to become by turns an object of admiration, pity, terror, but never of indifference.'

The latter portion of Chapter III. and the greater portion of Chapter VII. are reprinted, by permission, from the 'Atlantic Monthly' for September 1889, and the 'National Review' for January 1892.

CONTENTS

CHAPTER I

MYTHS

CHAPTER II

UTOPIAS

CHAPTER III

ADORATION OF THE MAGI

CHAPTER IV

PROPHETESSES AND VIRAGOES

CHAPTER V

CHILDREN

CHAPTER VI

THE REVOLUTIONARY TRIBUNAL

CHAPTER VII

WOMEN AS VICTIMS

CHAPTER VIII

THE PRISONS

GLIMPSES

OF THE

FRENCH REVOLUTION

—◆—

CHAPTER I

MYTHS

These lies are like the father that begets them,
Gross as a mountain, open, palpable.
Henry IV., Part I., ii. 4.

Cazotte's Vision—Mlle. de Sombreuil's Draught of Blood—The
Locksmith Gamain—Labussière's Paper Pellets—Girondins'
Last Supper—Famous Ejaculations—Last Batch of Victims—
Boy Heroes—Tanning Human Skin—English Emissaries—
the 'Vengeur'—Battle on the Ice—Robespierre's Wound—
Vendean Hero—Thomas Paine's Escape.

IF history, as Matthew Arnold says, is 'a Missis-
sippi of falsehood,' this is peculiarly applicable to
the history of the French Revolution. No epoch
has been the subject of more exaggeration, legend,
and deliberate lying, and this began at the very
beginning of the Revolution, frequently for the
purpose of inciting or justifying atrocities. The
story of Foulon having said that the famishing

B

people might eat grass is a specimen of legends of this class.   But passing over these ephemeral fabrications,[1] I propose to nail, like base coins to the counter, legends which still command more or less credence.   It is not indeed, even now, always easy to distinguish between fact and fiction, and it was less easy a generation ago, when original documents were rarely accessible.   Hence Carlyle stands excused for having been sometimes led astray by will-o'-the-wisps.   He cried *peccavi* for his account of the sinking of the 'Vengeur,' and he might perhaps, with a little vigilance, have detected other impositions.   At the same time he is to be acquitted of intentional misrepresentation or embellishment. Not so with Lamartine, whose 'History of the Girondins' is, next to Carlyle's, the book most widely known in England.   Experts, indeed, are aware that Lamartine is to be distrusted, but the general reader does not know, and can hardly be expected to know, that he not merely accepts any legend which is at all picturesque, but fabricates some of his own.[2]   Not a few people, consequently, were they asked to enumerate, say, the twelve most

---

[1] It was reported, and seems to have been believed in England, for it is recorded in the *Annual Register*, that Dr. Guillotin was one of the victims of his own machine, an engineer hoist with his own petard.

[2] He represents his father, in prison at Macon, as throwing a rope across the street to the rooms occupied by his wife, and thus paying her nocturnal visits.   His mother, he says, was then suckling him.   He was, however, nearly four years old.

striking incidents of the Revolution, would almost certainly include several of these 'mock pearls' of history.

I will begin with the legend earliest, not in origin, but in alleged date—Cazotte's prediction of 1788. Cazotte was a staunch royalist, who, having reached the age of seventy-two, had left off writing licentious stories, and had become a disciple of the mystic, St.-Martin. On the Revolution taking a serious turn he discerned in it a fulfilment of the Apocalypse, and after escaping the September massacres—his daughter, clinging to him, had excited the compassion of the mob—his esoteric letters to his secretary furnished one of the charges upon which three weeks afterwards he was tried and executed. In 1806 there appeared a posthumous work by Laharpe, describing how, in 1788, in a company of courtiers and philosophers full of glowing anticipations of the new era of liberty and enlightenment, Cazotte maintained a gloomy silence. Bantered by Condorcet, he said he saw terrible things in store. 'You, M. de Condorcet, will expire stretched on the floor of a dungeon; you will die of the poison taken by you to escape the executioner, a poison which the " happiness " of that time will oblige you always to carry about you. You, M. Chamfort, will cut your veins with twenty-two gashes of a razor, yet you will not die till several months afterwards.' Amid the increasing merriment of the guests, Cazotte told Malesherbes and Roucher that they would die on the scaffold, and the Duchesse de Gramont that she would be taken in a cart, her hands tied behind her back, to the place of execution. 'You see,' laughingly exclaimed the lady, 'that he will not even allow me a confessor.' 'No, madame,' gravely replied Cazotte, 'the last of the condemned to have a confessor will be'—he hesitated a moment—'the Queen of France.' At this the company shuddered, but the Duchess, wishing to dispel the gloom, asked, 'What will be your own fate, Mr. Prophet?' With downcast eyes and pensive look he replied, 'During the siege of Jerusalem a man went for seven days round the ramparts, crying with sinister voice, "Woe to Jerusalem!" On the seventh day he cried, "Woe is me!" and at that moment an enormous stone thrown by an enemy's hand struck him and dashed him to pieces.'

Will it be believed that Louis Blanc, who rejected the Hebrew prophecies, gravely inserts this prediction or vision in his 'History of the Revolution' as 'solemnly attested by serious witnesses'? The sole witness, or pretended witness, is Laharpe himself, but did he, in leaving this manuscript to be published three years after his death, expect even the simplest reader to believe it? Beuchot, moreover, got sight of the manuscript, and at the foot was a distinct acknowledgment that the whole thing was a fiction. The confession, however, was really unnecessary, for never was there a more transparent invention; yet, curiously enough, in literary merit it is superior to anything to be found among Laharpe's multitudinous productions.

A fellow-prisoner of Cazotte's, in September 1792, who also obtained a respite, was the Marquis de Sombreuil, Governor of the Hôtel des Invalides, and everybody is familiar with the story of his daughter saving his life by agreeing to drink a glass of blood, proffered her by the gang of murderers. Here is Lamartine's description of the scene :—

Sombreuil appears; he is condemned; the door opens, the bayonets glitter, his daughter darts forward, clings to the old man's neck, makes herself a rampart for him, conjures the assassins to spare her father or to strike her with the same blow. Her gestures, her sex, her youth, her dishevelled hair, her beauty, heightened by emotion, the sublimity of her devotion, the ardour of her supplications, soften these hired assassins. A cry of ' Pardon! ' rises from the crowd, the pikes are lowered, the daughter is granted her father's life—but at a horrible price. She is required—in sign of abjuration of aristocracy—to dip her lips in a glass filled with the blood of aristocrats. Mademoiselle de Sombreuil seizes the glass with intrepid hand, raises it to her mouth, and drinks to her father's deliverance. This gesture saves her; the people partake her joy; the tears of her assassins mix with her own.

The story will not bear examination. Sombreuil had been formally acquitted by the infamous

Maillard, who himself wrote against his name '*en liberté*,' and there is no instance of Maillard's decisions having been disputed by his gang of butchers outside the prison. Sombreuil, moreover, had not been acquitted without a hard struggle. He was charged with having helped to defend the Tuileries on August 10, but a man named Grappin obtained a suspension of the mock trial that he might go to the Invalides for further information. He went thither and found many of the pensioners exasperated against Sombreuil, but returning to La Force he pretended to bring back a favourable report. Acquittal followed, and all contemporary accounts agree that there was much emotion when the daughter threw herself into her father's arms and loaded him with caresses. The emotion was renewed when the white-haired man, supported by his daughter, passed out into the street. Alas! he, like Cazotte, had no long respite, for he was guillotined in June 1794. On taking leave of his daughter on his removal from Port Royal convent to Ste.-Pélagie, he pointed to Grappin, and said, ' If this good fellow were not already married I should wish you to marry him.' This is a proof not merely of Sombreuil's gratitude, but of the way in which imprisonment temporarily levelled down all social distinctions. His daughter remained at Port Royal, and some of her fellow-captives repeat the account she gave them of the scene at La Force, but not a word is said of the glass of blood. Verses, too, were addressed by them to her, in which she was held up as a model of filial affection, and Coittant apostrophised her in prose. Grappin shared in this prison ovation, but not an allusion is made to the draught of blood. In 1795, after her release, she petitioned the Convention for succour, and 1,000 francs was granted to her, on the report of a committee who expressed admiration for her conduct, but were equally silent on this harrowing episode. But in 1800, Legouvé, father of the present veteran Academician, in a poem entitled ' Le Mérite des Femmes,' mentioned Mademoiselle de Sombreuil, appending a note in which we hear for the first time of her quaffing blood. It is not to be supposed that Legouvé invented this ; he probably repeated a story already current. The poem in four years ran through nine editions, and was embellished with a picture of the Sombreuil scene. The heroine is alleged to have written to a Paris newspaper a letter in which she said : 'Seeing me pale, these men made me drink a glass of their wine, and that wine had drops of blood in it, and from that circumstance arose the legend with which I have been pestered for so many years.' The letter however has not been discovered. It would substantially agree with the version given to Louis Blanc by a lady acquainted with Mademoiselle de Sombreuil, viz. that she was fainting and received from one of the gang a glass of water into which a drop of blood had fallen from his hand. According to her son, Comte de Villelume, she struggled with the murderers and received three wounds, and blood spirted into the glass from the head of St.-Mert, who had just been despatched. She certainly, however, was not wounded, and St.-Mert had perished at least ten hours previously, so that this account, not given till half a century after her death, cannot be accepted. Another theory is that the glass contained water slightly coloured with red wine, which in her emotion Mademoiselle de Sombreuil mistook for blood. An account professedly given by her in 1796 to a M. Hochet, but only recently published, states that being told that all the pensioners demanded her father's death, she replied, ' It is impossible ; go and ask them ; ' that a messenger was accordingly sent ; that pending his return her father was taken back to the cell, that there she heard the vociferations of the executioners, who were quaffing beakers of wine mixed with gunpowder (!) ; that they cried out for victims, so that the judges could scarcely restrain them ; that her father was presently sent for, that she clung to him, that they vainly tried to force her away ; that one man at last said, ' Drink this glass of blood, and we will spare thy father ; ' that she emptied it at a draught, and that a man afterwards advancing to strike her father, she rushed forward and received the blow. But even if the lady gave this narrative in 1796, even if it was not concocted at a much later date in order to fit in with Grappin's mission, it would not be consistent with her silence in 1794.

French disputants have overlooked the testimony of the only eyewitness, Captain George Munro, who on the recall of Lord Gower remained for some months at Paris. In a despatch to the English Foreign Office he says :—

The Governor of the Invalides happened to be one of those (five) I saw acquitted. The street rung with acclamations of joy, but the old man was so feeble with fear and suspense, and so overcome with the caresses of his daughter, who was attending to know his fate, that they both sunk helpless into the arms of some of the spectators, who carried them to the Hôtel des Invalides.

A glass of water or wine may have been offered her either before Munro saw her come out into the street, or after she had passed out of sight.

Victor Hugo, in an ode written in his youth, but suppressed in his later editions, says :

> S'élançant au travers des armes :
> — Mes amis, respectez ses jours !
> — Crois-tu nous fléchir par tes larmes ?
> — Oh ! je vous bénirai toujours.
> C'est sa fille qui vous implore.
> Rendez-le moi, qu'il vive encore !
> — Vois-tu le fer déjà levé !
> Crains d'irriter notre colère ;
> Et, si tu veux sauver ton père,
> Bois ce sang. . . . — Mon père est sauvé.

A glass of wine figures also in connection with the secret cupboard at the Tuileries, the discovery of which sealed the fate of Louis XVI. and led to the ignominious expulsion of Mirabeau's remains from the Pantheon. Louis, as is well known, was fond of making locks, and when a young man had taken lessons in the art from Francis Gamain, son of the Court locksmith.   Francis succeeded his father in this post, but the Revolution was a great blow for him.   The King gave up a pastime which, on his removal from Versailles to the Tuileries, would have aroused suspicion; Court tradesmen were cut down or dismissed; aristocratic customers also failed him, and Gamain had to give up business. On November 19, 1792, when the King had been more than three months a prisoner, Gamain went to Roland, Minister of the Interior, and informed him that he had made for Louis a secret iron cupboard at the Tuileries.   He accompanied Roland to the vacant palace, pointed out the secret opening in the wall, the iron door was forced open, and startling documents were discovered which the poor King on August 10 had had no time to destroy.   A bunch of keys, handed over by Louis on that day to his chief valet Thiery, a victim of the September massacres, afterwards came into the possession of the revolutionary Government, and it was suggested that one of these keys might fit the lock of the iron cupboard.   Accordingly on

December 25—Christmas Day now stood for nothing —Gamain went again with Roland to the Tuileries and found that the key fitted.

Nothing more is heard of him till April 1794, when he petitioned the Convention for aid, and told a piteous tale. He alleged that on May 22, 1792, he fixed the iron door, which the King had himself prepared. It was a warm night, and when he had finished the task Louis brought him a glass of wine. Some hours afterwards he was seized with violent pain, which did not abate till he took an emetic. He was paralysed for nine months, and had no hope of being able to work again. In 1838 the Bibliophile Jacob (Paul Delacroix) published a different version, communicated to him by inhabitants of Versailles to whom Gamain had frequently related it. The Queen, it was said this time, entered by a secret door with a cake and a glass of wine. He drank the wine and pocketed the cake. On reaching the Champs Elysées he was seized with intense pain. A rich Englishman who was driving by took him up in his carriage and drove him home to Versailles, calling on the way at a shop in the rue du Bac for an emetic, a rather roundabout route from the Champs Elysées to Versailles. The Englishman handed him over, apparently dying, to his wife, and two doctors were sent for. The cake being found some days afterwards in his pocket was given to a dog, which immediately dropped down dead. He was paralysed and bedridden for fourteen months.

The Convention accepted Gamain's story, ordered that it should be published and circulated as a proof of Louis Capet's infamy, and conferred a pension of 1,200 francs on the victim. Had it taken the trouble to refer back to Roland's report, it would have seen that, so far from being paralysed for nine months, Gamain went to Roland within six months of the pretended poisoning, and again five weeks later, on neither occasion alleging illness, and indeed distinctly declaring himself ready to give any further attendance. Not till after the execution of the King and Queen, and the suicide of Roland, had Gamain told his story. Delacroix, however, believed that he had really been poisoned, but by an over-zealous servant, while Louis Blanc held that the evidence was insufficient either to acquit or condemn the King. It is urged as a suspicious circumstance that some of the documents of the affair are not to be found and must have been abstracted from the archives at the Restoration, but the more probable explanation is that the order of the Convention for printing them was never carried out. The reports, moreover, of the two committees on the case were drawn up by obscure deputies, whose spelling was defective. Gamain died in 1795, and it is admitted that his health had broken down and that though only forty-four he was prematurely old. Unfortunately we cannot assume that he was a prey to remorse for his treachery and calumny.

He was not the only man to 'exploit' pretended sufferings or services. When the Terror was at an end braggarts and intriguers claimed credit—or cash—for daring or ingenuity displayed in saving lives from the guillotine. Among others was Labussière, a popular comedian, who had been a copyist in the office of the Committee of Public Safety. He alleged that he used stealthily to stuff into his pockets the documents incriminating actors and other prisoners in whom he felt interested, that he then went to a bathing establishment on the Seine, soaked the papers into pulp, made pellets of them, and flung them into the river. When Fouquier Tinville would send for the documents affecting a particular prisoner in order to bring him to trial, they were unaccountably missing, and he had to relinquish his prey. Again and again did he inquire for the papers as to the imprisoned members of the Comédie Française, and he was just beginning to suspect something wrong when Robespierre fell and the actors' lives were saved.

It seems probable that this story originated in a desire to clear himself from the slur of having served the revolutionary committee. Like other stories it grew, and continued growing after Labussière's death. In 1805, a biographer named

Liénard held him up as a paragon of daring and devotion. He had saved 1,500 lives, he had risked suffocation by creeping into a wooden chest on the approach of a sentry, and so forth. Later on, the pretended memoirs of the actor Fleury repeated and magnified the story, except that the number of the saved was reduced to 1,100,[1] the future Empress Josephine, however, being included. Labussière, it was alleged, used to go before daylight to the Tuileries; the sentries, imagining that he was a very zealous clerk, suspected nothing; he would go into the room where the documents were lodged, and would abstract a number of them. As making a fire or bulky pockets would have excited attention, he soaked the papers in a pail of water till they were reduced to pulp, filled his pockets with large pellets of them, then went to a bath, divided a large pellet into small ones, and flung them out of the window into the river. One night, when he had thus abstracted the packet incriminating the actors, he heard footsteps and voices, and crept into a large chest used for storing fuel, at the foot of the staircase. He closed the lid over him, and presently St.-Just and three other committeemen came up and had an important conversation, reported verbatim in the memoirs, two of them sitting part of the time on the chest. When they had gone

---

[1] An average of ten a day, during his three and a half months' employment.

Labussière crept out, stiff and half-suffocated, but his troubles were not at an end. Resting on some steps in the street, to revive himself, he was arrested as a suspicious character by a Jacobin sectionist and taken to the lock-up. He would have been searched and detected had not his protests attracted a crowd, among them a fellow-clerk who vouched for his identity and got him released.

These memoirs passed muster with the general reader, but experts detected the fraud, for the names and doings of the committeemen were a tissue of blunders, and Laffitte, the real author of the book, privately confessed the imposition. M. Sardou, however, has made Labussière the hero of his drama 'Thermidor,' which was twice performed in Paris in January 1891, but was then suppressed in deference to Radical clamour. M. Sardou states that twenty years ago he made the acquaintance of a M. Pillet, mayor of Marly, son of the Fabien Pillet who was Labussière's chief in 1794. Pillet told him that he and his brother, when boys, could not understand why their father should ask to dinner a man like Labussière, ill-dressed, dirty, and a stammerer, whereupon the father replied— 'If you knew what that man has done, you would feel nothing but admiration for him.' And he told them how Labussière had saved 250 lives, he himself suspecting the stratagem, but shutting his eyes to it. This mayor was a conservative, and held a post in the Education Office ; he did not like to talk of his father's doings during the Revolution, and begged M. Sardou, if he carried out his intention of writing a play on Labussière, not to introduce his father into it. Fabien Pillet, however, did not die till 1855, and M. Sardou could easily about 1872 have found persons less reticent than his son who remembered him. There is no reason why 'Thermidor' should not have been written, nor why Labussière should not figure in M. Claretie's story of 'Puyjoli,' but M. Sardou must not expect those who have studied the Revolution to believe that it is founded on fact. A conversation held twenty years ago and of which no record was made at the time, giving recollections of another conversation about sixty years previously, is not very substantial evidence, and although Fabien Pillet credited Labussière's story, he apparently credited it on the authority of the Fleury Memoirs, for in his notice of Labussière in the 'Biographie Universelle' he cites the memoirs as his sole authority. It is true that those memoirs give a letter purporting to have been addressed by Fouquier Tinville, on July 23, 1794, to the Committee of Public Safety, who a month previously had directed him to bring the actors to trial. He pleaded in excuse the disorder during the past two months of the documents in the office, on account of the clerks being royalists in disguise, but he hoped by the end of that decade (that is by the 28th) to furnish a fresh report on the prisoners. But even if this letter is genuine the inference is that Fouquier Tinville was himself anxious to save the actors, and invented an excuse for delaying their trial; there is no reason, moreover, to think that Labussière, a mere copyist only twenty-five years of age, had the custody of documents on which hung the lives of thousands. It is urged, indeed, that in 1803 he was allowed a benefit by the Comédie Française, and that this story must therefore have been verified, but it appears that the benefit was allowed in a grudging fashion, doubtless because he had had a reputation even before the Revolution for hoaxing, so that little credence was given to his assertion that he had saved 1,153 lives. The benefit yielded 14,000 francs, but he wasted the money, and died a pauper and insane.

The 'last supper of the Girondins,' the twenty-one deputies executed on October 31, 1793, has been fixed in men's minds—for as Horace says, nothing is so thoroughly learned as by the faithful eyes—by Paul Delaroche's great painting of 1855. The trial was not over till ten at night, and as even the guillotine did not work by night the executions did not take place till next morning. Riouffe, then incarcerated at the Conciergerie, says:

The signal they had promised us ['us' means their

C

fellow-prisoners, who had gone to bed before the condemned were brought back from the court] was given.
It was patriotic songs, which simultaneously broke forth,
and all their voices joined in addressing last hymns to
liberty.   They parodied the Marseillaise after this
fashion :

> Contre nous de la tyrannie,
> Le couteau sanglant est levé, &c.

All that fearful night resounded with their songs, and
if they broke off, it was to discourse on their country,
and sometimes also for a sally by Ducos.

Ducos was lively to the last, and only a few days
before had composed comic verses on his arrest,
and on his persecutors.   Carlyle mistakenly sup-
poses that these verses were written or sung on
that last night.   Riouffe's account shows that there
was no supper at all, and that the twenty-one were
shut up in groups in their several cells, though
they could hear each other, and keep time together
in singing.   But Nodier, who had a turn for historical romances which he palmed off as real history,
published in 1833 'Le Banquet des Girondins.'
Lamartine in 1847 added further embellishments.
He represented that he had obtained all the details
from Lambert, a priest who, living near the prison
and having taken the oath to the civil constitution
of the clergy, was allowed to visit prisoners and may
possibly have seen the Girondins that last night,
though Lothringer, a priest who certainly saw them
next morning, gives no hint of it.   Lamartine, who

'saw' at the Carmelite monastery numerous inscriptions traced in blood on the walls by the Girondins, —the Girondins were never confined there, and though there were, and still are inscriptions, they are not written in blood—gives a truly artistic picture. A friend provides luxurious dishes, wines, and flowers; Vergniaud presides; Brissot, taciturn and gloomy, is vice-president; the younger prisoners indulge in light talk and jests; but towards morning the company become more serious. Brissot draws a mournful picture of the future of France, Vergniaud is more hopeful, the immortality of the soul is discussed, by-and-by the voices are lowered, the conversation is increasingly solemn, Vergniaud in thrilling terms sums up the debate, Lasource speaks next, the Abbé Fauchet compares their impending doom to Calvary; at last nearly all retire to their cells and throw themselves on their pallets; but thirteen remain—thus the 'nearly all' are only eight—and continue the conversation. At ten o'clock the executioner arrives to cut their hair and tie their hands. At the scaffold they sing the Marseillaise, the voices gradually getting fewer and the melody weaker as one after another mounts the steps, and lays his head on the block. All this is certainly a dramatic picture; unfortunately it is a pure fiction. But the Abbé Lambert could not contradict Lamartine; he had died the very year in which the book appeared. It is impossible to say whether he really furnished Lamartine with materials for this elaborate composition.

I may here remark that Madame Roland's last moments, though not the subject of actual legend, have been related with singular inaccuracy. The night before her trial, Chauveau Lagarde, the so-called 'officious' defender of the prisoner—that is to say he was appointed by the Court if the accused had chosen no counsel—spent some time with her, but she refused his services, telling him that he would merely risk his own life without saving hers. 'Let me not,' she said, 'have the pain of causing an honest man's death.' When he had left her she indited a defence, which, however, she was not permitted to read. Tissot, who saw her on her way to the scaffold, speaks of her flashing eyes, her winning smile, her endeavours to cheer her fellow-victim, Lamarche. She even extorted a smile from that dejected and timorous man. Her oft-quoted remark, according to her friend Helen Williams and the best authorities, was not 'O Liberty, what crimes are committed in thy name!' but 'O Liberty, how hast thou been duped!'[1] She is sometimes supposed to refer to the execution of the royal family, which, however, she had herself advo-

[1] Uncertainty rests on the last words and demeanour of the victims, for their friends were not allowed to accompany them, the military escort surrounded the scaffold, and newspapers seldom ventured to report anything tending to their glorification.

cated, or to the September massacres, which her husband had certainly condoned. What she really meant was that instead of the liberty anticipated by the Girondins there had come the sanguinary tyranny of the Jacobins, and that the despotism of the Court had been succeeded by the despotism of the mob. There is no foundation for the story accepted by Carlyle that she asked at the foot of the scaffold for pen and paper to write down her thoughts, no more foundation than for Lavoisier's alleged request for a respite, that he might finish a chemical experiment.[1] Pedantic as Madame Roland may have been, there was nothing theatrical in her last moments. Carlyle is also inaccurate in representing her as dying first, in order to encourage Lamarche. She really said to Lamarche, ' Mount first, you would not have nerve enough to see me die.' The executioner demurred to changing the order of the executions, but she said with a smile, ' Can you refuse a woman's last request ? '

Several of the most striking epigrams or utterances associated with the Revolution have, by the way, been distorted or invented. Vergniaud did

[1] During his imprisonment he and his fellow revenue-farmers had been busy drawing up accounts in self-justification, and at the Conciergerie, for the three days preceding the trial, they were in cells almost unfurnished, with no possible means of carrying on experiments or studies. Of course, therefore, Coffinhal did not refuse a respite with the words, ' The republic has no need of *savants.*'

not say that the Revolution, like Saturn, 'was' devouring its own children, which in October 1793 would have been a mere truism. In March 1793, on seeing the dissensions among the republicans, he expressed a fear that the Revolution, like Saturn, 'might' devour its own children. The passage is well worth quoting, for it was strikingly verified.

We have seen the development of that strange system of liberty according to which we are told: 'You are free, but think like us on such and such a question of political economy, or we denounce you to the vengeance of the people. You are free, but bow down to the idol to which we offer incense, or we denounce you to the vengeance of the people. You are free, but join us in persecuting the men whose enlightenment and integrity we dread, or we will style you by the most ridiculous names, or will denounce you to the vengeance of the people.' Thus, citizens, it may be feared that the Revolution, like Saturn, successively devouring all its children, will at last engender despotism, with its accompanying calamities.

Vergniaud was also the introducer of a phrase, frequently adopted or adapted by others. On September 17, 1792, quoting William Tell, ' Perish my name and memory, provided Switzerland be free ! ' he said ' Perish the National Assembly, provided France be free ! ' Hence Robespierre's ejaculation on negro emancipation, ' Perish the Colonies rather than sacrifice a principle ! ' The Abbé Edgeworth did not say to Louis XVI., ' Son of

St. Louis, ascend to heaven ! ' albeit French royalists still maintain that he did. A journalist named His is alleged on the day of the execution to have remarked that this is what Edgeworth ought to have said. What is certain is that it first appeared in print in the 'Annales de la République Française ' for January 28, 1793. That paper in its numbers of the 22nd and 25th had spoken of the execution without any hint of Edgeworth having uttered such words. In 1842 Lacretelle, then an Academician, claimed priority of publication, and half claimed— in private he wholly claimed—to have coined the phrase. Edgeworth disclaimed any recollection of uttering it, though under royalist pressure or cajoleries he was induced to believe that he might possibly have done so.

Did the drums silence Louis XVI. ? Edgeworth does not mention this. Santerre alleges that the drums ceased when the troops had all taken up their position, that Louis then exclaimed, loud enough to be heard six paces off, 'I desire that my blood may cement the happiness of France,' and that he then retired from the balustrade. Only when some cries of ' Pardon ! threatened to create a ferment did Santerre order the drums to recommence. Yet sensationalists have recently asserted, not merely that the unfortunate King was silenced, but that the order for this was given by his own *quasi*-uncle, General Beaufranchet. Now it is true that Beaufranchet was probably present at the execution, and it is true that he was the son of Maria Louisa Murphy, an Irish girl, mistress of Louis XV., and the first inmate of his Parc-aux-cerfs ; but he was the son, not of Louis XV. but of the husband, Beaufranchet, whom Louis found for her, after she had given birth to a child of uncertain sex and destiny. It is sufficiently striking to see a son of Louis XV.'s mistress a witness of Louis XVI.'s execution, without imagining any blood relationship between them. Maria Murphy, after burying two husbands and being divorced by a third, and after being imprisoned in the Terror, died in Paris on December 11, 1814, having in her life of seventy-seven years seen five French sovereigns.

The ineffectual attempt to rescue the last batch of victims of the Terror is a touching episode thus related by Carlyle :

We observe in the eventide, as usual, the death-tumbrils faring south-eastward [nearly due east], through St. Antoine, towards the Barrier [Barrière] du Trône. St. Antoine's tough bowels melt ; St. Antoine surrounds the tumbrils ; says it shall not be ! O heavens, why should it ? Henriot and gendarmes, scouring the streets that way, bellow with waved sabres that it must. Quit hope, ye poor Doomed ! The tumbrils move on.

Now it is clear from contemporaneous reports and depositions [1] that the forty-five victims of the

---

[1] Published in Combes's *Episodes Révolutionnaires.*

9th Thermidor left the Conciergerie between half-past three and four for the Barrière du Trône, a distance of about three miles, and that the Faubourg St. Antoine, through which they passed, was then perfectly quiet, for the simple reason that the decrees of the Convention against Robespierre were still unknown, if indeed they had yet been passed, for the sitting, after the arrest of Robespierre, was not suspended till 5.30. Young Sanson, one of his father's assistants at the executions, was back at the Faubourg St. Denis by 6.45 P.M. to take the command of his artillery company. The captain of the National Guards of the section in which the Barrière du Trône was situated, whose business it was to preserve order on the spot, had seen everything over and was also back at the headquarters of his section at 6.45. Debune, the Gendarmerie officer in command of the escort, sent in his report—in one deposition he says at seven, in another at eight —that the executions had taken place. They were certainly over by half-past six, but in any case there is not the slightest contemporary evidence of any attempt at a rescue. The inhabitants of the Faubourg St. Antoine watched the passing of the carts with their usual apathy or timidity. What seems to have given rise to the legend is that when Fouquier Tinville was prosecuted there was at first an idea of charging him with wantonly neglecting to save these victims, but this count was dropped.

He had joined in overturning Robespierre, and might doubtless before leaving the Conciergerie at half-past three for dinner have ordered the suspension of the executions. Sanson, the executioner, suggested, it appears, a postponement, on account of a reported ferment in the Faubourg St. Antoine; but Fouquier made light of the stir as merely a street brawl, and ordered Sanson to proceed as usual. Robespierre's fall, moreover, was in no way prompted by a desire to stop the daily butchery, but was solely instigated by self-preservation, and had not the following day been Décadi, the Jacobin Sabbath, there might have been another batch of victims. All that the Moderates in the Convention had stipulated for, as a condition of their joining in the overthrow of Robespierre, was that the number of executions should be reduced.

That overthrow nipped in the bud an apotheosis by which Young France was to have been taught heroism. At the very hour when the writhing ex-dictator was being led amid execrations to the Place de la Concorde, where so many of his victims had perished, he should have been marching to the Pantheon, perhaps to speak, at any rate to figure prominently, at the obsequies of two boys whom in his address two months previously, at the festival of the Supreme Being, he had declared worthy of immortality. The Jacobins fixed their festivals on Décadis, when even the guillotine was at rest, but

on that particular Décadi it rested not, for it
despatched Robespierre and ten of his satellites.

These two boys were Joseph Barra and Agri-
cola Viala. Barra, born at Palaiseau, near Sceaux,
on July 30, 1779, was on the staff of General
Desmarres, and was killed on December 7, 1793,
falling into an ambuscade and refusing to deliver
up to the Vendeans the two horses in his charge.
This very simple incident was embellished in the
customary fashion. Barra was represented as
declining to surrender, and as shouting with his
last breath, 'Vive la République!' and the honours
of the Pantheon were decreed him. Viala, a boy of
thirteen at Avignon, was said to have cut the ferry
rope by which Marseilles reactionaries were about
to cross the Durance, in order to march on Paris.
Shot while doing this, he cried : 'No matter, I die
for liberty,' and his mother, at first disconsolate,
was proud, like a Spartan mother, of her son's
glorious end. The Convention ordered that his
remains also should be placed in the Pantheon, and
David, the artist, was directed to arrange the
ceremony. On May 22, 1794, Viala's uncle, Moreau,
at the head of an Avignon deputation, thanked the
Convention for this honour, delivering a message
from the boy's mother that she had four other
children whom she loved dearly, but that she loved
her country still more. A professed eye-witness of
Viala's end was one of the deputation. On May 27,

Palloy, the Paris stonemason, famous for making a trade of selling relics of the Bastille, though there is no proof that he helped to capture it, appeared with a deputation from Sceaux, whither he had removed when Bastille relics fell to a discount. He offered statues of the two young heroes. Barra's mother, brother, and sister, as also Moreau, were with the deputation, and were honoured with seats beside the President of the Convention. There was also a troop of girls, headed by Palloy's daughter. She had often figured on girl deputations in Paris. In 1795, when she was nineteen, Palloy sent out a circular to every regiment of the army, inviting each to send a candidate for her hand. The suitors were to stay with him a fortnight, and the girl was to make her choice. This singular sweepstakes appears to have taken place, for the maiden shortly afterwards married a young captain. As for her father, flattering and soliciting pensions from every successive government, he lived till 1834.[1] The girls carried a statue of Virtue. Barra's mother and her children were kissed by the President, and a pension of 1,000 francs was accorded them.

David had made all the preparations for the apotheosis, but on the night of the 9th Thermidor, while the issue of its struggle with Robespierre was still uncertain, the Convention postponed it, and it was never held. On February 16, 1795, a letter to

[1] See Victor Fournel's *Héros de la Bastille*.

the Convention from Avignon denounced the Viala story as a ridiculous fable. The truth was that Viala did not attempt to cut the rope, and that the Marseillais crossed the river and ravaged Avignon. The Republic, said the writer, had too many real exploits to need absurd falsehoods. Nothing more was heard of the affair. Barère had probably supplied Robespierre with the materials of the legend, which—legends have nine lives—continues to this day to be repeated in popular books on the Revolution. In 1881 a statue of Barra was erected at Palaiseau.

I may pass rapidly over some minor myths. The story of human skins being tanned at Meudon to serve for soldiers' boots arose out of the secrecy observed in gunnery experiments and military balloons, but it would scarcely have arisen had there not been old anecdotes of the use of human skins for various purposes, and it may be mentioned that in 1887 the chief of the Paris detectives had a card case made out of the murderer Pranzini's skin. Deputies sent to Meudon by the Convention formally contradicted the tannery rumour. The report of two English emissaries being seated outside the Abbaye during the September massacres and regaling the murderers with drink was invented as part of a systematic attempt to trace all French troubles to English perfidy; yet Louis Blanc and

Michelet, both Anglophobes, credulously accept it.
It is a wonder they do not also believe that a hand-
kerchief dipped in the blood of Louis XVI. was
hoisted on the Tower of London, for this was also
asserted by Jourdain, the inventor of the story.   In
contemporary narratives and engravings of the
massacres, the two Englishmen are of course conspicuous by their absence.   The story of the crew
of the 'Vengeur' refusing to surrender and cheering
for the republic as they sank with the vessel, was
fabricated by Barère.   In reality 270 men were
saved by the English boats, while about 100 were
drowned.   Fifteen years ago, on the death of an
alleged survivor of the 'Vengeur,' the Paris papers
repeated the story, and more recently the erection
by a sailors' subscription of a statue of Captain
Renaudin was proposed, but the then Minister of
Marine discountenanced it, on the ground that
Renaudin had shown no exceptional heroism.   A
'Vengeur' panorama, however, was opened in
Paris in 1892, representing the 'heroic death
of 475 sailors.'   The legend that French cavalry
in January 1795 galloped over the ice-bound
Texel in which the Dutch fleet was set fast
and captured it after slight resistance, appears
to have originated in Paris caricatures.   Painters
followed suit, Jomini accepted the story, Thiers
and Alison gave it further currency, and a
Paris street still bears the name of the Rue du

Helder. Dutchmen, however, who resented an aspersion on their ancestors, showed in 1882 [1] that the French troops had been welcomed as allies at Amsterdam, and that the Batavian Republic formally ordered the surrender of the fleet, lying one hundred yards off Amsterdam, which accordingly took place without a shot being fired.

Robespierre, according to the best evidence, shot himself, and was not shot by Merda, who rose to a colonelcy on the credit of his alleged feat. Carnot's claims to strategy and to irresponsibility for the Terror are being roughly handled, and at the time I write a royalist legend is being criticised. Cathélineau, 'the peasant, was never commander-in-chief of the Vendean insurgents, the pretended appointment, still preserved by his descendants, being, says M. Port, a clumsy forgery. He played only a secondary part in the rising.

Thus far we have dealt with myths of French origin or fabrication; but England has made one contribution to the list. I may again quote Carlyle :—

In this set of tumbrils [9th Thermidor] there are two other things notable: one notable person, and one want of a notable person. . . . Paine has sat in the Luxembourg since January, and seemed forgotten, but Fouquier had pricked him at last. The turnkey, list in hand, is marking with chalk the outer doors of to-morrow's *journée*. Paine's outer door happened to be open, turned back on the wall; the turnkey marked it on the side next him, and hurried on; another turnkey came and shut it; no chalk mark now visible, the *fournée* went without Paine. Paine's life lay not there.

This story had evidently been told by Sampson Perry, a journalist who, convicted of libel, had fled to Paris, for on his death in 1823 there appeared in English newspapers an account of him which was copied into the 'Annual Biography.' It spoke of him as nine times imprisoned (he had been incarcerated in three different Paris prisons) and as condemned to death by Robespierre without trial! It added:

The door of his and Paine's cell swung on a swivel, which, by the least motion, would turn any way. It was the custom to mark with red chalk the cells of those who were to be executed, and the turnkeys went round to seize them. The turnkey accidentally let Perry's cell door swing back, the red mark was concealed, his cell passed unnoticed. Later in the day the keeper came round again, was astonished to find Paine and Perry there, but before he could take any steps he was shot by an infuriated mob, who had burst open the prison and liberated the captives just as Robespierre was being led to the scaffold.

Carlyle, apparently suspecting embellishments, toned down this account, omitting the condemnation without trial and the interposition of the mob, but even his reduced version is a tissue of absurdities. No chalking of the doors is mentioned by any other prisoner. The Luxembourg and other buildings were merely 'houses of detention,' and prisoners were never taken from them direct to the scaffold, very seldom even direct to the court. There was almost always a removal by night to the Conciergerie, which adjoined the court. One object doubtless of this measure was to prevent any attempt at rescue. At the Conciergerie the prisoners received a notice, usually served the night before, and satirically styled 'the evening paper,' that they were to be tried. Even Danton, in whose case there was exceptional expeditiousness, though at first taken to the Luxembourg, was next day interrogated and then transferred to the Conciergerie. There may be one or two instances of a person being summoned to a trial as a witness and suddenly placed in the dock, or of a wife in the court deliberately shouting 'Vive le roi' in order that she might be guillotined with her husband; but allowing for these few exceptions, the Conciergerie and the notice of trial were regular formalities. Now Paine had undergone neither of these, and was in no danger, unless indeed from an undated entry, of which he was blissfully ignorant, in Robespierre's note-book, viz., 'propose that Thomas Paine should be brought to trial, in the interest as much of America as of France.' That entry, on a par with the proscription tablets of Roman emperors, had probably been made on the discovery among Danton's papers

D

of a letter from Paine advocating the removal of the Convention to a provincial town. Had Robespierre lived, Paine in all likelihood would have perished, for though he had been expelled from the Convention as a foreigner, which logically implied the restoration of his American citizenship, it is doubtful whether this would have protected him. His 'miraculous escape,' however, as Perry styles it, is like that of the numerous persons who imagined or pretended that they were doomed to die on the very day that Robespierre met his fate, whereas the list of fifty-five prisoners for trial, not on the 10th but the 11th Thermidor, contained no name of note. These escapes are like that of Sir Roger de Coverley's ancestor at the battle of Worcester, who, the worthy knight explained, was sent away on a commission on the previous day. Paine's own account of his imprisonment is to be found in the preface to the second part of his 'Age of Reason.' He relates how at three on New Year's morning, 1794, he was arrested and taken to the Luxembourg, how on the way he contrived to call on Joel Barlow, to whom he entrusted his just completed manuscript of that work, how he was kindly treated by the keeper, Benoit, who, however, was soon superseded, and how, on January 27, the American residents in Paris went in a body to the Convention to solicit his release, but were told that he was an Englishman by birth. He continues:

I heard no more after this from any person out of the walls of the prison till the fall of Robespierre. . . . About two months before this event I was seized with a fever that in its progress had every symptom of becoming mortal, and from the effects of which I am not [October 1795] recovered. . . . I was then with three chamber comrades, Joseph Vanhuele, of Bruges, Charles Bastini, and Michael Robyns, of Louvain.

After speaking of their kindness, as also that of Dr. Graham and Surgeon Bond, members of General O'Hara's suite, Paine says of Robespierre's memorandum :

I have some reason to believe, because I cannot discover any other, that this illness preserved my own existence. . . . From what cause it was that the intention [of Robespierre] was not put in execution I know not, and cannot inform myself, and therefore I ascribe it to impossibility on account of that illness.

Illness, however, was no protection from the guillotine, as the case of Lavergne proves,[1] but how is it that Paine, who in October 1795 attributed his escape to this cause, afterwards gave a variation of Perry's story? In a pamphlet published by him in 1802 he says :

When persons by scores and by hundreds were to be taken out of the prison for the guillotine, it was always done in the night, and those who performed that office had a private mark or signal by which they knew what rooms to go to and what number to take. We, as I have said, were four, and the door of our room was marked, unobserved by us, with that number in chalk ;

[1] See p. 231.

D 2

but it happened, if ' happening ' is the proper word, that the mark was put on when the door was open and flat against the wall, and thereby came on the inside when we shut it at night, and the destroying angel passed by it.

In the same pamphlet Paine says :

A hundred and sixty-eight persons were taken out of the Luxembourg in one night, and 164 of them guillotined next day, of which (*sic*) I knew I was to be one.

These two paragraphs are equally inaccurate. There was no door-chalking, and even if there had been, Paine, on escaping in this way, would scarcely have been left undisturbed for three weeks. I say three weeks, for the Luxembourg prisoners were carried off to the Conciergerie on July 6, and were condemned, not in one batch of 168, but in three batches of 60, 48, and 36, 144 in all, on the 7th, 9th, and 10th, whereas Robespierre was not overturned till the 27th or 28th. Paine's version is even more absurd than Perry's, for Perry dates the escape on the eve of Robespierre's fall, when twenty-four hours' delay meant deliverance, whereas Paine, by connecting it with the Luxembourg batch, dates it on the 6th, when a day's delay would have been unavailing. One asks in vain why Paine, after publishing at the time a true account of his imprisonment, gave, ' in after years,' this utterly untrue account. Was he under some hallucination, or were his faculties impaired ?

CHAPTER II

UTOPIAS

This poet of the nations, who dreams on
And wails on (while the household goes to wreck)
For ever after some ideal good —
Some equal poise of sex, some unvowed love
Inviolate, some spontaneous brotherhood,
Some wealth that leaves none poor and finds none tired,
Some freedom of the many that respects
The wisdom of the few. Heroic dreams ;
Sublime to dream so, natural to wake,
And sad to use such lofty scaffoldings,
Erected for the building of a Church,
To build instead a brothel or a prison—
May God save France !
MRS. BROWNING'S *Aurora Leigh*, Book 6.

Equality—Classical Reminiscences—Imitation of England an America—Slaves—Aliens—Marriage—Illegitimacy—Academies—Animals—The Maximum—The Rebound.

JUST as privilege, that is to say inequality, had been the mark of the old monarchy, so by a logical reaction equality was the ruling passion of the Revolution. France had been divided into classes—the nobility, with its immunity from taxation and its monopoly of the highest posts in Church and State, the magistracy with its hereditary or purchasable admissions, the tradesmen and artisans with their guilds, the peasants with their feudal burdens, while in the colonies there was the further distinction of colour. The Revolution sought to efface all these dividing lines. It aimed at equality of status, rights, and duties, equality of eligibility in Army, Church, and Civil Service, equality in taxation, equality in political institutions in lieu of provincial disparities, equality of creeds, equality of colours, equality of prices, equality of children in the family, and at least an approach to equality of fortune and culture. All professions, all posts, were to be open alike to all. Convinced, moreover, that man everywhere and everywhen was naturally good, or like a sheet of white paper was capable of receiving any impress, the Revolution disregarded time and space.

> Rites and forms before its burning eyes
> Melted like snow.

Epochs and nationalities stood for nothing. A model once found, whether in classical antiquity or in contemporary nations across the seas, France was to be moulded to it. Undoubtedly there was much that was generous in this movement. War, slavery, poverty, were to disappear as by enchantment, and the earth was to become a paradise. Unfortunately these theorists took no account of history, heredity, political economy, nor indeed of human nature, and attributing all the obstacles encountered on their path to wilful perversity, they resorted to the most relentless tyranny to carry out the impossible. They heaped fallacy on fallacy, they committed blunder on blunder, and after five years of sanguinary anarchy France had to take the world as she found it, and to revert, not indeed to the abuses of the old system—that rotten edifice had collapsed and could not be restored—but to a recognition of the necessary inequality of conditions and capacities.

The Revolution originated no ideas. 'Books,' says Tocqueville, ' had furnished the theories; the populace undertook the practice, and adapted the ideas of writers to their own furies.' And again—'The contrast between the benignity of theories and the savagery of acts, which was one of the strangest features of the French Revolution, will surprise nobody who considers that that Revolution was prepared by the most civilised classes of the nation and carried out by the rudest and most uncultivated.' Rousseau's influence was, of course, preponderating, and Edgar Quinet has shown that the Revolution had not only Rousseau's ideas but his monomania:

Rousseau is to this Revolution what the germ is to the tree. He who thoroughly probed Rousseau's life would see the Revolution, in good and evil, enveloped in it; he bequeaths it not merely his ideas, but his temperament. He professes that all is good in man: he ends by finding mankind 'suspect.' A philanthropist, he daily advances towards an implacable misanthropy. Not a friend whom he does not immolate to his idol, suspicion. . . . He loses himself in a vision of mysterious spots in which his reason totters.[1]

Rousseau himself, however, was an effect as much as a cause. He was the man of his age. As early as 1755 Morelly had advocated the abolition of property, the building of towns on a uniform plan, the adoption by the State of all children at five years of age. The fathers of the American Republic had proclaimed equality of rights and Frederick the Great had drafted a scheme of popular government. These ideas of equality and symmetry were in the air, and the Revolution had no need to invent theories or even a terminology. The very term ' Supreme Being,' usually credited to Robespierre, had crept into use, and that among Catholics, without any feeling of irreverence or heterodoxy.

As Rienzi, to use Madame de Staël's felicitous phrase, ' mistook recollections for hopes,' so the French Republic regarded itself as the renovator of Greek and Roman traditions. It being the first Revolution in which oratory played a leading part, that oratory was steeped in classical allusions. Robespierre was the most pedantic of all its leaders, and these allusions are especially abundant in his speeches. What, however, may appear surprising is that this habit conduced to his political success. Nowadays, we should smile at a man who unrolled

[1] *La Révolution*, book v, section 3.

a manuscript and read in a jarring voice a disser-
tation full of references to the great personages of
antiquity, but such compositions then evoked the
admiration not only of legislatures composed
of men who had had a classical education, but
of the clubs, composed of the lower middle class
and of artisans. Mediæval preachers treated their
illiterate hearers to Latin quotations, and Robespierre frequently repeated or rehearsed his Convention speeches in the Jacobin Club, where Rome was
constantly cited. These discourses, smelling of the
lamp, and as shown by the multitude of erasures
very carefully revised, had greater effect than the improvised or at least unwritten harangues of Danton,
and when on the 9th Thermidor Robespierre was
refused a hearing, it was because his enemies had
reason to fear the result of his eloquence on
waverers. If he repelled the accusations of Louvet
(November 5, 1792) he compared himself to Cicero
denounced by Clodius for the illegality of his
measures against Catiline. If he proposed the
festival of the Supreme Being (May 7, 1794) he
recalled the Greek gatherings, where Miltiades,
Aristides, Epaminondas, and Timoleon were pointed
out by fathers to their sons as living examples of mag-
nanimity, justice, and patriotism, and he evidently
wished to be himself in like manner pointed out
—*monstror digito prætereuntium*—as the deliverer of

France. He looked forward to international festivals, in which the great men of all times and countries would be commemorated, and he assured Frenchmen that they had no reason to envy Sparta her matrons, for their own mothers, too, had given birth to heroes, and like them had proudly sacrificed those heroes to the country. In the same speech he extolled the Stoics, and drew a contrast between Socrates and Chaumette, Leonidas and Père Duchêne. If he had to complain of calumny (December 5, 1793) he remembered how Aristides was charged by Xerxes with pillaging the Greek treasury. On another occasion (April 24, 1793) he declared that he would rather be a son of Aristides, educated in the prytaneum at the expense of the Republic, than the heir of Xerxes, born in the corruption of courts to occupy a throne based on the degradation and misery of the populace. If he glorified honest poverty (April 24, 1793) he declared that the hut of Fabricius need not envy the palace of Crœsus. If he advocated the abolition of capital punishment (May 30, 1791), little foreseeing how his hands would hereafter be imbrued in blood, he remarked that under Tiberius death was the penalty of extolling Brutus, and under Caligula the penalty of disrobing before the image of the Emperor. He asked whether Rome had more crimes in the days of her glory, when the Portian law had repealed the severe punishments prescribed by the kings

and decemvirs, than under Sylla and the
Cæsars, whose rigour was as intolerable as their
tyranny.[1] In another debate (May 7, 1794) he
applauded Cato and Brutus, and spoke of Sparta
as shining like a star amid intense darkness.   He
urged (January 2, 1792) that the Emperor of
Germany must be hemmed in a circle, like Mithri-
dates by Popilius.   The calumnies cast on the
Convention reminded him (December 5, 1793) of
those heaped by Tarquin on the Roman Senate, of
the self-laudation of Octavius and Antony, their
hands reeking with blood and rapine, and of the
aspersions of Tiberius and Sejanus on Brutus and
Cassius. On another occasion (May 7, 1794) he eulo-
gised Cæsar's murderers, he cited Cæsar in proof of
the connection between tyranny and atheism, and he
contrasted his atheism with the piety of Cicero, the
dying discourse of Socrates, and Leonidas' invitation
to his companions at Thermopylæ to sup next day in
another world.   Robespierre, in short, as Taine says

---

[1] The Assembly almost unanimously decided to retain capital
punishment, contrary to the report of a committee, whose spokesman, Lepelletier de St.-Fargeau, doomed to assassination after
voting for the death of Louis XVI., urged the precedent of Tuscany,
the frequency of larceny in England, though visited with death,
the demoralisation of public executions, and the fallibility of
judicial decisions. Lepelletier proposed as a substitute solitary
confinement, with the admission of the public once a month as a
moral lesson. In the same discussion Duport described murderers
as *des malades*, and Pétion denied the right of mankind to take
away life. Of these four abolitionists three, Robespierre, Lepelletier, and Pétion had violent deaths.

of the Revolutionists generally, 'looked at the modern world through Latin [and Greek] reminiscences.' If he aimed at a dictatorship it was because Rome was his ideal. In his last speech of all, at the Jacobin Club (8th Thermidor), he ended by saying, ' If, notwithstanding all these efforts, we succumb, you will see me calmly drink the hemlock.' Whereupon the artist David fervidly exclaimed, ' I will drink it with thee ! '

Mirabeau in deprecating severities against the *émigrés* (February 28, 1791) urged that even in the hands of a Busiris such legislation could not be carried out, and on the same day he remarked that the Constitution Committee had not received from the Assembly the compliment paid by the Athenians to Aristides in making him the sole judge whether a project was moral ; but these are the only classical allusions to be found in those of Mirabeau's speeches included in Mr. Morse Stephens's ' Orators of the French Revolution.' His assistants, by whom many if not most of his orations were prepared, and several of whom were Swiss, must have been exempt from what we now call pedantry. They were too practical to indulge in rhetorical flourishes. So also with Talleyrand, who was assuredly as familiar with the classics as his middle-class colleagues in the Assembly, yet never quoted them. With Danton the rarity of historical allusions is just what we should expect ; it is bound up alike

with his failings and his excellences. He had a few
stereotyped similes, but we can count on the fingers
the speeches in which they occur, whereas with
Robespierre the difficulty is to find a discourse
devoid of any. Advocating national games in the
Champ de Mars (November 26, 1793) Danton could
not well refrain from referring to the Olympic games.
When the French troops had been driven out of
Belgium he declared (March 27, 1793) that Frenchmen, like the giants of the fable—was he unable to
recollect the name of Antæus ?—would recover their
strength on touching their native soil. On another
occasion (April 1, 1793) he boasted that his head,
like Medusa's, would make aristocrats tremble. He
likewise compared England to Carthage (March 10,
1793), a simile destined to become threadbare in the
mouth of Barère—Barère who, after Robespierre's
death, likened him to Pisistratus and Catiline.

Vergniaud, on the other hand, styled the
Demosthenes of the Gironde, resembles Robespierre
in his appeals to antiquity. Only once indeed
(March 13, 1793) could he make such a hit as to
express a fear that the Revolution, like Saturn,
successively devouring its children, would relapse
into despotism.[1] He then little imagined that his
own death would be an illustration of the remark,
nor did he live to see in Bonaparte the realisation
of the second part of his augury. A month later

[1] See p. 22.

(April 10, 1793) he repeated his forebodings in a
less felicitous form. He spoke of the reactionaries
as trying to make the republicans slaughter each
other, like the soldiers of Cadmus, in order to pave
the way for a despot. He compared (March 13, 1793)
the destruction of the Girondin printing presses to
that of the Alexandrian library. He held up to
imitation (July 3, 1792) the Spartans of Thermopylæ
and the Roman Senators who presented themselves
to the swords of the Gauls. The non-resistance of
most of the Girondins was a more or less conscious
imitation of these Romans and of Socrates. Vergniaud had previously (October 25, 1791) exhorted
Frenchmen to emulate the five thousand Greeks
who overcame the Persian host—fighting in the same
cause they would achieve the same triumph. He
compared the reactionaries to Catiline (March 13,
1793) and styled Lafayette (April 10, 1793) a pigmy
Cæsar. He urged Louis XVI. (October 25, 1791) not
to shrink from striking the *émigrés*, but to remember Brutus, who immolated treasonable sons. This
last comparison served Guadet (April 12, 1793)
in renouncing Dumouriez, and in defending the
Girondins Guadet had on the previous day contrasted Robespierre with Cicero. Louvet likewise,
in charging Robespierre with dictatorial designs
(October 29, 1792), dwelt on the family likeness between usurpers, from Cæsar to Cromwell, from Sylla
to Masaniello. When he pronounced an oration on
Féraud and his fellow victims (June 2, 1795) the

urn bore the inscription, 'They had the fate of
Cato, and Barneveldt, and Sidney,' a bust of
Brutus was placed beside it, and Louvet compared
the conspirators to Catiline. So also in the
Châteauvieux procession (April 15, 1792) the car
bore a representation of Brutus immolating his son
and of Tell shooting at the apple. Baudin, in an
eulogium on the Girondins (October 3, 1793) likened
their adversaries to Cæsar and Cromwell. Merlin,
complaining in November 1795, of the tardy proceedings against the Jacobins, said, 'What need of
these long formalities ? Did Brutus resort to them
before despatching Cæsar ? ' Other allusions to
Socrates, to Cato, to Claudius, and to Marius must
be passed over, but I must not forget to note that
Camille Desmoulins sealed his own doom, but re-
deemed his previous levities, by comparing the Terror
to the proscriptions of the Roman emperors.[1]

[1] Just as 1789 aped Rome so 1848 aped 1789. Alexis de
Tocqueville's recently published *Souvenirs* give some curious
illustrations of this. We see in the Fête de la Concorde, of May 27,
a second edition of July 14, 1790, and held on the same spot.
Emblems of all nations were displayed ; 300 girls in white, some
suspected to be boys in disguise, had each a bouquet, which
bouquets they flung, with a force which made them resemble a
hailstorm, on the members of the Assembly. One girl advancing,
recited verses in honour of Lamartine, and worked herself up into
contortions resembling epilepsy ; the mob insisted that Lamartine
should kiss her, and he, with ill-concealed reluctance, touched
with the tips of his lips her cheeks suffused with perspiration. A
decree, moreover, had ordered the members of the Assembly to
don the costume of 1792, white waistcoat à la Robespierre, but
only one obeyed this farcical order. Ulysse Trélat, a mad-doctor,
himself half mad, assured Tocqueville that the Revolutionary

Some of the Revolutionists not merely quoted the Romans, but imitated them. Clavière killed himself on the eve of his trial; Valazé stabbed himself in the dock; Condorcet, Buzot, Barbaroux, and Roland also committed suicide. Vergniaud had intended to do likewise, but at the last moment changed his purpose. Chabot attempted suicide. Madame Roland, who at twelve years of age regretted not being a Spartan or a Roman, had to be dissuaded from poisoning herself before trial, one reason, it is but fair to add, being that her property would thus have been saved for her daughter from confiscation. Charlotte Corday, in stabbing Marat, was manifestly acting under classical recol-

leaders, Blanqui, Barbès, Sobrier, Huber, were all mad, that some of them had been his patients, and that they ought to be in his asylum. Upon which Tocqueville writes: 'I have always thought that in revolutions, especially in democratic revolutions, madmen—not those figuratively so called, but real madmen— have played a very considerable part. What is at least certain is that semi-madness is not unsuitable in those times, and often contributes even to success.'

On a false rumour of the death of Louis Philippe, a man perched on a barricade pompously exclaimed 'Tarquin is dead,' and Lamartine's book had excited such admiration for the Girondins that people, says Tocqueville, seemed more bent on acting than on continuing the Revolution.

1848, indeed, resembled 1792, both in its horrors and its virtues. The Red Republican insurgents in June gave no quarter to prisoners, cut off their hands and feet, and hoisted the hands and arms of slaughtered captives on their barricades, yet they abstained from releasing seven or eight hundred criminals in La Force who would with alacrity have joined their ranks, and they forbade on pain of death any pillaging of shops.

lections. She took her favourite Plutarch with her on her journey to Paris, and she hoped to stab Marat in the Convention and to be torn to pieces— but possibly to be applauded—by his fellow deputies. She counted on meeting Brutus and other ancients in the Elysian Fields. One regrets the theatrical tone which some may attribute to her collateral descent from Corneille. When arrested she applied to the Committee of Public Safety for leave to have her portrait taken, as a bequest to her native department. At her trial, noticing that an artist, Hauer, was sketching her, she turned her head towards him that he might have a better view, and she obtained permission to give him a two hours' sitting in her cell while waiting for the tumbril. She suggested corrections in his sketch, and begged him to send a replica to her father. She presented him also with a lock of her hair. The Revolutionists, indeed, were too self-conscious. They felt that they were making history. If the highest genius is unconscious, so also is the highest statesmanship; but the French are nothing if not theatrical. Bonaparte, who had had the same classical training as his contemporaries, established the Consulate in obvious imitation of Rome, and his assumption of the title of Emperor was aping Rome rather than Germany, for at first his coins bore 'Napoléon Empereur' on the obverse, and 'République Française' on the reverse. Indeed, there

E

had been a proposal to style Louis XVI. Emperor. After Waterloo, on delivering himself up to the English man-of-war, Bonaparte, in his letter to the Prince Regent, compared himself to Themistocles soliciting the hospitality of Artaxerxes.

The Roman censors were held up for imitation by Lanthenas and St.-Just. Lanthenas, in August 1793, proposed that every branch of the Government, as also every army and every electoral constituency, should choose censors of manners and morals. They were to inculcate virtue, truth, forgiveness of injuries, reparation of wrongdoing, their only weapon being moral suasion; but the refractory were to be reported by them to a national censorship tribunal, which was to inflict punishment. Denunciations were to be made to the censors, as to the Council of Ten at Venice, but were never to be actuated by hatred, envy, or self-interest. The Convention itself was to have censors, and the members of that body, in order to get thoroughly acquainted with each other, were all to live at the Louvre, where they were to be periodically allotted into twelve groups, each having its saloon for reading and conversation, and its frugal mess, presence at which was to be at least once a week obligatory. This parliamentary lodging system, though without any obvious connection with the censorship, was included in Lanthenas' bill, which did not get beyond what we should call the first reading.

St.-Just, in his manuscript 'Institutions,' saturated with references to antiquity, proposes in like manner that every district and every army should have a censor, to denounce abuses and to prefer accusations against functionaries and public contractors to the revolutionary tribunal. He was to be paid 6,000 francs a year, and was to be forbidden to speak in public. The oldest inhabitant of a parish was to go every tenth day to the temple and proclaim whatever was faulty in the private life of functionaries and of young men under twenty. All irreproachable sexagenarians, wearing a white scarf, were to exercise a like duty. Women, one is relieved to find, were not to be subject to this censorship. And all this was not with St.-Just a mere dream. He had embodied the idea in a draft decree ready for presentation to the Committee of Public Safety and to the Convention. St.-Just likewise proposes that every adult male should once a year publicly designate his friends, and that renunciation of friendship should require a public explanation. Friends were to be debarred from litigation with each other, they were to be posted side by side in battle, they were to wear mourning for each other, and if a man committed a crime his friends were to be banished.

Babeuf, in advocating an agrarian law, borrowed from Rome, as he had already done by changing his name from Camille to Gracchus. He did not stand alone in such fashions, for John

Baptist Cloots became Anacharsis Cloots, and was often called, or called himself, simply Anacharsis, and Brissot gave that name to one of his sons. The infamous Chaumette (Père Dùchêne) styled himself Anaxagoras, and Couthon dubbed himself Aristides. A trace of this classical turn still remains in the commonness of the name Jules. The provisional government of 1870 had four Jules's—Trochu, Favre, Simon, and Ferry. Jullien, the Robespierrist pro-consul of eighteen, had no need to alter his name, for, born in 1775, he had been christened Mark Antony, but he officiated, ' wearing the red cap which is well worth the episcopal mitre,' at the abjuration of evil-sounding surnames, and at the celebration of civil baptisms.[1] At Quimper three *citoyennes* in his presence exchanged Chevalier, Baron, and Louise, for Victoire Nationale, Liberté Républicaine, and Aimée Liberté. At Vannes he named an infant Marat Montagne. Marat was Jullien's idol. At Lorient a Le Duc dubbed himself Sans Culotte Montagne, and a Le Comte became Pelletier-Patriote, while Catholic or royalist Christian names gave place to Sempronie, Lucrèce, Aissée, Fraternité, Liberté, Marat, Mucius, Libre, Publicola, Décius, Tell, Régulus, and Camille. Each of these changes gave Jullien an opportunity for political exhortations or classical reminiscences.

[1] Not only were infants named, and adults re-named, Marat, but thirty towns or villages proposed to take his name.

On the fall of Robespierre the Convention ordered the disuse of all these appellations.

Even the rooms in the Paris prisons were inscribed Cincinnatus, Brutus, Socrates, &c., sometimes also Marat, which was peculiarly appropriate, until, in June 1794, Payan urged on the municipality that the shades of these great men would be indignant at seeing the cells of conspirators called by their names. Thereupon the inscriptions were effaced.

Civic dinners, in imitation of Sparta, also became common in Paris a few weeks before Robespierre's fall. People had tables spread outside their houses in the street, and had their servants sit down to partake with them. A man would be heard haughtily ordering his servant on the staircase, and coming out to dinner would have that servant sit beside him and would drink his health. A fashionable lady would say to passers-by: 'Look how I love equality, I dine publicly with my servants.' This innovation, denounced by some as an intrigue of the Hébertists, by others as an aristocratic device for lulling patriotic suspicions, was, however, very short-lived.

Considering the analogy between 1648 and 1793, destined to be followed by the analogy between 1688 and 1830, one is surprised at the rarity of appeals to English precedents. At the beginning of the Revolution, indeed, there was an idea of imitating England by having two Houses and a royal veto, but this Anglomania did not last long. The clubs, however, were borrowed from England, at first from the parliamentary clubs of which the Jacobins was originally an imitation, and then from the London debating clubs, the importance of which was ridiculously exaggerated in France. The only thing besides these really borrowed from England was trial by jury, which was carried by Adrien Duport, but the permanent paid jurors of the Revolutionary Tribunal were a sorry travesty of an English panel. Mirabeau (September 1, 1789) cited the Long Parliament in proof of the danger of a single chamber making itself perpetual and tyrannical. He advocated (June 16, 1789) the term 'representatives of the people,' on the ground of the English and American use of the word people, and of Chatham's expression 'the majesty of the people.' Robespierre (June 2, 1793) coupled Sidney with Socrates and with Cato, but this is the only instance of his displaying hero-worship for an Englishman. Danton (April 1, 1793) had to repel a comparison with Cromwell. Guadet (September 18, 1793) likened the Jacobins to the Levellers, and the exclusion of the Girondins to Pride's Purge, and he foreboded a Cromwell, by whom he doubtless meant Robespierre. Vergniaud (December 31, 1792) warned the Convention against being enticed into unpopular measures as the Long Parliament was entrapped by Cromwell. St.-Just (July 9, 1793) compared Brissot to Monk, and deprecated a weak government because it was certain to be followed, as in England on Cromwell's death, by a Restoration.

Forced loans and the sequestration of royalists' estates were a repetition of what was done by the Long Parliament, but this was probably unconscious imitation. The trial of Louis XVI., however, was clearly copied from our 1649. A French translation of Charles I.'s trial had been widely circulated in Paris in November 1792. Robespierre, nevertheless, advocated a summary execution, in preference to the illusory forms under which Mary Stuart and Charles were put to death. Was Tarquin tried? he asked. Lefort ineffectually pleaded for the King's life, urging that Charles's death led to the Restoration, whereas James II.'s banishment evoked no sympathy for his son. Poor Louis himself at an early stage of the Revolution had begun studying Hume's history of Charles, and Bonaparte had studied Cromwell before imitating him on the 18th Brumaire; but Louis XVIII. in exile vainly tempted Bonaparte to copy Monk. Egalité, though little was said about it in print, was evidently looked upon as a possible William III., who might supplant Louis XVI., or succeed him, for the poor little Dauphin was very weakly, and Louis's brothers had disqualified themselves by quitting France and levying war upon her.

The United States were even less frequently cited than England, though the Committee of Public Safety of 1793 looks like an imitation, at least in name, of the Committees of Safety formed in the various states at the beginning of the war of Independence. The Girondins, indeed, wished to copy American federation. They were careful to say little on this ideal, yet their reticence did not save them from its being made one of the pretexts for guillotining them. They failed to see the difference between uniting states in a federation and splitting up a nation into states. The old provinces, owing to their fiscal vexations, had disappeared without causing the slightest regret, and their revival was impossible. As to Washington, his strict neutrality made him disliked. Moreover, there was as yet no Bonaparte to act as his foil, and the veneration now existing for him in France is of quite modern growth. Franklin, moreover, from his residence at Paris, was the representative in French eyes of American independence, though the French officers who had served in America must have been well aware of the political and moral superiority of Washington. In the eulogium delivered by the Abbé Fauchet at the instance of the Paris municipality in 1790, Franklin was represented as convening Congress, as appointing

Washington, and, in fact, as the leader of the movement. This ignorance on Washington is like-wise amusingly exemplified by a speech at the Jacobin Club in the autumn of 1792. America was spoken of as having made Washington presi-dent for life, and as running the risk of a heredit-ary presidency, which, in the hands of Washington's son (!), might prove a despotism.

Thus far we have seen the Revolution en-deavouring to imitate classical or contemporary examples. It was not, however, satisfied with this. It sought to convert dreams into realities. Human nature, like Pelias in the cauldron of Medea, was to undergo a palingenesis.

Disabilities of colour and race were to cease. The famous *cahiers*, statements of grievances or desires of the constituencies by whom the Assembly of 1789 was elected, contain twenty-three repre-sentations against negro slavery. Eight of these emanated from the clergy, three from the nobility, and twelve from the third estate, or commoners. The clergy of Mantes declared that slavery revolted every feeling mind, and that it was atrocious for a man to buy a fellow man, deprive him of liberty, subject him to continual hard labour, and make him till his death the victim of caprice and cruelty. They therefore called, not for emancipa-tion, but for the abolition of the infamous slave trade. The clergy of Melun, regarding liberty as a right affirmed by Christianity, irrespective of colour, demanded the abolition of colonial slavery. The clergy of Charolles, Metz, and Alençon prayed for the abolition of the slave-trade and slavery. The clergy of Paris asked for the abolition, 'if possible,' of the slave trade, or at least for the humane treatment of the slaves. The clergy of Péronne solicited the liberation of ' our unfortunate brothers the negroes in our colonies,' and asked the Assembly to effect this with all the precautions dictated by prudence and justice. The clergy of Rheims advocated reform of the abuses of the slave trade, so as to reconcile political advantages with the rights of nature; but, if this could not be effected, a barbarous policy should be sacrificed to the essential rights of mankind.

The nobility of Mantes asked for the abolition of the slave trade and preliminary measures for the liberation of the negroes, so that France might have the honour of priority in effacing this degradation. The nobles of Quesnoy asked vaguely for measures in favour of the negroes. The nobles of Châteauneuf-en-Thimarais wished colonial rights to be reconciled with the sacred rights of humanity.

The third estate at Alençon prayed for the abolition of the slave trade and the gradual abolition of slavery. Amiens, while regarding the slave trade as atrocious, and calling for immediate suppression,

admitted that emancipation could not be effected in
a day, as colonial interests had to be considered.
Vermandois asked for emancipation. Versailles
wished the feasibility of emancipation to be considered and for the exemption of freed men from a
special tax. Suburban Paris condemned slavery as
contrary to natural law. Rheims desired emancipation, for its third estate remembered that seven
or eight centuries ago it was itself in almost equal
bondage, but if there were political obstacles slavery
should be mitigated as much as possible. Rennes
remarked that ' if political interests of the greatest
weight prevent us from following the impulses of our
hearts by at once prohibiting the slave trade and
slavery, let the condition of the slaves be ameliorated,
let them be treated like men. Repeal barbarous
laws which impose heavy duties even on enfran-
chisement, and which may stand in the way of a
master's goodwill for his slave.' Villiers-le-Bel
wished political interests to be reconciled with the
sacred rights of nature. Mont-de-Marsan advocated
an investigation of the means of restoring to liberty
' fellow men as much entitled to it as ourselves.'
Senlis and Aval asked for the abolition of slavery.
Château Thierry, considering that France had
always been the asylum of kings—an allusion to
James II.—and the protector of oppressed nations,
and that the slave himself, on breathing the air
of its happy clime, found liberty, denounced the

slave trade and slavery as an outrage on humanity, but it desired safeguards for colonial labour.

The generous tone of these declarations commands admiration. If some of the constituencies contented themselves with demanding the suppression of the slave trade, it should be remembered that slavery was then thought to be dependent on continuous consignments of human merchandise. Nobody foresaw that, whether from acclimatisation or milder treatment, slave-breeding could be carried on, as in Kentucky up to thirty years ago, on a large scale.

The planters felt that amid this outburst of noble sentiments their system was doomed, for Guadeloupe instructed its deputies to withdraw from the Assembly if any proposals questioning their rights of property were presented.   The Assembly, however, found too much to do in France to give much thought to the colonies, and the negroes, impatient at the delay, rose in insurrection in St. Domingo in August 1791, committing atrocities for which Brissot, Grégoire, and the other abolitionists were held responsible by the planters and their sympathisers. But in May 1791, the Assembly had admitted mulattoes born of free parents to civic rights.   On September 9, 1792, a company of mulattoes volunteering for the army entered the Jacobin Club, declaring their determination to die a thousand deaths rather than see the revival of despotism. On June 4, 1793, the Convention rose as one man—as the Assembly had done in honour of the Jura serf, said to be six score years old—to greet a negress of 114, accompanied by a negro deputation. 'The humanity and philosophy of the Assembly,' said Bishop Grégoire, ' will efface the aristocracy of skin.' On February 3, 1794, the Convention admitted as a deputation for St. Domingo a negro named Belley, a native of Goree, first a slave and then a freed man in St. Domingo. He continued to sit in the Convention and the Council of Five Hundred till 1797, and then returned to St. Domingo. He served in 1802 in the army engaged in repressing the negro rebellion, and was captured and shot by his fellow-negroes. The Convention on February 4, 1794, unanimously decreed the abolition of slavery, whereupon the coloured deputies were embraced by the President and the members. A negress, or mulatto, who regularly attended the sittings, was so overcome by the spectacle that she fainted.

The disabilities of foreigners were also to cease, for were not all men brothers? The Crown had been the heir-at-law of aliens who, even if natura-lised, left no children or kindred in France. The Assembly, in August 1790, abolished this law of *aubaine* as contrary to international brotherhood, for free France invited foreigners to enjoy the sacred and inalienable rights of mankind. Indeed,

one of the *cahiers* of 1789 proposed that all tax-
payers should be citizens, and another advocated
that three years' residence should confer citizenship.   In the same spirit, all the world was invited
to offer suggestions for the constitution, and two
Englishmen—George Edwards and Robert Merry—
accordingly did so.   The Assembly, moreover, in
August 1792, on the eve of its separation, accorded
French citizenship to Priestley, whom persecution
by the Birmingham mob had commended to French
sympathy, and one of whose sons had settled in
France, though he was ere long driven out by fear
of the Terror ; to Paine, who had paid several
visits to France, and on the King's flight to
Varennes had openly advocated a Republic ; to
Jeremy Bentham, who had sent his treatise on
model prisons ; to Wilberforce and Clarkson as the
champions of negro emancipation, the latter having
visited Paris in 1789 to confer with French abolitionists ; to Mackintosh, applauded for the answer
to Burke, which he afterwards retracted ; to David
Williams, the Unitarian minister, who spent the
ensuing winter in Paris in the hope of helping
to frame the constitution ; to Count Gorani, a
Milanese, who had come over to Paris, published
insulting letters to European sovereigns, attached
himself to Robespierre, and on his fall withdrew to
Geneva, where he died in obscurity in 1819 ; to
Cloots, of whom I have already spoken ; to Campe,

the German educationist and disciple of Rousseau, who, in company with his old pupil William Humboldt, had visited Paris in 1789; to Pauw, Cloots's uncle; to Pestalozzi, the educationist; to Washington, Hamilton, and Madison, fathers of the American republic (why Hamilton and Madison were preferred to Jefferson and Adams is not very apparent); to Klopstock, whom Coleridge styled the 'German silver Milton'; to Kosciusko, the Polish patriot; and to Schiller. The selection was evidently made by the Girondins, who wished Priestley and Paine to sit in the Convention. Priestley, unsuccessfully nominated in Paris, was elected in the Orne and the Oise, but declined the honour on the plea of his inability to speak French. Paine was elected in the Seine-et-Oise and the Puy-de-Dôme, and sat for the Pas-de-Calais; Cloots being the only other foreigner. Madame Roland regretted that Williams had not been returned in lieu of Paine. Lord Brougham clearly mistook 1848 for 1792, when he applied for French citizenship in order to be a candidate for the Assembly, and he had to be reminded by the Minister of Justice—Crémieux—that renunciation of English nationality might entail inconveniences which he had not considered, such as the loss of his 4,000*l*. pension as ex-Lord Chancellor.

Not content with honorary or exceptional naturalisations, the constitution of 1793 offered citizenship to any foreigner having lived twelve months in France who earned a livelihood, purchased property, married a Frenchwoman, adopted a child, or supported an aged man.

In accordance with these ideas of universal brotherhood, the Revolution allowed foreigners to play a large part in it. I do not speak of Marat, who, though a native of Neufchâtel, and of Sardinian ancestry, had long been to all intents and purposes a Frenchman; nor of Miranda and other soldiers of fortune who joined the French army. On the Paris revolutionary committee of August 1792, there figured, along with Marat, Pache, also a Swiss, afterwards Minister of War and mayor of Paris; Gusman,[1] a Spaniard, eventually condemned with Danton, and the only one of fifteen prisoners allowed, 'out of politeness to a foreigner,' as Danton said, to deliver his defence; Dufourny, an Italian; Arthur,[1] an Englishman, though born in Paris; and Proly,[1] a Belgian, claiming to be a natural son of the Austrian statesman, Prince Kaunitz. Pereira,[1] though born in France, was the son of a Portuguese Jew; Wiltcheritz,[1] a shoemaker, and member of the Paris Commune, was a Pole; so, too, was Lazouski, another 'municipal'; the brothers Frey were Austrian Jews; Clavière, a Swiss, was Minister of Finance; Fleuriot-Lescot,[1] the mayor of Paris,

---

[1] All guillotined, and Clavière escaped guillotining only by suicide.

who supported and perished with Robespierre, was a Belgian ; Grieve, who hunted Madame Dubarry to death and boasted of having given the guillotine sixteen other victims, was an Englishman.

The Revolution, indeed, may be said to have commenced with one foreigner, Necker, and to have ended with another, Bonaparte, who as a youth hated France as an invader and tyrant in his native Corsica.

Religious strife, like international animosity, was to cease. In 1791 the Paris municipality, composed of Catholics, attended in state the *Te Deum* for the completion of the constitution at St. Thomas du Louvre, a church which had been purchased by the Protestants. The *Te Deum* consisted of passages from Racine, Voltaire, and Rousseau. At St. Jean du Garde, a region where religious animosities had been bitter, the priest and the pastor embraced at the altar, and there were instances elsewhere of priest and pastor attending each other's services and being honoured with the chief seat. This was an approach to St.-Just's idea that churches should be open to the rites of all religions, incense to be constantly kept burning in them by aged men, and new laws to be proclaimed in them. Nothing similar was again witnessed till the Paris Peace Congress of 1849, when the Abbé Darboy, the future archbishop and victim of the Commune, publicly embraced Pastor

F

Coquerel.   But kissing, too, was frequent in the
Revolution.   Some of the persons acquitted during
the September massacres were kissed by the mob
and escorted home in triumph.   Robespierre and
Dumouriez kissed at the Jacobin Club.   Bishop
Lamourette, whose very name suggested love, in
July 1792 induced the Assembly to have a general
kissing in token of oblivion of quarrels.   Alas ! the
guillotine awaited him, like so many others of the
kissers.

It would have been strange if, when all institutions and beliefs were passing through the crucible,
marriage had escaped, for in July 1789 several
women and girls had assumed male attire, and the
Paris municipality had had to threaten them with
a fortnight's imprisonment for the first offence, and
three months for the second.   Mary Wollstone-
craft's ' Rights of Woman ' was translated into
French in 1792, and she herself went over to Paris
in that year to make her unhappy experiment of free
love with the American Imlay.   St.-Just would have
allowed marriage to be kept secret as long as there
was no issue, and would have permitted divorce at
three months' notice.   He likewise proposes in his
' Institutions ' that every parish should annually
choose a rich young man who should be required to
select and marry a poor girl.   He apparently forgot
that he had elsewhere said ' there must be no rich
or poor.'   At the end of 1789 an ex-nun petitioned

the Assembly for the abolition of dowries, in order
that marriages might no longer be mercenary—on
the male side.　She also advocated—this was a more
practical idea—the employment of women in certain
government offices.　In July 1790, another female
petitioner suggested that a husband should add his
wife's surname to his own.　A wedded couple, she
urged, should join names just as they formerly
joined heraldic bearings.　A middle-aged bachelor
would thus be ashamed to have only a single name,
and married Lotharios would be labelled 'dangerous' by their double names.　The petitioner failed
to see that a Lothario might pretend to be a widower,
unless indeed the husband on his wife's death was
to drop her name, nor did she explain how com-
pound names were to be prevented from becoming
of interminable length, for if the first generation
had two names the second on her plan would have
had four, the third eight, and so on.　This would
have eclipsed Welsh nomenclature.　It is true that
in Switzerland a husband not unfrequently tacks
on his wife's name, to distinguish himself in a
country with a paucity of surnames from a multitude of homonyms, but I believe that if the son
does the same he drops his mother's name.

Another suggestion, offered in April 1794, by
Madame Cabarrus Fontenay, afterwards celebrated
as Madame Tallien, was that girls should be trained
for marriage by being taught in hospitals to tend

children and invalids. She herself, as a mother and widow of twenty, was anxious to devote herself to these 'sweet and delightful functions.' Fate had other things in store for 'Our Lady of Thermidor,' for whose sake Tallien helped to overthrow Robespierre.

The throwing open of convent doors, that all who chose might leave, was manifestly, like toleration for Protestants, an essential measure of religious liberty; but the tyranny of immuring girls in convents was succeeded by the tyranny of forbidding monastic life. All indeed that the Revolution could do for women was to allow divorce, even for incompatibility of temper, that is to say at the will of either party. Madame Tallien herself took advantage of this, and contracted a third marriage with the Prince de Chimay. Wives of aristocratic *émigrés* also found a convenience in it, for they could obtain a divorce on the ground of desertion, thus saving their property from confiscation, and when calmer times came they could re-marry their old husbands. John Hurford Stone, an English Radical who settled in Paris as a printer, though he obtained a divorce from his wife, did not follow it up, as he might have been expected to do, by marrying Helen Maria Williams, though they lived together and were ultimately interred side by side in Père La Chaise. Madame Roland and Buzot, though they regarded themselves as spiritually united, had too high a sense of duty to apply for divorces against their respective partners, albeit Madame Roland's sense of duty impelled her to disclose to Roland her affection for Buzot. It would be unfair, moreover, to ignore the many cases in which wives incurred the greatest dangers in order to rescue their husbands from the guillotine, or in which they refused to survive them. Delphine de Custine wanted to change clothes with her husband in prison, that he might escape, and the keeper's daughter had promised connivance, but he refused, knowing that her life would be forfeited. It would also be unfair to regard the loosening of conjugal ties as confined to France. Therese, daughter of Heyne, the great Homeric scholar, and wife of George Forster, who with his father went round the world with Captain Cook, formed an attachment about 1790 for L. F. Huber, and though it was apparently platonic, at least till Forster's departure from Mayence for Paris in July 1793, it embittered Forster's few remaining years. Yet with singular weakness of character, he kept up a correspondence friendly with Huber, affectionate with his wife. His death, in July 1794, was seemingly a relief for both, for Heyne styles her announcement of the event to him, a 'disgraceful letter.' Huber then married Therese, and strangely enough both professed to revere Forster's memory. He was ten years their senior.

All the local or general anomalies of the old laws of inheritance having necessarily to be swept away, there were some who advocated equality between legitimate and natural children. 'Legitimate!' exclaimed the ex-monk Chabot on September 20, 1793, 'we ought to banish that word. Should we not encourage unions which are the result of a pure and tender sentiment? There is no marriage but that of nature, and the offspring of a sentimental union are sacred by nature.' Cambacérès also regarded the distinction between legitimate and illegitimate children as a vestige of ignorance and superstition. The Convention, however, shrank from placing legitimate and adulterine offspring on the same footing. It confined itself to enacting that, failing legitimate issue, property should devolve on a mother's or, if there was written evidence of paternity, on a father's, natural child. An attempt to make this date back to July 14, 1789, occasioned such a multitude of suits that the retrospective clause had to be repealed. St.-Just, in the absence of lineal issue, would have had property devolve on the State. Primogeniture was of course abolished, but to ensure lineal issue he would have made divorce compulsory after seven years of sterility.

The Academies fell a victim partly to the cry for equality, partly to their close relations with the monarchy. It was not, however, till

August 8, 1793, that the Convention unanimously decreed their abolition. Grégoire, in proposing this, declared them to be institutions contrary to the principles of the Revolution; they established, he said, a kind of hierarchy, they pretended to a monopoly of talent, yet they preferred mediocrity to genius, and they had been the sycophants of Richelieu and Louis XIV. He did not fail to enumerate the great men to whom the Academies had never opened their portals, and he pointed to England, the country of Shakespeare, Dryden, and Milton, as a proof that genius needed no such institutions. Thus far Grégoire urged arguments which undoubtedly have a certain force and which are put forward in France even at the present day; but he truckled to the Jacobins by adding, 'Patriots are nearly always in a minority in these bodies. True genius is nearly always *sans-culotte.*' David, himself a member of the Academy of Painting, followed Grégoire with a tirade against his colleagues as enemies of progress, slaves to routine, and jealous of genius. He did not, however, go the length of his friend Marat, who in 1791, soured by their disregard of his communications, had said, 'The Academies, in the eyes of the philosopher, are merely ornamental establishments, monuments erected to the glory of princes, a kind of menagerie where, like rare animals, the most famous charlatans or pedants are collected at great expense.'   The Convention, while decreeing abolition, directed the Academy of Sciences, pending the formation of a scientific society, to pursue the investigations which had been entrusted to it; but whether from fear of the mob or from sympathy with the other Academies, that body declined to continue its sittings.   In October 1795 the Academies were restored, but meanwhile four members of the French Academy—Bailly, Malesherbes, Condorcet, and Chamfort, two of the Academy of Sciences—Lavoisier and Bochard de Saron, two of the Academy of Inscriptions—Laverdy and Lefevre d'Ormesson, had perished in the Terror, while a much larger number had sought safety in exile.   The Bar had also to be restored, for the decree of 1790 allowing a suitor or criminal to be defended by any person he might choose, lawyer or layman, had inevitably led to scandals, and to miscarriage of justice.

Even animals were to benefit by the new era. Among the numerous festivals proposed by the Revolutionists was one in honour of domestic animals, 'the companions of man,' and in October 1794, Ludot having suggested the establishment of veterinary colleges on the ground that the study of animal might help to cure human maladies, Coupé, an ex-priest interesting himself in agriculture and in potato cultivation, who had been expelled from the Jacobin Club as a Moderate, presented an elaborate report. After showing how man had made the brute creation his food and merchandise, he said :

We can consider them (animals) only from this unfortunate standpoint. Let us at least reconcile with this inevitable situation all the alleviations which are in our power. . . . These good creatures live and exist for us ; they are everywhere associates of our labours and efforts. Yes, they are such, and they are always sincere and ingenuous. How cruelly they are disappointed as to reciprocity from us, still more as to that sweet sentiment of gratitude of which they set us an example, and which they have even a greater right to expect from us !

After pointing out how polygamy has been imposed by man on flocks and herds, Coupé mentions that he has seen elderly peasants go to and from the fields on foot in order not to tire an aged horse, and he urges that in yoking animals together account should be taken of their mutual likes and dislikes. Man, he says, had become an evil genius for animals, yet Arabs, Tartars, and Hottentots use no whips, which should be carried only for show and for an emergency. Children, too, should be corrected of their habit of teasing or torturing animals. ‘ Let us strive,’ he says, ‘ to render life pleasant to all that breathes ; the life of animals is so short, and they know so well how to enjoy it.’ He advocated prizes for the cure of cattle diseases, and he concluded by suggesting the insertion in Ludot’s bill of this clause :

Every hired labourer or other person who ill-uses an animal with passion and fury is thereby stamped in the eyes of his fellow citizens with irrationality and ferocity.

The clause was not inserted, and it would obviously have been platonic, but Coupé anticipated by nearly thirty years 'Humanity Martin's Act.' Alas! that fondness for animals should not necessarily imply respect for human life. Robespierre, on the eve of his fall, in his walks in the Parc Monceau, in a field adjoining which the carts daily deposited their freight of decapitated corpses, was accompanied by a favourite dog, and St.-Just was accustomed to fondle a lap-dog. Still, Coupé's report is a refreshing bit of blue sky between the blackness of the Terror and the tempest of the Napoleonic wars.

After equality, or an approximation to equality, between men of different colour, between aliens and natives, between creeds, between the sexes, and between man and the brute creation, we come to equality of prices. The so-called *maximum* was certainly, next to the civil constitution of the clergy, the most egregious blunder of the Revolution. On September 29, 1793, the Convention decreed that the prices of thirty-eight articles, ranging from bread and wine to candles and tobacco, should be for a year in every department the same as they had been in 1790. It was an approach to Jack

Cade's decree: 'There shall be seven halfpenny loaves sold for a penny; the three-hooped pot shall have ten hoops.' Persons either selling or buying above such prices were to be fined double the value of the article, the fine to go to the informer. Delinquents were also to be inscribed on the lists of suspects, and treated as such. The wages of artisans and peasants were likewise fixed, but at 50 per cent. above those of 1790. This second enactment thus recognised that very depreciation of the currency which was ignored in the first. The effects of this system were inevitable. There was necessarily much clandestine trade at prices consistent with the law of supply and demand and with the varying value of the assignat *plus* the risk of detection. There was much prevarication among tradesmen, who, rather than sell at a loss, pretended, if offered the fixed price, to be out of stock. There was much requisitioning inflicted on farmers and on other producers. Thousands of persons were thrown into prison for violating an impracticable law. It is but fair to remark, that though political economy was already understood by thinkers, this *maximum* was based on precedents. The old monarchy in times of emergency—and a succession of bad harvests had caused a great emergency—had been accustomed to regulate prices, and it had systematically regulated manufactures. The economic blunder might moreover have done little mischief

but for the currency blunder.   Yet even in our own
day we have seen multitudes clamour for a paper
or a depreciated metallic currency, not seeing that
paper is worthless except so far as it is a promise
to pay in coin.   The Revolution, persisting in its
fallacy, closed the Bourse and prohibited dealings
between assignats and coin.   If the *maximum* would
not work, the fault was laid on conspirators and
speculators.   Not till after fifteen months was this
disastrous experiment abandoned.

Thus starting with Rousseau's doctrine that
unsophisticated man is naturally good, the Revolution undertook to regenerate France and the world.
All distinctions of race and colour, all separation of
classes, all political and social inequalities, all titles
of nobility, all prejudices and animosities, religious
or international, were to disappear as by the en-
chanter's wand.   Monarchs, aristocracies, State
churches, standing armies, were to be no more.
Even taxation was to be, at least in part, voluntary.
Children, altogether adopted by the State, or perhaps allowed to be lodged, fed, and clothed by their
parents, were to be trained for citizenship by participation almost from infancy in revolutionary
festivals.   Domestic animals were to become not so
much the bond-slaves as the friends of man, and
some thought that their use as food being unnecessary and repulsive, they might recover their pristine
liberty.   Condorcet even imagined that disease, if

not death itself, might be abolished. Legislation was thought to be omnipotent. The National Assembly accordingly drew up its declaration of the rights, not of Frenchmen, but of man, and in fifteen months it issued 2,559 enactments, the Legislative Assembly in eleven months issuing 1,712, and the Convention in fifty-seven months 11,210. When it was found that the millennium could not be established by mere paper and ink, all the compulsory measures with which the old monarchy had been reproached were revived and intensified. Municipalities or clubs—sometimes the two were practically identical—made arrests on a scale throwing far into the shade the old abuse of *lettres-de-cachet*. The Bastille having been improvidently destroyed, a multitude of smaller prisons had to be improvised in Paris, some of them so crowded and unwholesome that disease numbered more victims than the guillotine. Boycotting (the thing existed, though not the name), certificates of civism, passports, confiscation, imprisonment, death, were resorted to in order to overcome a resistance ascribed to conspiracy or perversity. Regulations as to dress (the tricolour cockade was compulsory for both sexes), as to trade, and as to religion (recusant priests were not merely ejected from their cures, but it was a crime to hold or attend their services), subjected every citizen to a tyranny compared with which the old despotism was liberty.

Had this experiment succeeded, France, if not

all Europe, would have been reduced to a monotonous uniformity unparalleled in history. There would have been a new earth, in which dwelt—uniformity. But the intolerable incubus was soon thrown off, and a revulsion ensued which in some important respects carried men back even beyond the point at which the Revolution had found them. Standing armies, so far from being disbanded, were enormously increased. Negro slavery, gaining a new lease from the bloodshed in St. Domingo, continued in the French colonies till 1848. The worship of the Supreme Being and Theophilanthropy were followed by a revival of sectarian fanaticism. The European monarchies were strengthened by the sanguinary failure of French republicanism. Napoleon's shoddy titles were as eagerly coveted as had been the peerages of the old dynasty.

Nevertheless, it is impossible not to admire the generous enthusiasms which were evoked by the Revolution. It was a splendid sunrise, though so soon to be darkened by the fury of the elements. It was perhaps necessary that the experiment of sudden transformation should be tried, and while witnessing a series of tragical failures we cannot withhold our sympathy and pity from those who experienced and suffered under them. 'It was a time,' as Tocqueville says, ' of youth, enthusiasm, pride, generous and sincere passion, whose memory, spite of its mistakes, will be perpetually cherished.'

CHAPTER III

ADORATION OF THE MAGI

Till the war drum beat no longer, and the battle flags are furled
In the Parliament of Man, the Federation of the World.
TENNYSON, *Locksley Hall.*

Cloots — Olavide — Miranda — Pigott — Vernon — Barlow—Paul Jones—Swan.

THE first anniversary of the fall of the Bastille struck a chord of sympathy throughout the civilised globe.

Schauten nicht alle Völker in jenen drängenden Tagen
Nach der Hauptstadt der Welt, die es schon so lange
     gewesen,
Und jetzt mehr als je den herrlichen Namen verdiente?

So asks the magistrate in Goethe's ' Hermann und Dorothea,' and the eagerness not merely to look towards Paris, but to share in the festival, gave rise to one of the most picturesque episodes of the Revolution.

On Saturday, June 19, 1790, the National Assembly, which had sat from nine in the morning till a quarter to three, reassembled, after dinner, at six, in the Tuileries Riding School—

young Louis XIV. learned horsemanship there —which it had occupied since the previous October, when it followed the King from Versailles to Paris. It usually met at nine, but on Sundays not till eleven, and rose at three or four, an evening sitting being held about every other day. The secretary read or summarised the usual batch of addresses of congratulation and sympathy from all parts of France, and deputations then advanced to the bar. Three of these had their say, and were followed—it being by this time sunset and the candles probably lit—by thirty-six men of the most varied complexions and costumes, Europeans, Asiatics, and Americans ; Africa was unrepresented. At their head was John Baptist Cloots, who read an address in these terms :

The imposing collection of all the flags of the French Empire about to be displayed on July 14 on the Champ de Mars, on the very spot where Julian trampled under foot all prejudices—this civic solemnity will be the festival not merely of the French but of the human race. The trumpet which is sounding the resurrection of a great people has resounded in the four corners of the world, and the songs of gladness of a chorus of twenty-five millions of free men have awakened the peoples entombed in a long slavery. The wisdom of your decrees, the union of the sons of France—this enchanting picture gives great uneasiness to despots, and just hopes to enslaved nations. A grand idea has occurred to us also, and we venture to say it will be the complement to the great national day. A number of foreigners of all countries on the earth ask leave to post themselves within the Champ de Mars, and the cap of liberty which they will raise with transports will be a pledge of the early deliverance of their unhappy fellow-citizens. Roman conquerors liked to draw conquered peoples fastened to their chariots. You, gentlemen, by the most honourable of contrasts, will see in your procession free men whose country is in chains, but whose country will one day be free through the influence of your indomitable courage and your philosophic laws. Our yearnings and homage are the bonds which will fasten us to your triumphant chariots. Never was an embassy more unimpeachable. Our credentials are not written on parchment, but our mission is engraven in ineffaceable characters on the hearts of all men, and, thanks to the framers of the Declaration of Rights, those characters will no longer be unintelligible to tyrants. You have legitimately recognised that sovereignty rests in the people. Now the people are everywhere under the yoke of dictators who, in spite of your principles, style themselves sovereigns. Dictatorship is usurped, sovereignty is inviolable, and the ambassadors of tyrants could not honour your august festival like most of us, whose mission is tacitly acknowledged by our countrymen, oppressed sovereigns. What a lesson for despots! What a consolation for unfortunate peoples, when we teach them that the first nation in Europe, by mustering its banners, has ensured us the signal happiness of France and of both the old and new worlds. We shall wait in respectful silence the result of your deliberations on a petition dictated to us by enthusiasm for universal liberty.

The president that evening was the Baron de

G

Menou, not the Abbé Sieyès, as Carlyle states, and as Cloots had anticipated, for which reason he had inserted the reference to Julian, in order that a priest might be obliged to respond to it. Menou, in a reply which was probably extempore, but may have been a little embellished when committed to writing, said :

Gentlemen, you have proved to-day to the entire universe that the progress made by one nation in philosophy and in the knowledge of the rights of man belongs equally to all other nations. There are epochs in the *fasti* of the world which influence the welfare or misery of all parts of the globe, and France ventures to-day to flatter herself that the example just set by her will be followed by peoples who, appreciating liberty, will teach monarchs that their real greatness consists in commanding free men and in executing the laws, and that they can be happy only by ensuring the happiness of those who have chosen them for their rulers. Yes, gentlemen, France will feel honoured in admitting you to the civic festival the preparations for which have been ordered by the Assembly, but as the price of this benefit she thinks herself entitled to require of you a signal testimony of gratitude. After the august ceremony, return to the localities where you were born ; tell your monarchs, your rulers, whatever name they bear, that if they are anxious to be remembered by the most distant posterity they have but to follow the example of Louis XVI., the restorer of French liberty. The National Assembly invites you to be present at the sitting.

We may fancy what curiosity had been aroused,

and how it increased when a Mahometan priest uttered some sentences—almost unintelligible from his nervousness or ignorance of French—on the happiness of the universe being ensured by the French constitution. The president, felicitously interposing, remarked :

Arabia formerly gave Europe lessons in philosophy. It was she who, having preserved the deposit of the exact sciences, spread through the rest of the world the sublime knowledge of every department of mathematics. To-day France, wishing to pay the debt of Europe, gives you lessons in liberty, and exhorts you to propagate them in your own country.

The deputation were invited, as usual, to the honours of the sitting—that is to say, to remain during the debate ; but Cloots first repaired to a committee room, where he banded in his oration, and dictated a list of the nationalities represented by his motley company. That list, very inaccurately given by the newspapers of the time and by historians who have copied them, I quote from the official minutes :

1. Arabs.	8. Dutch.	15. Brabanters.
2. Chaldeans.	9. Swedes.	16. Liegeois.
3. Prussians.	10. Italians.	17. Avignonais
4. Poles.	11. Spaniards.	18. Genevese.
5. English.	12. Americans.	19. Sardinians.
6. Swiss.	13. Indians.	20. Grisons.
7. Germans.	14. Syrians.	21. Sicilians.

As Cloots left the committee room a diplomatic *attaché* exclaimed, ' I protest against it on behalf of my nation ! '—which nation, says Cloots, was groaning under a rigid despotism. On re-entering the hall, he found a warm discussion going on, raised, or at least hastened, by his deputation. There were proposals to remove the inscriptions and chained figures commemorating on public monuments the subjugation of foreign peoples, and to abolish all titles of nobility. National and class barriers were to disappear. ' Nobody,' said Noailles, son of the Duc de Mouchy, ' talks of Duke Fox, Count Washington, or Marquis Franklin ; they are acknowledged to be great as Charles Fox, George Washington, and Benjamin Franklin.' Lafayette, himself a marquis, supported the proposals. The Abbé Maury vainly pleaded for further consideration, and suggested that the abolition of titles might be a sign of pride, just as Plato—when Antisthenes, trampling on his carpets, exclaimed, ' Thus I trample on the pride of Plato '—retorted, ' But with greater pride, O Antisthenes ! ' The Assembly was in a fervour like that which had produced the surrender of class privileges ten months previously : and, after a debate prolonged till eleven o'clock, it enacted the abolition of all titles and armorial bearings. The vote required the royal sanction, which was not given, so that titles were not really abolished till the constitution of 1791 was adopted; but the newspapers, and doubtless a portion of the public, did not wait for this. Mirabeau was not present that night, though he had been there in the morning, soliciting and obtaining the release of his brother, Mirabeau-Tonneau (his corpulency had earned him the nickname), who had been unwarrantably arrested by the Perpignan municipality. Mirabeau impatiently exclaimed, ' You have puzzled Europe for three days with your Riquetti,' for the ' Moniteur,' which had the best reports of the Assembly, had begun styling him—and styled him till his death—' M. Riquetti l'aîné,' sometimes considerately adding, ' dit Mirabeau.' Lafayette in like manner had become ' M. Motier.' Death alone restored to Mirabeau the name under which he had achieved fame. People shrank from speaking of the illness or death of Riquetti. The foreign ambassadors had claimed exemption—as, indeed, was allowed to foreigners generally—from that erasure of armorial bearings on carriages and house fronts which had furnished sport for Parisian urchins.

But to return to Cloots's deputation. Camille Desmoulins, an eye-witness—for he was a member of another deputation which offered a memorial to be placed in the Versailles Tennis Court—declared with his usual exuberance that since the Tower of Babel no such gathering of peoples had been known. They were plenipotentiaries, he said, for concluding the Abbé de St.-Pierre's universal peace. Others, however, mocked, and alleged that Cloots had dressed up some French valets out of place in oriental robes borrowed from a theatre; but the ' Actes des Apôtres,' usually so eager in ridiculing revolutionary ceremonies, was in this case silent. A pamphleteer alleged that the Englishman had been thrice bankrupt, that the Dutchman was an absconding debtor, the Sicilian a thief, the Spaniard a parricide, the Russian—Cloots, however, did not name Russians—a Siberian brigand, the Italian a scandalous libertine, the Pole a dishonest servant, the German and the Swiss deserters, and the Liegeois a Spa swindler, while the pretended Indians and Americans were Frenchmen born beyond the seas but living and owning property in France. Beaulieu, who at the time in his newspaper had briefly but gravely mentioned the deputation, says in his history of the Revolution, published in 1801 :

It consisted of the Prussian Baron Cloots, a kind of madman, a revolutionary fanatic, who, indeed, assumed the title of Orator of the Human Race, and it was he who spoke; of an Italian named Pio, who in the course of the Revolution was usefully employed in more than one intrigue; of an Armenian, long settled in Paris, and connected as interpreter of foreign languages with the National Library ; of two Englishmen, one of them editor of a London Opposition paper; of some Swiss porters, a negro and other valets dressed up in costumes from old clothes shops, and to whom twelve francs were given. All the newspapers gave an account in respectful terms of the deputation of the human race ; the inventors alone of this masquerade took the liberty of laughing at it.

Beaulieu proceeds to speak of a member of the deputation applying by mistake for his promised twelve francs to Biencourt instead of the Duc de Liancourt. It is likely enough that this was a current story, but Liancourt, Arthur Young's chief French friend, was not the man to stoop to a ridiculous fraud. An anonymous pamphleteer, professedly a foreigner, described the deputation as consisting mostly of outlaws and swindlers, and he asserted that the foreigners in Paris, at a gathering in the Palais Royal gardens, had indignantly repu-diated the sentiments of Cloots's address, for though sympathising with the Revolution they respected their own sovereigns. The death of Franklin, for whom the Assembly had ordered three days' mourning, seems to have suggested the idea of the deputation, the credit of which Cloots must divide with Liancourt, the man who, as Master of the Wardrobe, awoke Louis XVI. to announce the fall of the Bastille. 'Why, it is a revolt,' said Louis. 'Sire,' replied Liancourt, 'it is a revolu-tion.' An ardent advocate of a liberalised monarchy, Liancourt had eventually to flee from France. He travelled in England and America, and returned in 1797, but refused to recognise the Empire and busied himself in agricultural and manufacturing improvements. A liberal peer under the Restoration, he died in 1827 at the age of eighty, and a painful scene occurred at his funeral. Old pupils of his technical school at Chalons insisted on carrying the bier. The Paris police drove them away, and in the scuffle the coffin fell into the mud. This estimable man survived most if not all of the members of the deputation which he had helped to organise.

I have taken some pains to identify these eighteenth century Magi, whom, like other foreigners episodically connected with the Revolution, French historians have scarcely deigned to notice. No list of them was published at the time, which is not surprising, for some might not have wished their sovereigns to hear of their figuring on this self-imposed embassy. Others, even if at first proud of their performance, may have afterwards looked back on it with chagrin. Hence it is impossible to compile a complete list. Cloots's categories show neither alphabetical nor geographical arrangement, and though he uses throughout the plural form we may be certain that some of these nationalities had only a single representative. Others may have had two or three, and the Dutch, Belgians, and Genevese were the most numerous, for recent revolutions, or attempted revolutions, in their countries had made

Paris a place of refuge. Those risings seem at first sight precursors of the French upheaval, yet it is not easy to trace in them any intelligible principle. The Dutch rose simply against the Orange dynasty, the Belgians against the premature reforms of Joseph II.; the Geneva ferment had more of a democratic tinge, being a contest of classes. Cloots, as might be expected, was twitted with the fact that so large a proportion of his band, far from representing their respective nations, were outlaws, and he could only reply that many were voluntary visitors. It would have been well had some of the latter taken Menou's advice and gone home to tell what they had seen. They would thus have escaped evil days. As it was, two of them 'went the way of all revolutionary flesh,' to use George Forster's expressive euphemism for the guillotine; others were imprisoned; and one at least abjured his sympathy with the Revolution.

The antecedents and subsequent fortunes of these men form a curious chapter in psychology, but a word should first be said on their welcomer, Menou. He was second in command at the Tuileries on August 10, 1792, and escorted the royal family to the Assembly. He afterwards served in Vendée, and, failing to put down the Paris rising of Vendémiaire 1795, was superseded by Barras, who chose Bonaparte as his chief subordinate. He went with the expedition to

Egypt, married an Arab girl, and pretended to turn Mahometan, attending the mosque services in oriental dress. He capitulated to the English in 1801, and died at Venice in 1810 at the age of sixty.

Cloots was not only the convener and spokesman of the deputation, but was the most striking, which in no way means the most estimable, personage in it. His paternal ancestors were Dutch, and the great-great-uncle after whom he was named John Baptist was a ship-owner at Amsterdam, but for four generations they had been Prussian barons, possessing an estate at Gnadenthal, a few miles from Cleves. His father, a privy councillor to Frederick the Great, translating the name of his property into French, had dubbed himself Baron du Val-de-Grâce. His mother claimed descent from De Witt, and her brother Cornelis de Pauw, Canon of Xanten near Dusseldorf, was one of the first to apply the wand of scepticism to Greek history. He questioned the very existence of Lycurgus, and depicted the early Greeks as barbarians and pirates. Frederick, on his old companions having died out, sent for Pauw among others as substitutes on trial; but, after hanging on six months at Potsdam, Pauw retired with the pension allowed by Frederick to his 'failures.'

The future 'orateur du genre humain' was born on Midsummer day 1755. As a child he saw French officers taking French leave to his father's hospitality in the Seven Years' War, but conducting themselves so well that the boy acquired a craving for Paris. Thither he was sent after a little schooling at Brussels and Mons, and Lafayette was among his comrades at Plessis college. Destined for the Prussian army, he was next despatched to the Potsdam military school, but regimental tyranny disgusted him, and his father having died in 1767, he was able, with an income of 4,000*l*. a year, to realise his ambition of living in Paris. I must pass rapidly over his acquaintance with Franklin, Rousseau, and Voltaire, his long readings at the King's (now the National) library, his return to Gnadenthal to write his ironical defence of Mahometanism,[1] his return to Paris in the hope of martyrdom, his disappointment at the lack even of notoriety, his anonymous denunciation of himself to the Paris authorities, their obdurate disdain, his plunge into the vortex of horse-racing and gambling, and his anti-religious harangues at the famous Café Procope and at lecture halls. These harangues having at last gained him notoriety, he was called upon in 1784 to choose between silence and the Bastille, whereupon he fled to England. Lord Shelburne, who had met him at the Duc de Liancourt's, had invited him over, and he was enrap-

---

[1] Printed anonymously at Amsterdam in 1779, though with the imprint of London. Cloots, by birth a Catholic, had at Potsdam become a deist.

tured with Burke, with whom he talked late into the night at Beaconsfield. Burke was then in a flame against the power of the crown and the peerage. He sent Cloots to hear David Williams preach, but Unitarianism did not suit a man on the eve of turning atheist. A second visit to Paris was cut short by the scheme of walling-in the city. Though the walls were simply meant to prevent smuggling, Cloots felt that he could not breathe in a fortress, and vowed not to return till Bastille and walls had both disappeared. He next visited an uncle in Holland, printed his eulogium on the French, 'Vœux d'un Gallophil,' was egregiously duped by a sham Albanian Prince Castriotti,[1] and travelled in Italy and Spain—everywhere, according to his own account, denouncing abuses and narrowly escaping arrest.

Enchanted with the news of the French Revolution, he arrived in Paris shortly after the fall of the Bastille; the city walls, however, were still standing, and proved very useful to his Jacobin friends. He went to preach the new gospel in Brittany, and he harangued in public and private in Paris, especially in the saloons of Fanny Beauharnais, Josephine's aunt. He was much elated at the prominence he acquired by his

[1] The divorced Duchess of Kingston is said to have had him for her last lover. He committed suicide in prison while awaiting trial.

deputation, and shortly after the festival of July 14 he altered his name from John Baptist to Anacharsis, on the strength of a fanciful analogy between the Scythian philosopher, to whom the Abbé Barthélemy's romance had drawn attention, and himself, a sojourner in the modern Athens, Paris. He little thought that there was to be a more tangible resemblance—a violent death. He also furnished the following certificate to his colleagues, in order that they might receive the ribbons distributed among those who had taken part in the festival:

Capital of the globe, February 5, year 2.—I certify and make known to all the free men of the earth that ——, a member of the oppressed sovereign of ——, had the honour of attending the Federation of July 14, by virtue of a decree emanating from the august French Senate, June 19, year 1.—Anacharsis Cloots, Orator of the Human Race in the French National Assembly.

It is needless to enter minutely into his revolutionary career, which can be traced by his rhapsodical pamphlets and the equally rhapsodical biography published in 1865 by M. Avenel. He again appeared before the Assembly in December 1791, to read an address in favour of war. He was naturalised, as we have seen, in August 1792, his uncle Pauw sharing the honour from the safe distance of Xanten. Through the influence of his

friend Villette he was elected to the Convention by
the Oise, for which Villette also sat, and he was
likewise elected by the Saône-et-Loire. He was a
candidate, too, at Paris, but was hooted down at
the Jacobin Club, and, in spite of his patriotic gift
of 12,000f., was denounced by Marat as a Prussian spy. He ultimately, however, gained Marat's
friendship, though at the cost of a rupture with
his aristocratic and Girondin acquaintances. In
November 1792 some Dutch and German Moravians,
who contemplated settling in France, asked him to
be their protector. He was an active member of
the Foreign Affairs Committee of the Convention,
and was president for a month of the Jacobin Club.
He voted ' for the death of the tyrant Capet, pending that of the other tyrants,' and wrote to a
Jacobin Club at St. Omer: 'I have had one
monarch's head cut off, but my regicide appetite is
insatiable; my hands, baptised in the blood of
Louis XVI., I shall wash in the blood of the last
European tyrant.' He joined Chaumette in getting
up the religious masquerade and priestly abjurations
which brought even the conformist clergy into contempt. Robespierre steadily disliked him, and in
December 1793, by a torrent of invectives to which
Cloots had not the presence of mind to reply, drove
him from the Jacobins. Expulsion from the
Convention as a foreigner followed, with imprisonment first at the Luxembourg, then at St.-Lazare,

and ultimately at the Conciergerie, the last stage before the guillotine. While at St.-Lazare he wrote, on March 1, 1794, a letter which has found its way to Mr. Alfred Morrison's great collection of autographs, and in which he says:

The aristocratic prisoners with whom I am ignominiously mixed remind me by their invectives of a number of civic acts which reflect honour on me and which I had forgotten. . . . The infected mass of prisoners regard me as a monster. I approve as much as ever the great measure of incarcerating suspects. It is not unknown to the prisoners that I was one of the first instigators of that salutary measure. The wretches would willingly bite my eyes out.

Atheism had now, in Robespierre's view, become ' aristocratic,' and three weeks after writing this letter Cloots was tried, if trial it can be called, with Hébert and seventeen other Jacobins. There was really no evidence against him, but a juror, in reply to his protests of innocence, actually asserted that his idea of a universal republic was a trap for bringing all Europe down on France. Carnot, passing the tumbril on its way to the guillotine, heard him exclaim to the crowd, ' Do not confound me with these scoundrels,' viz. his Hébertist fellow-victims. Vain and flighty, perhaps not altogether sane, Cloots reaped what he had sown. He was probably regretted by none but his mother, who had fruitlessly urged his return home, and his uncle Pauw, who lived till 1799. Cloots anticipated—did he inspire ?—Victor Hugo's idolatry for Paris and his dream of the United States of Europe. Madame Roland gives a repulsive picture of his inviting himself to dinner while the September massacres were going on, defending the butchery amid the silence of the rest of the company, picking out the best morsels, and continuing his obtrusive visits until too plainly shown by being helped last at table that he was unwelcome ; but Madame Roland had strong prejudices, and was probably repelled by his lank ungainly figure and unpleasing countenance as much as by his ferocious sentiments. The good fare which is said to have made him associate with Hébert could scarcely have drawn him to her house, for she was assuredly no epicure. He must have possessed some good qualities, or he would not have been admitted to the friendship of Liancourt. Unmarried, he left an illegitimate child, and she, according to his biographer, had a daughter who became an actress at the Porte St. Martin. In 1795 a kinsman, who had apparently come over in hope of recovering the farm at Crépy-en-Valois, whither Anacharsis intended ultimately to retire, was arrested in Paris.

Spain was represented by Pablo Olavide, Count Pilos, famous for his persecutions and imprisonments. He was born at Lima in 1725, and after the great earthquake of 1746, in which his parents and sister perished, he devoted, as town auditor, the money unclaimed by heirs of the victims to the erection of a church and a theatre. The priests wanted a second church instead of the theatre, and accused him of malversation. He was summoned to Madrid and thrown into prison. A generous citizen, Jauregny, hearing that unless he had change of air he was in danger of death, became bail for him, and he was allowed to go to Leganez, where a rich widow, touched by his misfortunes, offered him her hand. The accusation against him being thereupon withdrawn, he entered into partnership with two merchants, Gigon and Almanza, made an annual visit to Paris, and was introduced by the Spanish ambassador Aranda, a correspondent of Voltaire's, to the Encyclopedists. He visited Madame de Warens and Rousseau at Les Charmettes, for his name is still inscribed there, and he spent a week with Voltaire. Interested in literature, science, and art, Olavide fitted up a theatre in his Madrid house, and translated and performed Voltaire's tragedies and Grétry's operas. The nobility eagerly attended these private entertainments. About 1760, after a visit to Italy, he was appointed governor of Andalusia and director of the Sierra Morena settlement. This mountain pass, on the highway from Madrid to Cordova, had been a prey, since the expulsion of the Moors, to sterility and banditti. It is not clear whether

H

Olavide formed the plan of colonising the region or whether the work had already been commenced, but he was the virtual founder of the settlement. German Swiss formed the bulk of the colonists, but there were some French artisans from Lyons and Beauvais, some survivors of the Guiana expedition, and some Italians, as well as some Catalans. The first settlers were decimated by epidemics, but the colony soon became flourishing. Richard Twiss, in 1773, found cornfields, olives, and vines, with the best country inn in all Spain. Major Dalrymple in 1774 gives an equally favourable picture, but heard some grumbling; and Swinburne, who ‘ never saw a scene more pleasing to the eye,’ likewise listened to a tale of grievances. Still it was evidently, compared with its former condition, an Eden.[1] Unfortunately there was a serpent in it. Romuald, a Bavarian Franciscan, who had the spiritual charge of the community, was ambitious of a Spanish bishopric ; he excited religious animosities against the few Protestants who had slipped in, and he resented the prohibition of the passing bell during an epidemic, as also the annulling of bequests for requiem masses. He even won over Olavide’s wife. The

---

[1] The three towns Carolina, Carlotta, and Guarroman have now 14,000 inhabitants, nearly the number in Olavide’s time ; and there are still some faint traces of foreign origin. Longfellow in 1827 found Carolina, where he passed the night, ‘ the first Spanish village which had anything of rural beauty about it,’ but apparently heard nothing of its history.

Spanish Court, moreover, had undergone a clerical reaction ; Aranda, ousted from the premiership, had been sent back to the Paris Embassy, and a storm was manifestly brewing.

Olavide was summoned to Madrid in November 1775, and by intercepted letters ascertained that he had been denounced to the Inquisition, a tribunal anxious to reassert its recovered influence. In November 1776 he was arrested, his papers were seized, and for two years he was in close confinement. About forty leading personages, whom it was desirable to terrify, were then invited to his trial. Seventy-eight witnesses had deposed against him. He was charged with speaking contemptuously of Catholic rites, with possessing heretical books, with holding the Copernican theory, and other offences. He had clearly talked, with a freedom very dangerous in Spain, of the opposition of the priesthood to intellectual and material progress. He fainted while the long indictment was being read. Several judges are said to have voted for death. He was sentenced to spend eight years in a convent, there to peruse certain pious books ; he was deprived of his property, debarred for life from holding any public post, was never to approach within fifty miles of Madrid or Seville, was never to mount a horse, and was to wear nothing but coarse serge.

Allowed, in the winter of 1780, accompanied by a familiar of the Inquisition, to go to Cauterets to take the waters, he escaped to Toulon, but his old friend Aranda was ordered to demand his extradition. It seems likely that the Spanish Court, while thus humouring the Inquisition, counted on a refusal, and the then rulers of France were not likely to surrender a heretic who had warm friends to plead for him. Olavide, however, warned by Colbert, Bishop of Rodez, fled to Geneva. After a while he obtained permission to live in Paris, frequenting liberal *salons*, and investigating, at first with interest but afterwards with incredulity, the performances of Cagliostro and Mesmer. He naturally welcomed the Revolution, but the September massacres were a great shock to him, and foreboding the worst he retired to a small property purchased by him at Meung. In April 1794, by order of the Committee of Public Safety, soldiers one night surrounded the house and carried him off to prison to Beaugency. Confinement seems to have completed the conversion to Catholicism which the atrocities of the Revolution had begun. Not long after the termination of the Terror, he published ' The Triumph of the Gospel,' a series of letters in which a sceptical man of fashion relates his conversations with a priest and his acceptance of Catholic dogmas. The book has the stamp of sincerity, all the more so as theologians have detected minute heresies in it, but unfortunately it is not autobiographical. It gives the reasoning by which Olavide would have convinced libertine freethinkers ; it does not describe his own transformation. It strongly condemns Voltaire, and justifies sovereigns for not tolerating avowed infidelity, but has no direct allusion to his own persecutions. It speedily ran through eight editions in Spain, and in 1798 Olavide, pensioned and invited to return, settled at Baeza in Granada, where he died in 1803. He presented to the Orleans Hospital in 1800 a small farm, which, on the confiscation of its property in the Revolution, he had bought with the intention of restoring it. His treacherous persecutor is apparently the Romuald Mon y Velarde who became Archbishop of Tarragon in 1804, was translated to Seville in 1816, and died in 1819. Did he and Olavide ever meet again ?

Another Spanish American, General Miranda, who probably figured in the deputation as the representative of America, had almost as many vicissitudes as Olavide, but was far his inferior in moral worth. He was born at Caraccas about 1752, went to Spain at seventeen to complete his education, entered the Spanish army, and fought in the Spanish corps serving under Rochambeau for American Independence. He wished the New World to throw off the Spanish as well as the English yoke, and after being engaged in an unsuccessful plot in Cuba, he wandered over Europe. He paid several visits to England, and was in Russia when the French Revolution broke out, whereupon he hastened to Paris. Through an intimacy with Pétion, he entered the French army. He had mastered the theory of war, but had not had an opportunity of practising it. His stern, imperious manner did not suit the soldiers of the Revolution. In October 1792 he was sent as lieutenant-general to the Army of the North, but was unfortunate in several engagements. He threw the blame on his chief, Dumouriez, at whose instigation, apparently, he was arrested. He was brought to trial at Paris in May 1793, but was triumphantly acquitted. Thomas Paine was one of his witnesses to character —that is, to Republicanism; but Paine afterwards suspected that he had been all along in the pay of Pitt. He retired to a village near Paris to arrange his papers, but his servant was a spy of his enemy, Pache, and in July he was again arrested. He obtained leave to appear before the Convention, and addressed it in his defence, but it declined to interfere, and he was not released till January 1795. One of his staunch friends and admirers was Thomas Christie, from Montrose, who was deputed by the Convention to translate the new Constitution into English, but handed over the task and the pay to his friend George Forster, Captain Cook's naturalist.[1] Miranda, charged with

---

[1] Christie went to Paris for six months at the end of 1789, and probably joined Cloots's deputation.

complicity in the rising of September 1795, was sentenced to transportation, but on the way to the coast he escaped, and he applied to the Directory for a fresh trial. The matter was still pending when, in 1797, again suspected of conspiracy, he was once more placed on the transportation list, whereupon he fled to England. On the Peace of Amiens he ventured to return, but was arrested and sent to Cayenne. In 1806 this restless adventurer concerted a rising in Spanish America, and had to conceal himself till 1810, when he reappeared in his native town, offered his services to the authorities, and obtained some public post. Eventually he was inveigled into the hands of the Spaniards, was sent as a prisoner to Spain, was confined at Carthagena and Cadiz, and died in captivity in 1816. Possessed of undoubted military talents, either he had turned them to little account, or fortune had been studiously froward. His name, however, is inscribed on the Arc de Triomphe at Paris, and his belt was sent by the Venezuela republic to the Paris Exhibition of 1889.

Coming to men of much less note, I may begin with Robert Pigott, a friend of Miranda, and the only Englishman positively known to have accompanied Cloots. Beaulieu, indeed, speaks of two Englishmen, one of them the editor of a London paper, who must have been the man mentioned by the anonymous pamphleteer as thrice bankrupt, but him I cannot identify. Pigott's family had for three centuries been settled at Chetwynd Park, Shropshire. In May 1645 Charles I., on his way from Oxford to Naseby, stayed three nights with Pigott's great-grandfather, whose wife, Anne Dryden, was the poet's cousin, and his bedroom— or alleged bedroom, for the house has undergone many alterations—is still shown. Among the heirlooms, moreover, preserved by the family is a gold ring, in which is set a miniature portrait of Charles, together with a death's head, the date ' January 30, 1648,' and the words ' Martyr Populi.' The ring is said to have been one of four given as mementoes by Charles on the eve of his execution. A fragment of the Royal Oak is also preserved. The Pigotts were staunch Jacobites, and the Pigott who was concerned in the escape from the Tower of Colonel Parker, the conspirator, in 1696, and who immediately afterwards repaired to Paris, was probably one of them. In 1697 Robert Pigott, grandfather of Cloots's Pigott, was High Sheriff of Salop; in 1720 the Old Pretender, on his visiting Rome, gave him his portrait, and in 1729 Pigott was elected M.P. for Huntingdonshire.

Robert, the grandson, in 1770 lost a bet of 500 guineas under very peculiar circumstances.[1] This did not cure him of betting, for he is doubtless the Pigott who, in September 1789, lost 400 guineas on

[1] See page 179.

a bet that a Colonel Ross could not ride a horse from London to York in forty-eight hours. Ross accomplished the feat in forty-five hours.

In 1774 Pigott was High Sheriff, but about two years later—sharing the belief of croakers that England was on the brink of ruin—he disposed of his estates and went to live on the Continent. Chetwynd Park passed into the hands of the Borough family, but the rectory was held till his death in 1811 by Pigott's brother William. His sister, Honor, died near Bristol in 1816, aged eighty-one, and Harriet Pigott, his niece, born at Chetwynd in 1766, died in 1846; Harriet, the clergyman's daughter, embraced Catholicism, had aristocratic royalist friends in Paris, and published several books, including a kind of autobiography.

In 1782, as a letter to Franklin shows, Pigott was at Geneva. Shortly before the French Revolution he was staying in London (as appears from Brissot's memoirs), was a zealous vegetarian— Pythagorean was then the name—and was a disciple of the quack doctor Graham, who was then making a show of Emma Lyon, the future Lady Hamilton. Pigott was evidently just the man to be enraptured with the Revolution and to fraternise with Cloots. When some royalist deputies sent an usher acquainted with English—probably Rose, a man of Scotch extraction—to test the genuineness of the deputation, Pigott answered him ' in good

Miltonic English,' and the usher retreated in confusion. Four months previously Pigott had read or sent to the Assembly a protest against Sieyès' bill to restrict the liberty, or rather the licence, of the press. This protest was read at a meeting of the revolutionary club at Lyons—where Pigott resided when not at Geneva. He printed it, and in an appendix he incidentally condemned John Howard for multiplying prisons, and advocated for prisoners a vegetarian diet, ' that wholesome and natural regimen of bread, water, and vegetables,' in order to soften their hardened natures and render them milder and more tractable. At Lyons he doubtless made Madame Roland's acquaintance ; and in her letters to Bancal she repeatedly mentions him as an ' oddity,' anxious to buy or build a mansion in the south of France, but so fickle that she expected him to be looking about all his life and to build only castles in the air.

Addressing a club at Dijon in 1791, Pigott, inspired by Rousseau, condemned bread as indigestible, especially for children, and he extolled potatoes, lentils, maize, barley, and rice. The Irish, he urged, flourished on potatoes, the Scotch on oatmeal, and the Sardinians on maize, which last would furnish sugar and excellent beer. Cabbage was the chief food of the early Romans, who required no doctors. As a transitional measure bakers should be compelled to use less leaven, to retain part of the bran, and to mix some barley and rye meal with the flour. At the beginning of 1792 Pigott issued a pamphlet advocating the use of caps instead of hats, whether cocked or chimney-pots. Hats, he maintained, were introduced by priests and despots, concealed the face, and were gloomy and monotonous, while to salute by raising the hat was degrading servility. Caps, on the contrary, did not obscure the face, added to its natural dignity, and were susceptible of various shapes and colours. For about six weeks the cap movement was a great success, but a sensible letter against external signs of republicanism, sent by Pétion to the Jacobin Club, put an end to it. When the Châteauvieux insurgents, three months later, entered Paris in triumph in the red caps worn by prisoners at the galleys, their headgear was adopted by the Jacobins, but this does not seem to have had any connection with Pigott's campaign. Pigott, who published in 1792 and 1794 two scurrilous pamphlets on London society, died at Toulouse on July 7, 1794. He left a widow, Antoinette Bontau, probably a Genevese, and had had a child who predeceased him.

The other members of the deputation, as far as they can be traced, were comparatively common-place people. The three Orientals were professors or curators at the King's Library. Chavis, the Arab, furnished Cazotte with the outlines of his

'Eastern Tales,' written in an Italianised French ; no wonder, therefore, that his short speech was unintelligible. The Chaldæan was Behenam, the Syrian Cajadaer Chammas. One of these was doubtless the ' Armenian at the National Library ' who was denounced at the Jacobin Club in October 1792 as an anti-revolutionist. The Pole was probably Zalkind Hourwitz, also of the Library, who on the previous New Year's Day figured on a Jewish deputation to the Paris municipality, and who had promised one-fourth of his salary as a patriotic gift. Cloots, in a quarrel with the Abbé Fauchet, named Hourwitz as an arbitrator. General Wittinghoff may have accompanied him. Trenck was mentioned by some of the newspapers as among Cloots's band, and Madame Tussaud remembered dancing with him on the night of the Federation, but the waxwork lady ' remembered ' much that had never happened, and Trenck at that time was busy pamphleteering in Hungary. He did not reach Paris till the winter of 1792. Madame Tussaud's uncle Curtius, whose original name was Kreutz, may as a Bernese have represented Switzerland, or it may have been Charles Haller, grandson of the great Haller. Charles Haller was certainly in Paris in 1790, full of enthusiasm for the Revolution, and if he joined Cloots he was the last survivor of the band, for he lived till 1854, to the age of eighty-six, having long before abjured democracy and embraced absolutism and Catholicism. Germany was represented by Goy, probably a clerk in Lafarge's tontine office, who published in a Paris newspaper some German verses on the Federation. He may have been accompanied by Prince Charles of Hesse Rothenburg, nephew of the Duke of Hesse, who sat at the Jacobin Club between his tailor and his shoemaker, was implicated in Babeuf's conspiracy, and was 'interned' by the Directory. The Sardinian must have been Cerutti, an ex-Jesuit who helped to write Mirabeau's speeches and delivered a eulogium on him at his death. Cerutti sat in the Assembly of 1791, and died in February 1792. Rotondo, another Sardinian, must likewise have been there. A restless agitator, prominent in the Champ de Mars affray of July 1791, he is last heard of as being arrested for conspiracy in April 1793, at Geneva. As for the Genevese, they were so numerous in Paris that it is impossible to say which of them figured on the deputation. The Sicilian was Pio, who in the previous February had been dismissed from the Neapolitan Legation on account of his sympathy with the Revolution. In March 1790 he solicited employment from the Paris municipality, and was naturalised on the spot. He obtained a post at the passport office, and died in obscurity. The Swede was doubtless a man dismissed from the Swedish Legation in March

1790, for having joined the Paris National Guard. If it was Curmer, he was arrested by the mob, on Louis XVI.'s flight to Varennes, as a suspected accomplice. The Italian was probably Stamati, whose claim to a pension was submitted to the Assembly by Cloots on July 17, 1790. He may have been joined by Dufourny de Villiers, an architect who, on the fall of the Bastille, was deputed to search for secret cells—the populace refusing to believe that there had been only seven prisoners—or by Doldy, a Florentine. The latter was guillotined, and Dufourny, though an ardent Jacobin, narrowly escaped. Holland was represented by Baltasar Abbema, ex-commandant of Amsterdam, the Baron de Capellen, Boetzlaer, Van der Pol, Staphorst, and John Conrad de Kock, all of whom were anti-Orangist refugees. Kock, who in 1792 started a bank, was guillotined with Cloots, and his widow gave birth to the gay, licentious, prolific novelist, Paul de Kock. Liège was represented by Van der Stenne, and Brabant by Balsa, Raet, Dubuisson, and Nyss, afterwards aide-de-camp to Dumouriez and his partner in flight. Some of these Low Country delegates returned home on the overthrow of Austrian and Orange rule, and held office under Napoleon. Of the Avignon, Grison, and Indian deputations nothing positive can be ascertained.

The United States were not represented in

Cloots's deputation. The Americans in Paris evidently did not think that the tone of Cloots's address befitted the representatives of a people who had been assisted by Louis XVI. in gaining their independence, and they preferred to appear by themselves. At the morning sitting of July 10 the president, the Marquis de Bonnay, accordingly announced that 'Paul Jones and other North Americans' had solicited admission to the Champ de Mars, and he was directed to reply that the Assembly would be glad to see them there. Some misunderstanding must, however, have existed, as to this semi-private or perfunctory application, for at the evening sitting a deputation presented itself, consisting, according to the official minutes, of G. Howell, Alexander Contee, N. Harrison, James Swan, Benjamin Jarvis, John Anderson, Joel Barlow, W. H. Vernon, Samuel Blackden, F. L. Taney, Thomas Appleton, and Paul Jones.

The spokesman was Vernon, whose courtly manners, which earned him in his native Newport, Rhode Island, the *sobriquet* of 'Count Vernon,' had evidently recommended him for this distinction, but the address had in all probability been drawn up by Barlow, and it was in these terms :

Struck with admiration at the development and extension of their principles in this happy country, the citizens of the United States of America now in Paris ardently solicit the favour of approaching the sacred altar of liberty, and of testifying to the National Assembly the warm gratitude and profound respect merited by the founders of a great people and the benefactors of the human race. The western star which is shedding its light on distant shores unites its rays with those of the glorious sun which is pouring floods of light on the French Empire, to enlighten, eventually, the universe. The force of truth is irresistible, and the celerity of its progress is beyond all calculation. We believed and we sincerely desired that the blessings of liberty would be one day appreciated ; that the nations would emerge from their lethargy, and would claim the rights of man with a voice which could not be stifled. We believed that the luxury and passion of ruling would lose their illusory charm ; that those chiefs, those kings, those gods of the earth, would renounce the idolatrous distinctions lavished upon them, in order to mingle with their fellow-citizens and rejoice at their happiness. We believed that religion would divest itself of its borrowed terrors, and would reject the murderous arms of intolerance and fanaticism, in order to take up the sceptre of peace. These events are now hastening on in a surprising manner, and we experience an inexpressible and till now unknown delight at finding ourselves in the presence of this venerable assembly of the heroes of humanity, who with so much success have fought in the fields of truth and virtue. May the pleasing emotions of a satisfied conscience and the benedictions of a happy and grateful people be the reward of your generous efforts ! May the patriot king who has so nobly sacrificed with you upon the altar of the country ultimately share the fruits ! The monarch who, in beginning his career, poured his blessings on distant regions was well worthy of exchanging the seductive lustre of arbitrary power for the love and gratitude of his fellow-citizens. (In regenerated France he may well be called King of the French, but in the language of the universe he will be the first King of Men.) We have but one desire: it is that you would kindly grant us the honour of attending the august ceremony which is to ensure forever the happiness of France. (When the French fought and shed their blood with us under the standard of liberty, they taught us to love it) Now that the establishment of the same principles brings us nearer together and tightens our bonds, we can find in our hearts only the pleasing sentiments of brothers and fellow-citizens.) It is at the foot of the same altar where the representatives and citizen soldiers of a vast and powerful empire will pronounce the oath of fidelity to the nation, to the law, and to the King that we shall swear everlasting friendship to the French,— yes, to all Frenchmen faithful to the principles which you have consecrated; for like you we cherish liberty, like you we love peace.

The president replied :—

(It was by helping you to conquer liberty that the French learned to understand and love it) The hands which went to burst your fetters were not made to wear them themselves; but, more fortunate than you, it is our King himself, it is a patriot and citizen king, who has called us to the happiness which we are enjoying,— that happiness which has cost us merely sacrifices, but which you paid for with torrents of blood. Two different paths have led us to the same goal (Courage broke your chains; reason has made ours fall off.) Through you liberty has founded its empire in the west, but in the east also it has innumerable subjects, and its throne now rests on the two worlds.) The National Assembly

I

receives with pleasing satisfaction the fraternal homage rendered by the citizens of the United States of America now present. May they ever call us brothers! (May Americans and French be only one people !) (United in heart, united in principles,) the National Assembly will see them with pleasure united in that national festival which is about to furnish a spectacle hitherto unknown in the universe. The National Assembly offers you the honours of the sitting.

How deceptive, alas, were the expectations thus indulged in ! Scarcely a year had passed before the Marquis de Bonnay was a fugitive. Formerly page to Louis XVI., a ready versifier, popular in fashionable society, he soon took alarm at the serious character assumed by the Revolution, and on the King being brought back a virtual prisoner from Varennes he joined the *émigrés* at Coblenz. He left behind him a sealed packet, not to be opened, according to the label on it, till his death, but the Assembly broke the seals. It proved, however, to contain love letters of 1787, from a married princess, whose name, with more delicacy than might in such times have been expected, was kept secret. The Assembly laughed contemptuously on learning the real nature of these apparently important documents. One is reminded of the love letter which, brought to Cæsar in the Senate, he was forced, in order to dispel suspicions, to hand over to the mockery of an adversary. Bonnay remained in exile till the fall of Napoleon, and was afterwards ambassador at Berlin; but in 1820, when a second time a widower, he dressed up a young secretary in woman's dress and passed him off as his wife. This freak, inexcusable in a septuagenarian, cost him his place, and he died at Paris five years subsequently.

How Bonnay must have sighed over his illusions of 1790! With the exception of Paul Jones, who died before the Terror set in, and who, Gouverneur Morris assures us, all along detested the Revolution, the deputation also must have been rudely disenchanted. Of its twelve members two are so well known that little requires to be said of them, while most of the others are scarcely heard of again. John Paul, who in 1775 added the name of Jones, was the son of a gardener at Kirkbean, Kirkcudbrightshire. After an apprenticeship at Whitehaven he served on board slave ships, next smuggled on his own account, was then a merchant at Tobago, and then a Virginia planter. From 1775 to 1781 he was an American privateer and commodore, and his daring made him the dread of English merchantmen, and of English and Scotch ports. He next joined the French navy, and in 1788 became a Russian admiral, taking part in an engagement against the Turks in the Black Sea; but he quarrelled with Prince Potemkin; the British officers in the Russian navy refused to serve under a man they scorned as a pirate, and, after a fruitless negotiation with Austria he settled in Paris. He enjoyed a pension from the Empress Catherine, to whom in March 1791 he sent, through Grimm, a plan for attacking British India; but she told Grimm that Jones had been allowed two years' leave of absence to escape a trial for rape, that he was a quarrelsome fellow, and that India was too far off to count in a European war. He died in Paris, in neglect and poverty, in 1792, at the age of forty-five, and the Assembly sent a deputation, including a Catholic dignitary, to his funeral. Colonel Samuel Blackden, one of the deputation of 1790, was present at it.

Joel Barlow, born at Reading, Connecticut, in 1755, had, like Paul Jones, played many parts. First, an army chaplain, then a briefless barrister, he went in 1788 to Paris as agent for an Ohio colonisation scheme. The Revolution soon, however, stopped the emigration movement, and Barlow left for London, handing over the agency to William Playfair, brother of the Scotch geologist. Realising subsequently a fortune in France, Barlow returned to America in 1805. In 1811 he was appointed ambassador to France, and was on his way to confer with Napoleon at Wilna when he was attacked with inflammation of the lungs, and died in 1812 near Cracow. He was early a versifier, and in 1808 published an ambitious poem, the 'Columbiad,' in which the discoverer of America has visions of its future destiny.

Of Vernon it is sufficient to say that he was the son of an opulent merchant, a friend of Lafayette, that he was admitted to the French court, and that being once mistaken by the Paris mob for a French aristocrat, he was being dragged to a lamp-post for strangulation, when a French acquaintance came up and convinced the mob of their mistake. He returned to America with a fine collection of paintings, and died at Newport in 1833 at the age of seventy-four.

Alexander Contee, a Baltimore man, reappears in March 1791. He complained to the police that at a gaming house forty-six louis won by him had been snatched from him, and that a roll of a hundred louis had been abstracted, a roll of lead being substituted. It would evidently have been better had he, in accordance with Menou's advice to Cloots's deputation, returned at once to his native country to report what he had seen.

But I now come to James Swan, whose career is much more curious than that of any of his companions. He was born in Fifeshire in 1754, but went in his teens to America, and was clerk to a Boston merchant. Indignant at the inhumanity on board slave ships, he published in 1773 'Dissuasions from the Slave Trade.' The dispute with England aroused his enthusiasm, and he was one of the sham Indians who threw the tea-chests into Boston Harbour. He joined the force raised by

General Joseph Warren, who made him his aide-de-camp, and Swan was by his side when Warren fell at Bunker's Hill. After holding some fiscal offices, he rejoined the army in September 1776 as major of artillery, and distinguished himself in the occupation of the heights of Dorchester, whereby the English fleet, busy in honouring St. Patrick's Day, was obliged to evacuate Boston harbour. He also fitted out a privateer, the 'Boston.' He was next secretary to the War Committee, then a member of the Provincial Congress, then again in the field. In 1784 he wrote on the fisheries, and in 1786 he published 'National Arithmetic,' an argument for a closer federal union.

On the cessation of the War of Independence he had begun trading with France, and he visited that country in 1787, where his old friends, Lafayette and others, assisted him in procuring favourable terms for American commerce. During the dearth of 1789 he sent large consignments of wheat to France. Shortly after this he established a rum distillery at Passy, just outside Paris, rum being a spirit which had hitherto been imported from England. How long he remained in Paris is not clear. He had a partner there, apparently a Frenchman, named Dallard. In 1795 he was back at Boston, where he succoured the distressed French garrisons which had been driven from Martinique and Guadaloupe.

He is said to have been agent to the French government for supplies from foreign countries.

In 1798 he returned to France, where he had a
protracted dispute with a Hamburg firm, Lubbert
& Dumas, with whom he had had dealings since
1792. In 1803, Dallard, Swan & Company acknowledged a debt of 235,000 francs, Lubbert agreeing
that payment should await a settlement of claims
by Swan against the French government. In 1807
an arbitration took place, which resulted in Swan
being adjudged debtor to the amount of 625,000
francs. In that year a law was passed whereby
foreigners not domiciled in France might be imprisoned for debt, and might be arrested pending the
suit if they had not sufficient property in France to
cover the claim, or if they did not give security.
Imprisonment for debt had been abolished since
1793, but this new law was based on the plea that
foreigners were able to leave their creditors in the
lurch. In 1808 Swan was arrested under it. He
had signed bills for 600,000 francs, some of which,
amounting to 58,000 francs, had been discounted by
Paris bankers, Audinet & Slingerland. He disputed
the validity of the arrest, arguing that the law was
not retrospective; but on March 22, 1809, the
Supreme Court confirmed the arrest.

Swan accordingly remained in prison at Ste.-
Pélagie, and nothing more is heard of him until
1816, except legends of his fitting up his room

luxuriously, and of his hiring a house just opposite for his family, who kept their carriage, went to theatres, and gave dinner parties, at which a vacant chair was a reminder of the absent host. A discount must evidently be taken off these stories. In February 1816 Swan petitioned the Chamber of Deputies, publishing his petition, as also a letter to the newspapers in support of it. Hyde de Neuville, in presenting the petition, stated that Swan had been eight years in confinement, and that there had been conflicting decisions as to whether foreigners enjoyed after five years, like natives, the right of release. Piet replied that the case had been decided by a Paris court, an Orleans court, and the Court of Cassation, and that Swan's refusal to give sureties was the cause of his detention. A third speaker, Pasquier, recalled the case of Lord Massareene, who, though possessing 8,000*l.* a year, was obstinate enough to remain twenty years in prison in Paris rather than find sureties. The Chamber refused to interfere, but some months later Hyde introduced a bill entitling male debtors to release at sixty-five years of age, and females at sixty, instead of both having to wait till they were seventy. Gambling and usury, he had been told, he said, by the Ste.-Pélagie authorities, were the principal causes of incarceration.

The bill was taken into consideration (equivalent to the first reading); but in January 1817 the government took the matter out of Hyde's hands by submitting a measure which raised the allowance to imprisoned debtors from their creditors from twenty to forty francs a month, entitled them to release after three years on payment of one third of the claim and giving security for the remainder, and made foreigners, like natives, entitled to release after five years. This last provision was objected to by Piet, who stated that a Chinaman, released after five years, had gone home. Other objections were taken to the bill, which was referred back to the committee, and was not heard of again.

Swan, meanwhile, twice petitioned the Chamber. He cited the case of a Portuguese named Matheus, who, losing 5,000 louis in a gaming-house, was coerced into signing bills for twenty times the amount, and though he offered to pay much more than the real debt, was at Ste.-Pélagie with him for five years, but was then released. His own imprisonment he attributed to usury. He denied the representations of the Paris newspapers that he was very rich, insisting that payment of the 700,000 francs demanded of him would ruin his large family. Lubbert, moreover, he insisted, owed him a larger sum, though the cross-suit had not been tried, and had rejected very fair proposals for a compromise. Swan took his stand upon principle : ' Considerations far superior to interest can alone dictate such conduct, and can make a man prefer to liberty an obstinacy instigated by honour and the goodness of his cause.' He spoke of himself as a sexagenarian whom culpable intrigues had deprived of his liberty, and whom legal quibbles had prevented from recovering it. He was determined that the claims on both sides should be fully investigated, relying for this on the kindness of the sovereign and the wisdom of the Chamber. He reproached Piet, his opponent's counsel, with not having observed in the Chamber the silence maintained by his own advocate, Perignon, and he twitted Lubbert with having had a relative, Timothy Lubbert, convicted of custom-house frauds.

Lubbert wrote a reply, and Swan a rejoinder, after which there is a silence of twelve years. Swan, who in 1817 had published at Boston a pamphlet on 'Agriculture, Manufactures, and Commerce,' issued in 1828 'Observations on the Present State of European Manufactures, Commerce, and Finances.' In 1829 the duel was renewed, Lubbert this time dealing the first blow, and Swan retorting with 'A Word in Reply to the Pamphlet published by M. Lubbert, styling himself of Bordeaux, but a Citizen of Hamburg.'

The Revolution of 1830 set Swan at liberty. On July 28, twenty-two years after he had entered Ste.-Pélagie, a mob assailed the prison in order to release the political captives, while a rising took place inside. Of the two hundred and fifty-seven debtors, one hundred and sixty-eight forced their way out, Swan among them ; sixty-three waited till the next day ; and twenty-six preferred remaining within the walls. On the 31st, nineteen gave themselves up again, and Swan was on his way to do the same,—perhaps, like the prisoner of Chillon, he said,

Even I
Regained my freedom with a sigh,—

when he was struck with apoplexy in the Rue de l'Echiquier. He was carried into a house in that street, and expired there. His will, proved at Boston, mentions a son and three daughters, and he has many descendants in America.

Like Lord Massareene, he had a patriarchal beard, and must have been a conspicuous object in the streets of Paris during his three days of liberty. He had left the prison with his comrades by way of protest, but scorned the idea of foiling his antagonist by unfair play. Fifteen of his old companions were almost immediately re-arrested on the restoration of order, one hundred and one were gradually apprehended, and ninety-five retained their liberty.

Thus the man who had witnessed and exulted over the first Revolution just lived to see and benefit by the second. Had he survived two years longer, he would have profited by a new law, which fixed ten years as the maximum term of imprisonment for foreigners, and accorded release to septuagenarians. It would be interesting to know what sort of life was led by him during his long captivity. He must have made the acquaintance of Béranger and Courier, and must have seen a curious succession of political offenders,—Napoleon's state prisoners, sixty-eight of whom were released in 1814, a crowd of Russian deserters in 1815, and so forth. If his family were in Paris, they doubtless had free access to him. As for his implacable creditor, he was bound to advance twenty francs a month towards Swan's maintenance, so that in twenty-two years he must have paid more than 5,000 francs. This was throwing good money after bad, but in point of pertinacity the two litigants were on a level. *Par nobile fratrum,*—or rather *hostium.*

These magi of the Revolution were assigned a prominent position at the Federation. Cloots, who, like many volunteers, including probably other foreigners, had worked for a week with spade and wheelbarrow in preparing the ground, fancied that the regular ambassadors looked askance on him and his colleagues as interlopers. If, however, they condescended to look at all, it was probably with complacency at their being themselves protected by an awning from the rain which must have soaked the deputation. The ambassadors had been originally invited by the mayor, Bailly, but had declined this as not sufficiently official. Bailly then issued invitations to them in the name of the municipality. Thereupon they consulted the French Foreign Office as to whether the King wished them to go, and were told that he would be glad to see them. 'It seems to be a general opinion,' wrote Lord Gower, 'that our absence might have occasioned serious consequences.' They were accordingly escorted by sixty cavalry from the Papal Nuncio's house. As for the magi, they were blissfully ignorant alike of the future of the Revolution and of their own destinies. They took the celebration seriously, and would have been shocked had they heard the then Bishop Talleyrand, on mounting the altar steps to celebrate mass, whisper to Lafayette, 'Do not make me laugh.' Little did they foresee the greatest disenchantment in human annals, or their enthusiasm would have been turned into anguish. Little did they imagine that two at least of their number would be slaughtered by a liberty degenerating into anarchy, that several others would have experience of French prisons, and that one would end his days in a Spanish dungeon. They doubtless expected that July 14 would be a permanent festival. They did not foresee that in 1791 there would be no celebration, that in 1792 it would fall very flat, and that after some languishing commemorations it would fall into desuetude till 1880. They doubtless expected that the Revolution would retain its cosmopolitan character, that like a religious revolution it would spread by preaching and propaganda, that it would, in fact, as Tocqueville says, be ' a sort of new religion, a religion imperfect it is true, without a God, without a ritual, without a future state, but nevertheless like Islamism flooding the whole earth with its soldiers, apostles, and martyrs.' They did not foresee that the Revolution would be plausibly construed as having converted the comparatively cosmopolite Europe of the eighteenth century, in which a Voltaire was as much at home at London or Berlin as at Paris, into the divided and nationalised Europe of the nineteenth. The rights of man, argues M. Albert Sorel, were transmuted into the rights of nations. There is some truth, but also some paradox, in this view, for Napoleon drafted Germans, Italians, and Netherlanders into his service, and he encountered a really national resistance only in Spain and Russia, the two countries manifestly the least affected by French ideas.

CHAPTER IV

PROPHETESSES AND VIRAGOES

The oyster women locked their fish up,
And trudged the streets to cry ' No Bishop !'
BUTLER, *Hudibras.*

Patriotic Gifts—At Versailles—Louise Chably—Théroigne de Méricourt—Louise Audu—At the Federation—Fishwives' Blackmail—Clubbists—Rose Lacombe—Olympe de Gouges — At the Convention—Pillage—Aspasie Carlemigelli.

WHAT was done and suffered by women is one of the most characteristic chapters of the Revolution. It comprises every degree of fanaticism, heroism, and constancy. We see women in the vanguard of mobs, women at the bar and in the galleries of the Assembly, women in the clubs, women in bread riots, women in the prisons, women on the scaffold. There were furies and heroines, viragoes and victims. The most striking martyrs of the guillotine are two women—Marie Antoinette and Charlotte Corday; the most pathetic are the nuns of Compiègne and the virgins of Verdun; the bravest is Madame Roland, the most craven is Madame Dubarry. Women were the most sanguine at the

outset, the most despairing at the close; the most
admirable, the most repulsive; the most generous, the most callous. We find, moreover, among
women, and this is especially significant, two clear
cases and several presumptive ones of mental de-
rangement.

The first appearance of women on the scene
commands unmixed eulogy. Three weeks after the
fall of the Bastille, fifteen women and six girls,
wives and daughters of Parisian actors and tradesmen, repaired to Versailles to offer their jewellery
and other ornaments towards clearing off the
deficit. A patriotic subscription had been suggested for this purpose twelve months previously
by Olympe de Gouges, of whom we shall hear more
presently. This deputation, however, was not
headed by her but by a Madame Moitte. She had
written an address, but it was read not by herself
—the time had not quite come for female orators—
but by Boucher, in which she spoke of the offerings
of Roman matrons to Camillus, and her address,
or an expansion of it, was afterwards published
under the title of ' The Souls of Roman Matrons in
French Women.' The deputation, she said, would
be ashamed to wear these ornaments when patriotism dictated the sacrifice of them, and they suggested the opening of a voluntary fund. The then
president, Bishop de la Luzerne, made a gallant
acknowledgment. ' You will be more adorned,' he

said, ' by your virtues than by ornaments.' Although several gifts had previously been made, it was this which set the fashion. Jewellery and money flowed in freely. On October 3, a Parisian *demi-mondaine*, as she would now be called, forwarded 1,200 francs in lottery tickets. ' I have a heart for love,' she said ; ' I have amassed money by loving. I offer it to you for the country. May my example be followed by my comrades of all ranks.' The usual ' honourable mention ' was accorded to this offering. The movement led to the so-called ' patriotic contribution,' and it was enacted that every citizen should pay one-fourth of his or her income for 1790, on the distinct understanding that this special impost should not be repeated. Gifts were not, however, invariably actuated by the most laudable motives, and in September 1791 the Assembly refused to accept the property of a widow named Mellican, whose object had been to spite her indigent kindred, for it declared that ' true patriotism cannot exist without love of kin.'

The next appearance of women at Versailles was of a very different character. Seven or eight hundred, mostly of the dregs of the Parisian population, but including some respectable women met on the way and compelled to join, marched thither on October 5, 1789, ostensibly for the purpose of imploring the King and the Assembly to ensure

K

Paris against famine. There were a few hundred men, but the women marched in front in order that the soldiers might shrink from firing on them. There were even men in female dress, for six of these were arrested at Versailles. Some of the women levied blackmail at shops and houses on their way, and the Paris municipality on the 11th decreed silver medals to twelve fishwives who had arrested these freebooters. In December 1793 the same body ordered that these medallists should be assigned seats at all public ceremonies, together with their husbands and children, and that they should bring their knitting. Some among the women boasted at starting that they would bring back the Queen's head on a pike. What they did bring back were the heads of two slaughtered guards, which heads, on passing through Sèvres, they had powdered and curled by a barber, and on the following day two women, escorted by a drummer, went about Paris announcing that the heads were on view in the Palais Royal. How the women invaded the Assembly, how, on the president at length in despair vacating the chair, a woman took his place, how orgies went on that night in order to seduce the soldiers from their allegiance, it is needless to repeat, but I may quote an account, which has escaped the notice of historians, given by Louise or Louison Chably, the only member of the deputation allowed an audience of the King. The daughter of a wood-carver, she was sixteen years of age, be it premised, and sold bouquets in the Palais Royal.

Louise Chably, 16½ years of age, and of interesting appearance, started for Versailles with 600 women on Monday, towards noon, and arrived at 4.30 P.M. The girl Rollin accompanied Louise Chably, also three women. In the courtyard of the National Assembly they met M. Mounier, with four deputies. The girl Rollin taking M. Mounier's arm, and her companions the arms of the deputies, they presented themselves thus at the railings of the palace. There was at first a refusal to open the gates, but Comte d'Estaing, perceiving at their head the President of the National Assembly, immediately bade them enter. The King had gone out hunting, and they awaited his return. M. Mounier presented himself alone, and informed his Majesty that a large number of women had arrived from Paris, five of whom begged to be admitted to the honour of speaking to him. The King said one would be enough. Louise Chably then entered, and throwing herself in tears at his Majesty's feet, she repeated to him that it was very trying for working men, earning mostly only 24 francs a day [week] to lose part of their day at the bakers' doors, at the risk of being crushed in the crowd, and to return without being able to procure bread for themselves and their children, and she begged his Majesty to exert his authority for having Paris supplied with corn and flour. The King was touched, and graciously replied that he had already made sacrifices and retrenchments, that he was ready to make any more that might be necessary for the welfare of his people, that he was about to give the strictest orders for supplies to be sent to Paris. The girl Chably also said that the black cockade occasioned great murmuring, and the King was gracious enough to point out to her that he was not wearing one. M. Necker, by the King's good pleasure, bade her sit down, and she says that refreshment [wine] was given her in a fine gold goblet. His Majesty passed into another room, and Louise Chably went into the palace courtyard to rejoin her companions. They wrongfully accused her of having received money, and wanted to hang her. MM. Mounier and Mirabeau prevented this, and led her back to the King, who at the request of these two gentlemen went out on the balcony to justify the girl in the eyes of her companions, and announced that he had given orders that they should all be taken back to Paris in court carriages. His Majesty asked the girl Chably, who again appeared, what she had hidden in her apron, whether it was a bouquet. 'No, sire,' she ingenuously replied, 'it is my *sabots*.' Reckoning on the King's kindness, she said, 'I shall never be believed, sire, unless the good news which I take to Paris is confirmed in your own handwriting.' His Majesty immediately drew up, in his own handwriting, an order which showed his tender solicitude for his people, and he directed the girl Chably to deliver it to the municipality. Filled with gratitude, she threw herself at the King's knees, and would have kissed his hand. His Majesty said it would be much better to kiss his face. She took advantage of that happy impulse, and said, 'What a happiness for me ! I have kissed our good King at his bidding.' Towards eleven at night Louise Chably and her companions all set out in court carriages, and arrived at the Hôtel de Ville at two in the morning. Officers who were there when they alighted from the carriages, and were already aware of what had passed, asked to see Louise Chably, and the carriage conducted her to M. Bailly. The mayor and representatives of the commune gave her as gracious a reception as she had had at Versailles, and she was conducted home, escorted by soldiers.[1]

What an exciting day for a poor flower-girl! What a tale she must have had to tell her parents and her four brothers and sisters! How she came to be selected as mouthpiece of these hundreds of women is not very clear, either from her own account or from other narratives. It appears that two fishwives were the persons who threatened to strangle her. She evidently mistook some other deputy for Mirabeau, who, though in 1790 he had formed secret relations with the Court, could not in 1789 have ventured to present himself at the palace, and who was, moreover, disliked by Mounier.

Before quitting Versailles let me speak of the woman most prominent in the scene, albeit she had not planned the march. Anne Josèphe Théroigne de Méricourt, commonly known as Mademoiselle de Théroigne, was born at Marcour, in Belgium, in 1762. Her father, Peter Théroigne, or Terwagne, became a widower in 1767, married again in 1773, and died in 1776. Anne, left in charge of a harsh stepmother, was seduced in girlhood, and, unable to remain at Marcour, went to

---

[1] *Journal de la Municipalité*, October 16, 1789, which vouches for this being her own account.

England, and next to Paris. The Duke of Orleans (Egalité) is said to have introduced her to the Prince Regent, afterwards George IV., but it is difficult to distinguish fable from fact. She lived in Paris on an allowance from the Marquis de Persan, and styled herself Madame Campinados. She revisited England in 1787, and was enamoured of the Italian singer, Tenducci, whom she brought to Paris ; and they went together to Italy, living a year at Genoa and mixing in the best society. She sent also for her two brothers and her half-brother. When the States General met she was at Rome, but hurried back to Paris in June 1789. The day before the attack on the Bastille she was in the Palais Royal gardens when Desmoulins summoned the people to arms, and next morning she headed the mob which procured arms from the Invalides. She took part in the attack, and in June 1790 was one of the recipients of swords of honour from the municipality. In October 1789 on horseback, with sword and pistols, she was among the mob who fetched the royal family from Versailles. When the Assembly followed the King to Paris she attended the sittings, held receptions of deputies and journalists, spoke at the clubs, and formed at her own house a club called 'Friends of the Law.' Romme was the chief member, and his pupil, the young Russian Count Strogonoff, was in love with her, but she had bidden farewell to gallantry. Curiously enough, the club blackballed her brother, ostensibly because of his imperfect knowledge of French, but probably because of his shamelessly living at her expense. The club did not ' draw,' and was soon amalgamated with the Cordeliers. Mademoiselle's circumstances became straitened, and in twelve months she pawned jewels to the amount of 7,691 francs. On February 4, 1790, she was one of the *citoyennes* in the gallery, who after the King's visit joined the deputies in swearing to the constitution. She harangued the Cordeliers Club, and Camille Desmoulins enthusiastically compared her to the Queen of Sheba visiting ' the Solomon of districts.' The club, however, while inviting her to address it whenever the spirit moved her, declined to admit female members. Threatened with arrest as one of the Versailles mob, she retired to Belgium in order to revolutionise that country. But in January 1791 the Austrian troops, reinstating the Bishop of Liège in his dominions, captured her and imprisoned her at Küffstein. The Emperor Leopold, however, pitied or was amused with her, and released her in the following November. She returned to Paris with the halo of martyrdom, and figured again in clubs and processions. In April 1792 she formed a female club in the Faubourg St. Antoine, which met thrice a week till the husbands complained to brewer Santerre, who advised her to close it, as men on leaving work liked to find a comfortable home, instead of seeing their wives frequent gatherings where they did not always learn amiability. She took part in the capture of the Tuileries, and was one of the three women to whom the Marseillais presented wreaths. Although she did not herself kill Suleau, the royalist pamphleteer, who had scurrilously abused her, she was 'consenting unto his death,' for she headed the band which forced open the guardhouse where he and three others were detained, and massacred them. Yet she had by this time broken with Robespierre, and had begun to advocate union and moderation, and the September massacres horrified her. On May 15, 1793, on going to the Convention, she found a mob of Jacobin market women, who had collected there to prevent the admission of women with tickets from Girondin deputies. On their stopping her she first remonstrated, and then scolded or even threatened. Thereupon they seized and flogged her. This indignity is generally supposed to have affected her mind; but Forster, the Mayence deputy, speaks of her in July as loquacious, enthusiastic, and sagacious. She had, however, become subject to headaches, and looked pitiable, though traces of beauty yet remained. She could still afford to keep a carriage, and talked of retiring into the country, and of engaging a tutor to complete the deficiencies of her education.

But in the autumn she had to be placed in a lunatic asylum, whence she implored passers-by from the windows for release, and she also sent appealing letters to prominent politicians. Her malady increased and was hopeless. The great lunacy doctor, Esquirol, published an account of her. In 1810 her ravings diminished, but she still refused to wear clothes, and her condition remained most distressing till her death in 1817.[1]

One of Théroigne's fellow-laureates in August 1792 was Louise Reine Audu, styled—perhaps as a pun on her second name—'la Reine des Halles.' This hater of Marie Antoinette, who yet bore the name Reine, is believed to have been prominent in the march to Versailles. She was arrested and detained for some time. She at first denied having been at Versailles at all, but as fifty witnesses had deposed to her presence she was obliged to admit it. She maintained, however, that she was compelled to go by some women who told her that their object was to ask the King and Queen why they had no bread. Witnesses alleged that she had boasted at starting that she would bring back the Queen's head on a pike, but she insisted that her sole weapon was a broom handle. She was also charged with having distributed money, but she asserted that she had only three sous, not being allowed to go home to fetch more money for her

[1] *Life*, by Marcellin Pellet, 1886.

journey. She was likewise accused of attempting to seduce soldiers from their allegiance and of taking part in the slaughter of the guards, but she stated that she was drenched with rain on reaching Versailles, that one of the stablemen of Comte d'Artois (the future Charles X.) allowed her and some companions to sleep in a loft in the Count's stables, that on sallying out, impelled by hunger, she met a wounded guard who gave her all he had, viz. a bag of plums and a decanter of water, and that she was at another spot drinking with some guards when the massacre occurred. Like the rest of the accused, she was released without trial. Nothing more is heard of her till the capture of the Tuileries in which she figured, and she then disappears from the scene.

Women of all ranks, from a princess to seamstresses, took part in preparing the Champ de Mars for the Federation, or Feast of Pikes, on July 14, 1790. The procession formed on the boulevard, between the St. Martin and St. Denis gates, relics of the Paris boundaries under Louis XIV., which are still standing. It started at ten in the morning. Many of the men had had no breakfast, and on the way some began to fall out of the ranks to buy food; but women, among the spectators who lined the windows, hastened to go and offer them refreshments which were paid for in kisses, received with the utmost grace and sometimes returned. The procession, on passing the Assumption Convent, was applauded by the nuns, whereupon an opera singer went forward and addressed them, exhorting them, as they were now free, to leave their cells, each choose an honest National Guard and give birth to charming little National Guards, thus fulfilling the duties of true citizens. The nuns repeated their plaudits, and one of the youngest and prettiest waved him a kiss. Some of the spectators, seated on the oval tiers of earth raised for the occasion, had arrived as early as sunrise. Heavy showers fell during the day, and the effect of these was that women went home without shoes or with shoes encased in mud, their hair in disorder, bareheaded or with handkerchiefs on their heads, escorted by horsemen also bespattered with mud.

A Madame Mouret, claiming descent from Lafontaine and conducting a girls' school, fired with enthusiasm for the festival, had waited a month before on the municipality to suggest a Woman's Federation, but that body evasively referred her to the Assembly. There was also a proposal for a Woman's Banquet to the Federalists, but these plans came to nothing.

About this time and for several years afterwards the market women in Paris and elsewhere presented compliments or bouquets, and expected, or even demanded, *largesse*. This was not

altogether a new practice. St.-Simon tells us that
in 1701, when the Dauphin, Louis XIV.'s son, had
a ten days' illness due to over-feeding on fish, the
Paris fishwives, with whom that insignificant prince
was a favourite, perhaps because he was a good cus-
tomer, sent four of their number to Meudon to inquire for him. He admitted them to his bedside,
and one of them, falling on his neck, kissed him on
both cheeks. The other three ventured only on
kissing his hand. He had them shown over the
palace and supplied with dinner. He dismissed them
with a present of money, and the King also following
suit, they spent it in a *Te Deum* at St. Eustache and
a banquet. The fishwives had been accustomed to
compliment Marie Antoinette on her 'name-day,'
and to receive fifty louis from her, but in 1787, sid-
ing with the banished Parliament, they kept away.
Earl Gower, the English ambassador, need not therefore have been so surprised in April 1791, when
calling at the Foreign Office on the Marquis de
Montmorin, to find fishwives 'taking leave of him
with the most cordial embraces, having already performed that ceremony on most of the *corps diplo-
matique* who had the misfortune of dining there.'
Later in the year Mrs. Damer, the sculptress, was
presented with a bouquet by fishwives, who, it is fair
to say, refused six francs proffered in payment;
but she did not think it safe to decline a kiss from
one of them, and was only thankful that the other

half dozen and the crowd below did not demand the same courtesy. Lady Rivers, passing through Lyons, was advised to wait on the fishwives, who had recently forced the Comtesse d'Artois to turn back on her way to Italy, and she was civilly received. Charles Wollaston and James Frampton had their carriage door opened by fishwives at the last stoppage before Paris, and had to 'pay their footing' to the tune of five francs. The three Mayence deputies, Forster, Lux, and Potocki, on reaching Paris, with very scanty purses, in January 1793, were kissed by the market women, and had to pay twenty-five francs in paper money for the honour; but paper money had been so lavishly issued that it was at about 50 per cent. discount.[1]

The market women's visits were not always so complimentary. In February 1791, exasperated at the departure of the King's aunts for Rome, they resolved that 'Monsieur,' the future Louis XVIII., should not also give them the slip. Followed therefore by a male mob, 6,000 persons in all, they forced their way into the Luxembourg, and sent a deputation of thirty to ask him for a pledge to

[1] It is but fair to say that the fishwives were donors as well as recipients. On August 27, 1791, their two guilds presented to the Assembly for public purposes their corporate plate of the value of about 1,550 francs, hitherto deposited in a church, for as patriots they now needed no guilds, nor any religion but liberty. The president, Victor de Broglie, a future victim of the guillotine, complimented them on thus helping to make all France one family, without class or trade distinctions.

remain at Paris. Monsieur had just returned from a farewell visit to his mistress, Madame de Balbi, to whom he had announced his projected flight. He blandly assured the deputation, however, that he was too much attached to his royal brother to think of quitting him. ' If the King left us,' they asked, ' would you remain ? ' ' For sensible women you seem to me rather stupid,' was the evasive rejoinder, and there was laughter on both sides. Monsieur with difficulty escaped being kissed, and the mob outside insisted on escorting him to the Tuileries. Vainly did he urge that he went at eleven every night to the King's *coucher*. He was forced to comply. Women mounted the box, and the mob, with torches, accompanied him to the Tuileries. The result was that he postponed his departure till June, starting for Belgium the same night that Louis XVI. started for Varennes.

Madame de Staël, though no royal personage, but simply Necker's daughter and the Swedish ambassador's wife, was beset, on attempting to leave Paris on September 2, 1792, by a swarm of women. She had mistakenly started in a grand carriage, thinking that diplomatic pomp would awe the mob, but the women stopped the horses, declaring that she was carrying away the gold of the country and was joining the enemies of France. She had to drive, first to the section, then to the Hôtel de Ville, through a howling mob, and after a

whole day of danger and fasting, she had to post-
pone the journey.

At the sections, at the clubs, at the Convention
itself, women were eager listeners, talkers, or
demonstrationists.

At many of the ' sections ' which met twice a
week, on Sundays and Thursdays, women were
constant attendants, though not apparently entitled
to the two francs per sitting which was frequently
the inducement with male patriots. Indeed towards
the end of the Terror they outnumbered the men.
They do not seem to have been allowed to speak, but
they indulged in comments and exclamations. Thus
at the Indivisibility section on February 7, 1794,
a cock-and-bull story of bullocks and sheep having
been nocturnally driven into La Force prison led
the women to say, ' This is how we are duped.
Meat is supplied to rich prisoners, while we poor
devils get none. What need of all these aristocrats
who are starving Paris? Ought they not all to
have been guillotined long ago ?' Again, in the
ex-church of St. Nicolas des Champs, the meeting-
place of a section, four proud mothers brought their
children, the oldest only four years old, and bade
them recite the Declaration of Rights. There was
a storm of plaudits, the children were kissed all
round, and the mothers were complimented on so
early inculcating the principles of republicanism.

At the Jacobin Club women appear to have had

from an early date a special gallery allotted them, and it was an easy step to form mixed or female clubs in the same building, a partially and later on wholly disused monastery. Accordingly there was formed in 1790 a ' Fraternal Society of patriots of both sexes,' which met twice a week in the library, whereas the Jacobins met in the refectory. When, however, library wished to send a deputation to refectory, the latter stipulated that it should not include women. 'Nothing would please us more,' said the Jacobins, 'than to give the excellent *citoyennes* chosen by you proofs of the special esteem felt by us for their virtues and patriotism, but weighty considerations overrule our inclinations.' The time was not yet ripe for petticoat politicians, for the Cordeliers, as we have seen, refused to enrol Théroigne, and in October 1791 some *citoyennes* who complained before the Assembly of clandestine marriages and baptisms by recusant priests, were curtly told by the president that nature designed women for the solace of men and not to meddle in politics. The guillotine had not yet placed the two sexes on a political equality. This Fraternal Society was probably composed of the occupants of the Jacobin gallery, who occasionally sent down proposals or presented memorials. Thus on Thursday, December 27, 1792, *citoyennes* submitted to the Club an address to the Convention demanding the death of Louis XVI., as

the assassin of their fathers, husbands, and sons,
and all the women in the gallery were invited to
descend and take it to the Convention. There,
however, the 300 women were told that Sunday
was the only day when petitioners were permitted
to harangue at the bar. They applied again next
day, describing themselves as widows and orphans
of the victims of the attack on the Tuileries, but
received the same answer. On the Sunday they
were accompanied by deputations from eighteen
Paris sections and by men said to bear the scars
or wounds of that attack, one man indeed being
carried on a litter, and after some demur they
were allowed to parade round the hall. The presentation of republican emblems to Cooper and
Watt—the son of James Watt—on December 18,
1792, was likewise the act of the women's gallery,
and its acknowledgment a few days afterwards was
probably made to a gathering in the library. The
library club appears to have existed till October
9, 1794, when the *muscadins* or *jeunesse dorée*,
exasperated by the boast of Billaud Varenne at a
meeting of the Jacobin Club a few nights previously, that the lion (Jacobinism) was not dead
but only asleep, and would soon awake and tear its
enemies to pieces, besieged the building, smashed
the windows, and after two hours forced an entrance.
Women were knocked down in the scuffle and
trailed in the mud, and there was a complaint of

L

one emerging with ruffled hair and bleeding head, but quiet citizens, who had apparently gone merely for amusement or from habit, offered their arms to the women in order to protect them. The women, however, were plainly told that they had no business to be in the gallery either of the Club or the Convention, but ought to stay at home. Yet there were women on the other side, if we may believe the Jacobin version given to the Convention next day, that several were captured in the early part of the affray, and that their pockets were filled with stones. Carlyle, placing too much reliance on a history of the Revolution by 'Deux amis de la liberté,' has adopted and even exaggerated an account of women being 'fustigated in a scandalous manner,' which would have been a retaliation in kind for the indignities undergone on an October Sunday of 1791 by women who had been attending a recusant service at the Irish Seminary; but in the heated discussion in the Convention, when both sides gave their accounts of the disturbance, there was no hint of flogging. The four committees ordered the club to be closed, and the Convention endorsed the decision.

A women's club, entitled the Revolutionary Republican Society, was formed in May 1793 by Rose Lacombe. She was one of the three 'heroines' presented with wreaths by the Marseillais for their prowess at the capture of the Tuileries

in August 1792, and she was the leader of the
furies who daily attended the Convention. When
Robespierre stood on his defence on November 10,
1792, the galleries contained 800 women to 200
men. They refused ingress, as we have seen in
Théroigne's case, to non-Jacobins, and with pistols
and poniards in their belts, are said to have
demanded 1,800 heads as the condition of everything going well. Rose Lacombe, born in 1767,
had been an actress in the provinces, and had
come up to Paris in 1789, intending to continue
her profession, but she found the Revolution a
more attractive stage. Her club, according to
Buzot, a Girondin, and therefore prejudiced, consisted of the dregs of Paris. It met originally in
the disused charnel-house of the Cemetery of the
Innocents, but latterly in the library of the
Jacobins, though the Fraternal Society repudiated
any connection with it. Its first sign of life
was the sending of a deputation to the Paris
municipality, with a request that it might share
in the deliberations of the so-called revolutionary
committee; but the municipality, while commend-
ing its patriotic zeal, explained that the committee
was not a club, but a delegation of the forty-eight
sections of Paris. We hear nothing more of the club
till August 26, 1793, when the deputation, headed by
Rose Lacombe, asked the Convention to ' weed out '
aristocrats from all public posts, and to decree a

'levée en masse,' that is, to make the whole population soldiers. On September 18 a second deputation urged the arrest of the wives of *émigrés*,
and the reclamation of loose women in public
reformatories. Its next step brought the club into
trouble. Seven or eight hundred women collected
outside the office of the Committee of Public Safety
to solicit the release of one Salvandy, wrongfully
denounced, as they alleged, by the Marseilles
Republicans. They even had the audacity to ask
permission to inspect all the prisons and ascertain
what persons ought to be released. Bazire went
out into the street to parley with them. He told
them that the first preliminary was to obtain testi-
monials for Salvandy from the Marseilles deputies ;
but they expressed contempt both for the deputies
and for Robespierre, and warned Bazire that they
would make 'a beardless boy like him' repent of his
refusal. They next went to Moise Bayle, and had
a similar scene with him. Bayle, in reporting the
affair to the Convention, stated that the club
meant well, but was led by intriguers and needed
purging. Complaint was also made that at the
unveiling of busts of Marat and Lepelletier in one
of the Paris sections, a woman made a speech
which began promisingly, but ended by advocating
the dissolution of the Convention. Such, moreover,
was her habit at all the sections. This was probably
Citoyenne Lesage, who, as early as December 27,

1792, had presented to the Jacobin Club a
memorial for fresh elections, on the ground that
the Convention had disappointed the patriots.
The women in the gallery, incensed at her
audacity, clamoured for her expulsion, and the
Jacobins, regarding the memorial as a Girondin
manœuvre, debated whether she should be expelled
or merely censured. Trembling in every limb she
awaited her fate, and her trepidation probably
saved her, for the club let her off with a fright.
Rose Lacombe, it was stated in the Convention,
was herself sheltering a Royalist journalist named
Leclerc, and she was suspiciously interesting herself in a young man named Rey, who, with his
uncle, ex-mayor of Toulouse, had been sent under
arrest to Paris as anti-revolutionists. While the
discussion was still going on she arrived in the
gallery, and, pressing forward, claimed a hearing.
This was too much, even for the not too orderly
Convention. Twenty deputies were on their legs,
protesting that an outsider could not take part in
the debates, and such was the uproar that the
president put on his hat, to signify a suspension of
the sitting. On quiet being restored he sharply
rebuked Rose, telling her that by such conduct she
justified her accusers. It was agreed that the Committee of Public Safety, without making any invidious
distinctions, should write to all the clubs to recommend a purge. As for Rose, she threatened to cane

an editor who had erroneously announced that she was under arrest, and on October 7 she reappeared with a deputation at her heels, to remonstrate against having been compared to the Medici queens, to Elizabeth of England, and to Marie Antoinette. The female sex, she admitted, had produced one monster, Charlotte Corday, who, however, had never belonged to the club, but women had for four years been betrayed and assassinated by numberless male monsters. On October 26 a deputation from the club went to the municipality to represent that grocers and other tradesmen were hoarding up goods and pretending that they had none, so that a general searching of shops was expedient. Two days later there was a scuffle between the clubbists and the market women, the latter refusing to be forced into wearing the red cap. Women, by a decree of the previous month, occasioned by some royalist women having snatched off the tricolour cockades of their republican sisters, had been required to wear the cockade on pain of a week's imprisonment for the first offence, and imprisonment till the peace for the second, but the clubbists insisted on the red cap also. The combatants numbered nearly six thousand, the clubbists were defeated, and some of them were flogged. The police had to quell the tumult, and they temporarily closed the club. Next day the aggrieved market women went to the Convention to plead for liberty of dress. Fabre d'Eglantine there-

upon denounced women's clubs as composed of
adventuresses and 'female grenadiers!' The deputation was dismissed with assurances that nobody
should be molested on account of dress, but one of
them, on second thoughts, re-entered the hall to
suggest that all female clubs should be closed. She
gave as a reason for this the fact that a woman,
Marie Antoinette, had caused the misfortunes of
France. Next day Amar, on behalf of the Committee
of General Safety, made a long report, which might
now serve the opponents of woman suffrage. He
argued that women were too excitable and too easily
misled to mix in politics, and that home was their
proper sphere, where they might instil patriotism
into their husbands and children. Charlier urged,
indeed, that women had the same legal right to form
clubs as men, but the Convention was inexorable, and
ordered the closing of all women's clubs. A week
later, the Convention refused to hear the protest of a
female deputation, who thereupon, apparently apprehensive of ignominious ejection, hurriedly withdrew.
From the Paris municipality they encountered a
like rebuff. Going thither at the head no longer of
a club but of the women of the Gravilliers section,
Rose Lacombe and her companions were denounced
by Chaumette as abjuring their ' sex, neglecting
their domestic duties, and taking foreign pay. At
his instance, the municipality declined to receive
any more female deputations. Thus banished from

politics, Rose was reduced to selling candles and bouquets at a lean-to stall by the Luxembourg. Even this refuge failed her when the Directory, taking possession of the Luxembourg, cleared away the stalls, and nothing more is known of her.

The earliest female club orator is believed to have been Olympe (originally Marie) de Gouges. As early as 1788 she advocated a patriotic subscription to clear off the deficit, and in the summer of 1789 she flooded the Assembly with pamphlets. She was born at Montauban in 1748, her mother being a dealer in old clothes, and her father, as she hints, being Lefranc de Pompignan, a judge, poet, and dramatist, who died in 1784. At fifteen she married a retired eating-house keeper, named Aubry. At sixteen she was a widow, with an infant son, and in the possession of a competency. She came up to Paris, led a gay life there, and though unable to read or write, dictated numerous dramas. One of these, directed against negro slavery, was brought out in 1788, but was unsuccessful, and a visit to London, in order to get it performed there, was fruitless. Speaking and pamphleteering henceforth absorbed her, and at times she was really eloquent. She was a fervid humanitarian, and looked confidently forward to a millennium. One of her suggestions was that the Assembly should adjourn for six months, so that the constituents might send up fresh statements of their views. She

wrote to the Convention offering to defend Louis
XVI., and she denounced Marat and Robespierre.
In June 1793 she was arrested for printing a bill in
which she proposed the convening of the electors
throughout France, in order to choose between
monarchy, an indivisible republic, and a federal
republic. The printer had refused to post this on
the walls, her usual mode of publication. She was
arrested, imprisoned five months, and then tried
and executed, her plea of pregnancy being rejected.
'Woman,' she once exclaimed, 'has the right of
mounting the scaffold, she should also have the right
of mounting the tribune.' She little imagined that
the converse was to apply to herself. Her son, an
officer in the army, was cashiered, but petitioned
the Convention for reinstatement, protesting that
he did not share his mother's opinions.

The Convention was more than once coerced or
ousted by women, like the Assembly at Versailles
in October 1789. On May 20, 1793, the mob
which invaded it to the cry of 'the maximum or
death,' included many women, who forced some of
the deputies to yield their seats to them. Fleury,
a Breton deputy, describes how he found a woman
on each side of him, armed with daggers, how they
asked him whether he was a Jacobin, and how on
his replying in the negative they began drawing
their daggers from their belts. Fortunately for
him the president at that moment put the motion

for the maximum, and though the Jacobins alone rose to vote for it, nobody ventured to vote against it, consequently it was declared to be carried. Upon this the deputies retired, while the women remained all night in the hall, ordering a bountiful supper at the public expense, and leaving such traces of their orgies that the necessary cleaning and fumigating delayed next morning's sitting by three hours. In 1795 the 'Megæras,' as the Girondins had styled them, had their last innings. On All Fools' Day, maddened by famine, the women in the galleries of the Convention hissed and interrupted the speakers, broke down the partition, and, joined by a mob of both sexes, invaded the floor. One of them even mounted the tribune, but was immediately ordered to descend by the mob. Prominent among these furies was Aspasie (her real name was Marie Fran-çoise) Carlemigelli, who in her twenty-three years had had strange vicissitudes. Her father, a groom to the Prince de Condé, turned her out of doors when a child, to shift for herself. She entered domestic service, and while still in her teens, her ill-balanced brain necessitated her confinement as a lunatic. The Revolution intensified her insanity. At one time she raves against the Revolution, is arrested, is discharged penniless, the jailers having stolen her purse, and goes about the streets shouting 'Vive le roi!' for the purpose of being guillotined, but her provocations are pitifully or contemptuously ignored. At another time she brings an unfounded accusation of royalism against her unnatural mother, but the denunciation is dismissed. She next raves with the Terrorists, joins in the rising on All Fools' Day, 1795, and on May 20 she is with the mob invading the Convention. She vows that she will kill Boissy d'Anglas, the president, and she tramples on the body of the murdered deputy Féraud. This time she could not be left unnoticed, but instead of being sent to an asylum she was arrested, and after a year's imprisonment was guillotined. The Convention ordered that until quiet was restored women should be excluded from the galleries, and that at no time should they be admitted unless introduced by a citizen.

Provision carts from the country were sometimes stopped by women on their way to the market, and their contents appropriated at a low price or without payment. Disturbances, too, by women outside bakers' shops were for several years of frequent occurrence, but the scarcity was not always confined to bread. On February 24, 1793, a deputation of washerwomen waited on the Convention to complain that soap and starch had become so dear that clean linen would soon be an unattainable luxury, and they demanded the punishment of death against shopkeepers guilty of hoarding. President Dubois-Crancé assured them that the Convention was considering the matter, but admonished them that to go about the streets threatening shopkeepers was the very way to raise prices. Next morning, however, *citoyennes* invaded the grocers' shops and commenced selling goods at what they considered reasonable prices. Some of the money went duly into the till of the helpless tradesmen, but many articles disappeared without payment. When the Convention met in the afternoon it was informed that the bakers' stocks of flour had been examined and a week's supplies found, but it agreed to advance 3,000,000 francs to the municipality to insure six months' supplies. 'It is shameful,' vainly remonstrated some of the deputies, 'to subsidise one town at the expense of the nation.'

The provinces also had their female fanatics. Dijon and Lyons had their women's clubs, and at Besançon we hear of a women's club which asked to be affiliated to the Paris Jacobins. Except at Paris, however, women were mostly content with attending or joining the clubs of the other sex. At Les Sables, in Vendée, *citoyennes* were admitted in February 1792 to membership of the club, though without votes; but even there two boys, six and eight years of age, were admitted at the request of their proud father, the elder child having first delivered a speech in which he said, 'Admit me among you, that I may grow up under your auspices. I promise one day to be a staunch upholder of the constitution.' The boy may have grown up, but the constitution in six months came to a violent end.

We have seen that royalist women in Paris once declared war against the tricolour cockade. In the isle of Yeu, in Vendée, they went further, and effected a counter-revolution. On January 2, 1792, irritated at the increase of taxation, they assembled, deposed the municipality, forced a priest to act as their secretary, and restored the old institutions. The male population tacitly encouraged them. But in a few days seventy-five soldiers arrived, and the women submitted without resistance. Two of them were prosecuted, but were acquitted.[1]

The moral of this chapter may be found—who would have expected it?—in the rebuke or remonstrance addressed by Chaumette on November 17, 1793, to some women, who, wearing the red cap, presented themselves before the Paris municipality. Usually sanguinary and fanatical, but for once speaking the words of truth and soberness, Chaumette said:

How long has it become decent for women to abandon the pious cares of their homes, the cradles of their infants, to appear in public squares, in tribunes, and at the bar of the senate? . . . Imprudent women, who would fain become men, have you not already your fair share? What more do you want? Your despotism is

[1] Chassin, *Guerre en Vendée*, 1892.

the only one which we cannot overturn, because it is the despotism of love, and consequently the work of nature. Remain what you are, and so far from envying us the perils of a stormy life, be content to make us forget those perils in the bosom of our families by resting our eyes on the spectacle of our children made happy by your care.

CHAPTER V

CHILDREN

The fathers have eaten sour grapes, and the children's teeth are set on edge. . . . Ye shall not have occasion any more to use this proverb in Israel.

EZEK. xviii. 2, 3.

Theories on Education—Disorganisation—Offerings and Addresses—Jullien—George Sand's Mother—Toy Guillotines —Descendants of Revolutionists—Intellectual Sterility— Napoleon's last Conscripts.

IN education the Revolution unsettled everything and settled nothing. It aimed at much, it accomplished little. It found village schools deficient in quality rather than in quantity. In few cases had there been buildings erected for the purpose. The schools were mostly held in convents or monasteries, or in cottages bequeathed by charitable persons or belonging to religious orders. The furniture was of the barest description. The schoolmaster was frequently the leader of the choir, the bellringer, beadle, or gravedigger, entirely under the orders of the priest. The school year lasted only seven or eight months. The revolutionary leaders were laudably anxious to render education universal, but their intentions were better than their acts. In April 1792 Condorcet, on behalf of a committee of the Constituent Assembly, submitted a scheme which, though it never came on for discussion, served as a basis for later legislation. He proposed that every village should have its school for both sexes or its separate school for each sex. Every child between the ages of six and ten was to be entitled but not compelled to attend. There was to be a school library and museum, the latter containing natural history and mineralogical specimens, models of machines, and appliances for the rudiments of technical training. There was to be no religious instruction. Every Sunday the master was to give a public lecture on morality or physics, thus enabling ex-scholars to continue learning; and experiments with magnets were to show how apparent miracles could be naturally explained. The town was to have its college for secondary education, and some of these colleges were to be situated on the frontier, thereby promoting international brotherhood, diffusing the principles of liberty and equality, and making the French language universally known. Gymnastics were to be taught, and the exact sciences were partially to supersede the dead languages.

Michel Lepelletier de Saint-Fargeau, who was assassinated just after he had voted for the death of Louis XVI., left behind him a scheme which was warmly approved by Robespierre. All children between five and sixteen were to be lodged, boarded, clothed, and educated by the State. On this being referred, however, to a committee, parental rights found strenuous defenders. Bishop Grégoire urged that peasants required their children's help, that an enforced separation would be seriously detrimental to both, and that reckoning the annual cost at 100 francs a head, 300 millions would have to be added to the budget. Danton, who felicitously described education as the 'bread of reason,' and as next to bread the greatest necessary, replied—' I too am a father, yet my son does not belong to me, but to the republic. It is for it to dictate his duties, so that he may serve it well.' With his usual practical sense, however, Danton agreed to give parents the option, not of keeping their children away from the school, but of boarding and clothing them, and this was adopted, but the measure was never carried out.

If St.-Just, with Robespierre and Couthon, had established the triumvirate the design of which was attributed to them, he would perhaps have attempted to put in operation the scheme of education contained in his manuscript 'Institutions.' While girls would have been left to their mothers, boys from the age of five would have been State property or a State trust. They would not have been allowed to eat meat, or to drink wine, they

M

would have been dressed alike all the year round in cotton fabrics, they would never have been either fondled or chastised, they would have slept on mats, eight hours being the time prescribed, and while permitted physical recreation they would have been debarred games giving scope for pride or declamation. In other words no 'pretending' would have been allowed. From ten to sixteen their training would have been chiefly agricultural and military. In harvest time they would have been lent out to assist farmers, and they would have been drilled in companies.

Thus much for theories. In point of fact, schools almost disappeared or were nearly deserted during the interminable discussions and ephemeral enactments of the Convention. Where schools were still carried on the masters in general threw little zeal into the revolutionary teaching which they were admonished to give. The Catechism, indeed, had given place to the Declaration of the Rights of Man, or to Jacobin parodies of the Lord's Prayer and the Ten Commandments. As a rule, however, schoolmasters evinced no zeal for these innovations, and, if forced to accept them, did not welcome them.

The Revolution had nevertheless a considerable influence on the rising generation, especially in Paris, by inciting or encouraging a premature introduction to public life. Children not merely danced round trees of liberty and recited revolutionary compositions, they speedily followed the example of women in offering patriotic gifts. On September 21, 1789, a boy of thirteen presented to the Assembly six foreign coins, his entire fortune. Next day a girl of Nimes sent an offering, and on October 2 Adolphe de Montfort, a boy of eleven, did likewise. On November 26, 1789, a dancing-school at Lyons, in January and on February 7, 1790, the boys of three Paris colleges, tendered their gifts. In August 1790 the Dijon collegians resolved to forego prizes, and send the money thus saved to the Assembly. Though too young to defend their country they wished to show themselves its sons. 'A fortunate chance,' said the head boy, 'has placed me at the head of my comrades to offer my first possession to my country. May I, when of age, be in the same rank in shedding my blood for it!' The second boy said he had been distanced in ability, but not in love of country. The band struck up *Ça ira*, and there was much enthusiasm. Numbers of Paris schoolboys helped in the digging and shovelling on the Champ de Mars in preparation for the federation of July 14, 1790; and at the ceremony a battalion of boys, with a banner inscribed 'The Hope of the Fatherland,' was posted near the altar.

Schools and colleges had by this time begun sending up addresses to the Assembly. On June

16, 1791, the boys of the parish of Notre Dame, Paris, after having been confirmed, went, escorted by priest and schoolmaster, to the Jacobin Club, and then to the Assembly. Thanks to their military drill they marched with the precision of a regiment. ' Just emerging,' said their spokesman, ' from the ministrations of religion, we have come to offer you the homage of the religious patriotism which animates our minds. What gratitude should this wonderful Revolution inspire in us, who are about to emerge from that happy age where distinctions of honours or fortune are unknown, in us who, thrown into the world, were about to be doomed to the infamy of slavery, and could have risen only by servility ! . . . We are free, we can be virtuous; we thank you for it, fathers of the country, creators of liberty. . . . God and liberty ! such is our device, and it will soon be that of all nations. Till now we have been the children of religion ; if you deign to admit us we shall be the children of the country. We shall be men, we shall be citizens; let us swear to be faithful to the nation, the law, and the king.' The boys all exclaimed, ' We swear it.' President Treilhard kissed them, and, in reply, spoke of the rising generation as imbibing with their mothers' milk patriotism, religion, and virtue. The boys were invited to the honours of the sitting, that is, to seats of honour in the hall; but on a proposal to print the two speeches, Folleville sarcastically remarked that this 'infantine ceremony' had been rehearsed at the Jacobins, and that the report would be incomplete without the speech of the chairman of that club. Uproar followed, and the royalist champion, Abbé (afterwards Cardinal) Maury, exclaimed, 'It is not an infantine, but a puerile ceremony.' Chabrond thereupon denounced the insolence of the Right, at which fifty of them rushed to the floor, threatening an onslaught on the Left. Upon order being restored, Foucault lamented that the boys had been seduced on the day of their confirmation into a sacrilege, but he was shouted down, and the two speeches were ordered to be printed.

On the day of the fall of the Bastille a school-boy of fourteen, Marc Antoine Jullien,[1] scattered in the streets bits of paper on which he had written, 'The overthrow of the Bastille is no great thing, the throne must be overturned.' This precocious youth left school full of honours in 1792. He began reporting the debates of the Assembly for Robespierre's organ, the 'Anti-Federalist.' He joined the Jacobin Club, and made a speech there on January 22, 1792. Robespierre sent him in September 1793 into the provinces to 'enlighten the people, support the clubs, watch enemies, and thwart their plans.' In later years he claimed credit for having, at the risk of his life, denounced Carrier,

[1] See p. 52.

and he told a circumstantial story of his letter to
Robespierre from Lorient being intercepted by
Carrier, of his being arrested immediately on
arriving at Nantes, of his being taken into Carrier's
bedroom, of Carrier drawing the letter from under
his pillow and threatening him with instant death,
and of his cowing that sanguinary monster by
warning him that, as the son of a deputy, his death
would not be unavenged. The truth is, as proved
by his own letters, published in 1893, that no letter
was intercepted, that he had an altercation with
Carrier on reaching Nantes, but remained there
five days, and that on proceeding to Angers he
wrote to Robespierre urging Carrier's recall, on
account, not of his barbarities, but of his feud with
his colleague Tréhouard. Yet Jullien's inex-
haustible loquacity, his ability to deliver four
speeches a day, his celebration of civic baptisms,
his composition at odd moments in three days of a
Jacobin play, render his nine months' mission a
wonderful feat for a lad of eighteen. He lived just
long enough to witness the Revolution of 1848,
priding himself to the last on his intimacy with
Robespierre, and reciting in London drawing-
rooms, with the profuse tears of senility, mediocre
verses on the first Revolution. His son, an actor,
assumed the name of Lockroy, and his grandson,
retaining that name, was Renan's secretary in
Syria, married Victor Hugo's widowed daughter-

in-law, and has been a member of French Cabinets.

Another boy of fourteen, who had run away from home to join the army, but had been rejected as too young, and who was afraid to return to his parents, was introduced to the Jacobin Club on November 17, 1792, and a collection was made for him. His parents were apparently expected to forgive him if he did not reappear penniless.

Girls, as well as boys, processionised and perorated. George Sand's future mother, Sophie Victoire Delaborde, daughter of a bird-seller and ex-billiard keeper, was selected as the prettiest girl in the quarter—this was probably in the autumn of 1789, when she was about fifteen—to present wreaths of flowers at the Hôtel de Ville to Bailly and Lafayette. She was dressed in white, and her powdered hair was decked with roses, other girls in like costume accompanying her. She had to recite some verses by Collot d'Herbois. Lafayette took the wreath, but gallantly placed it on Sophie's brow. 'Lovely child,' said he, 'these flowers are more becoming to you than to me.' A banquet and dancing followed. Sophie, in the crowd, lost her grandmother and her younger sister, and was escorted home at night by patriots. Four years went by, and Sophie as an actress sang a stanza of an anti-revolutionary song, composed by a priest. Next day she was arrested, together with her sister, now a seamstress, and they spent a twelvemonth in various prisons, one of these being the English Austin nunnery, where her future mother-in-law, a countess, was also an inmate. But actress and countess did not then become acquainted with each other. Nor did the youth Maurice Dupin imagine, as he regarded from Passy, by agreement with his mother, the dome of the Pantheon, their common cynosure, that his future wife was under the same roof as his mother. Sophie may have been one of the 500 girls who, in 1790, decked with flowers and ribbons, carried to the Pantheon a picture of the Federation. Nearly two years later forty maidens in white figured in the triumphal procession of the liberated Châteauvieux soldiers, each carrying a fragment of the prisoners' chains.

If we are to believe a story related to the Jacobin Club in February 1794, a girl of thirteen, concealing her sex, joined the army of the North, had two horses killed under her at Hondschoote, and after three years' service applied to the club for assistance. Collot d'Herbois exclaimed that he did not rank her among women, for she had shown all the virile intrepidity of a warrior; the chairman kissed her; 141 francs were immediately subscribed for her, and she was invited to honour the club frequently with her presence. The collection casts a shadow of doubt over the whole business.

Let us turn to another side of the picture. Guillotines became children's toys, with which they operated upon birds, mice, and insects. Even as late as 1801 the Arras authorities had to order the seizure and destruction of these toys, as ' suggesting ideas of death which might render children ferocious and sanguinary.' And at Paris in 1795 a commissary suggested that children should not be allowed to approach the scaffold just after an execution (two murderers had then been guillotined), as this was calculated to impair their proper horror of blood. It is, however, dangerous to generalise from isolated facts, and Taine attached undue importance to Anne Plumptre's talk with a gardener at Nîmes, who told her, ' We never dared to scold our children during part of the Revolution. The self-styled patriots held as a fundamental principle that children should never be punished. This made them so unmanageable, that often when a parent began scolding his child, the latter told him to mind his own business; " We are free, we are equal, we have no father and mother but the Republic. If you are not satisfied I am; you can go elsewhere and find a place more to your liking." Children,' added Miss Plumptre, (this was in 1803), ' are still very impertinent, and it will take years to make them bearable.'

Children born or brought up during the Revolution might have been expected to bear through life the marks of its storm and stress, but whereas the founders of the American republic were, with the exception of Washington, founders of families, none of whom, however, save the Adams's have attained distinction, the majority of the French leaders were celibates or childless husbands. Mirabeau's only legitimate son died at five years old. His 'adoptive,' that is to say his illegitimate son, Lucas de Montigny, became after a fashion his father's biographer, for he published a mass of undigested documents, but he showed no trace of Mirabeau's genius. Mirabeau's brother, 'Barrel Mirabeau,' as he was nicknamed on account of his obesity, was decidedly commonplace. He left three sons, also commonplace, but a grand-daughter, the Comtesse de Martel, has acquired not unmixed fame as the novelist 'Gyp.' Robespierre was unmarried. Marat left no children by his *quasi* wife.

Barère, Barnave, St.-Just, Couthon, Vergniaud, Barras, and Carrier, seem to have been unmarried, or at least childless. Lindet, an excommunicated bishop, had a wife but no children. Hébert, of Père Duchêne notoriety, had a wife, an ex-nun, who was executed shortly after him, but we hear of no issue. Buzot, Madame Roland's 'elective affinity,' had a wife but no children. Billaud Varenne was divorced by his wife, a German ex-Protestant, who after her marriage had continued to enjoy the state pension allowed to converts. On being banished to Cayenne he cohabited with a negress. He had no children. Collot d'Herbois was married, but seems to have been childless. So also was Sergent Marceau, the last survivor of the Revolutionists, for he died in 1847 at the age of ninety-six. Latterly blind and unable to recollect names, he was to the last a great talker, and Mrs. Simpson (*née* Senior) published in 1889 his conversations and papers, too readily accepting his own version of his revolutionary career. Pigott, who, as we have seen, represented England on Cloots's deputation, had lost his only child. Thomas Paine, twice married, had no issue. George Grieve, who hunted Madame Dubarry to death, was unmarried, as also was Arthur, a fanatical member of the Paris Commune.

Roland, Danton, and others, however, left posterity. Madame Roland had an only child, Eudora, who was eight years old when the Revolution broke out. An orphan in 1793, she married in 1799 Léon Champagneux, the son of her guardian, who was the head of Roland's *bureau de l'esprit public*. It was a *mariage de convenance*. She had two daughters, Zelia, who in 1826 married Joseph Chaly, and Malvina, who married Dallemagne, and died of cholera, without issue, in 1832. Zelia had three daughters, but they left no issue. Eudora survived till 1858, thus witnessing three revolutions and living under five sovereigns. After Malvina's death she became a strict Catholic. The Rolands have thus no living descendants. This is also the case with Danton. His first wife bore him two sons, the first in 1790, the second in 1792. She died during his absence in Belgium in the winter of 1792, and on his return a week after the funeral, he is said to have had the body exhumed for a last embrace. Yet in four months he took a second wife, a girl of sixteen, whom his first wife, it is said, aware of Danton's liking for her, had wished to be her successor. The only son by this second marriage died in infancy. The second wife marrying again, the two boys, George and Antoine, were brought up by their maternal grandfather, and seem to have had little communication with their step-mother, for in 1844, when they defended their father against accusations of embezzling public money, they were uncertain whether she was still living. They had a cotton factory at Arcis, their father's native place. Both were unmarried. In 1848 a deputation went to congratulate them on the new Revolution, but Antoine, whose mind must have been already unhinged, took fright at its appearance, and committed suicide. George survived till 1858. One of them had adopted a girl, who appears to have left descendants, for on the unveiling in Paris in 1889 of the statue erected on the site of Danton's house, a so-called representative of the family was present, presumably her son, but the Danton line is really extinct. The tribune had only one sister who grew up. She became a nun, and died of fright in 1814 on the entrance of the allied army. Brissot, whose grandmother became imbecile at sixty, and whose mother was subject late in life to religious monomania, left a widow and children in poverty, to be pensioned by Napoleon. One of his sons, Anacharsis, had a subscription opened for him in 1830. This, or another son, had a son, a painter of little note, who died in July 1892, at the age of seventy-four. Camille Desmoulins left an infant son. Desmoulins wrote from prison to his wife : 'Live for my Horace ; talk to him of me, I shall not kiss him again, and he will not again say *adi, adi* (adieu) ; he will not again call me back on my way to the Convention.' Alas ! Lucile was quickly to follow her husband to the scaffold. Little Horace, whom Robespierre had been accustomed to fondle, was brought up by his maternal grandmother, Madame Duplessis, and by her daughter Adèle, who had refused the hand of Robespierre, though she could not have foreseen that that hand would be imbrued in her brother's blood. Horace took a legal degree in Paris in 1813, accepted a decoration from the Bourbons, and practised as a barrister. In 1817 he emigrated to St. Domingo, married there, and died in 1825, at his father's age of thirty-three, 'the age of the sansculotte Jesus,' as Camille told the revolutionary tribunal when asked his age. Horace left a daughter, Madame Boom, who in 1875 was still living.

Carnot had two sons, Sadi, a promising mathematician who died young, and Hippolyte, not born till 1801, when the Revolution was well over. Hippolyte was in early life a St.-Simonien, became Minister of Education in 1848, returned to public life on the fall of the Empire, and lived just long enough to vote for his son's election to the Presidency of the Republic. Santerre, the brewer visited by Dr. Johnson and Thrale, left a son who, as already mentioned, tried to clear his father from the reproach of silencing Louis XVI. on the scaffold. Fouquier Tinville left a widow and a daughter. Fouché had two sons, who went into exile with him in 1816, and nothing more is heard of them. Tallien had a son and three daughters, one of the latter named Thermidor. Fabre d'Eglantine had a son, who became a naval engineer, and who had two sons; one was a government clerk, respectable and commonplace, the other was prosecuted as a drunken vagabond about 1860. They left no issue. Boissy d'Anglas had a son, and when the Tennis Court at Versailles was restored in 1884 I remember hearing Jules Ferry compliment his grandson on his grandfather's bust having been placed there. Adam Lux, the deputy for Mayence, published a pamphlet proposing a statue of Charlotte Corday, with the device 'greater than Brutus.' He forced himself as it were on the guillotine, though his colleague Forster thought he should have been dismissed as insane, for during a week he had been half-starving himself on a quarter of a pound of bread a day. In a farewell letter to his wife in Germany he said, ' I cannot help you in the education of our daughters, but I leave them as an inheritance my way of thinking and the recollection of my life and death.' The letter was intercepted by his jailors, but the elder daughter, Mary, born in 1789, evidently inherited his way of thinking. Too plain, as she thought, to hope for marriage, she was enchanted with Richter's works, wrote him passionate letters, received kind but discreet answers—Richter had already a wife and children —and disappointed with these she resolved on suicide. Her attempt, however, being frustrated, she waited for her mother's death and her younger sister's marriage, and then in 1814, at her father's age of twenty-six, she threw herself into the Rhine. She was rescued and brought back to consciousness, but persistently thwarted all medical attentions, and succumbed. Kock,[1] a Dutch banker in Paris, and an ardent Revolutionist, was executed after a week's imprisonment on March 24, 1794. On May 21, his widow, in custody in her own house, gave birth to the future novelist, Paul de Kock. She was his second wife, and he was her second

[1] See p. 110.

husband. She was a Swiss, Mary Kirsberger, from Bale, and her first husband had been Claude Perret. She married Kock in December 1789, at the age of twenty-five; their first child did not live. In 1799 she took a third husband, a Frenchman, and an inveterate gambler. Paul, like his father, was a Protestant, but he married a Catholic, and his children—including Henry, also a novelist, were brought up as Catholics. Paul had two half-brothers born before the Revolution—Henry, a Dutch general and statesman, who died in 1845, and John Peter, a French officer, who died in 1858·

On the whole the effect of the Revolution on the children of its celebrities is not very evident, and the great writers of the first half of this century were almost without exception born some years before or after the Revolution. Thus Madame de Staël was thirty when the Revolution broke out. Guizot, whose father fell a victim, was born in 1787. Thiers was not born till 1797, Michelet and Philarète Chasles not till 1798, Alfred de Vigny in 1799, Victor Hugo in 1802, Dumas in 1803, Musset not till 1810. It is true that David, the sculptor, was born in 1789, Lamartine in 1790, Victor Cousin in 1792, and Casimir Delavigne in 1793, but these are not enough to vindicate the years of the Revolution from the reproach of intellectual sterility. The sterility, moreover, of adult talent under the Empire is notorious. Napoleon could not find a single great writer to extol him, and he would fain have drawn Goethe from Weimar to Paris to fill up the void. The Terror was partly responsible for this barrenness. Condorcet, Bailly, André Chénier, and Lavoisier had perished, and who knows how many men whose powers were still latent or immature also fell under the axe? As for the mass of children born in the height of the Revolution, they must have been the conscripts of Napoleon's later campaigns, the physical inferiority of whom is notorious. Had not the Paris lists of 1890–91 an exceptional proportion of conscripts incapacitated, because born during the siege and the Commune?

CHAPTER VI

THE REVOLUTIONARY TRIBUNAL

O unfortunate Frenchmen, what good will you have done in overthrowing Bastilles, if brigands come and dance and slaughter us on their ruins ?
                                                    BEAUMARCHAIS, March 6, 1793.

Sir W. Codrington—General Dillon—J. J. Arthur—Judges and Jurors—No Remorse—Apathy of Spectators—Commiseration dangerous—Stoicism of the Victims—A Chinese Parallel.

WE do not get to understand the Reign of Terror by simply shuddering at it. To understand it we must study the psychology of the jurors of the Revolutionary Tribunal, the temper of the auditors, the frame of mind of those who witnessed the executions. But before entering on this too much neglected field, it is well to comprehend the organisation and working of that dread tribunal, and for this purpose I have selected from the national archives three cases all the more interesting to us inasmuch as the prisoners were Englishmen, though they were dealt with precisely in the same way as natives. One illustrates a dismissal without trial, another a trial and conviction, and the third an execution without trial.

William Codrington, elder son of a Gloucester-shire baronet, was born in 1737. In May 1770 he and a boon companion, Robert Pigott,[1] were dining together at Newmarket, and they agreed to 'run their fathers' lives one against the other' for five hundred guineas. In plain English, each betted that his father would live the longest. This was not an unheard-of wager, for in 1754 Lord Powers-court's son made and won many bets of the same kind. What, however, was unprecedented was that Pigott's father had died in Shropshire a few hours before this bet on his longevity. On learning this Pigott insisted that the wager was null and void, but Codrington had meanwhile trans-ferred his interest in it to Lord March, afterwards the notorious Duke of Queensberry. March went to law, and Lord Mansfield gave judgment in his favour, holding that the impossibility of a contin-gency did not vitiate a bet, provided both parties were unaware at the time of that impossibility. Codrington, one of the *roués* who clustered about the Prince of Wales (afterwards George IV.) was an inveterate gambler, and was not usually so fortunate as in this instance. His father, Sir William (M.P. for Tewkesbury in 1769) extric-ated him from his liabilities, but despairing of his son's reformation, he stipulated the second time that the entail should be cut off and that

[1] See p. 104.

N 2

the estates should descend to his nephew Christopher.[1] William, on a moderate allowance from his father, retired to France about 1780, with his wife Mary Kirke, of Derby, who died at Dinan in 1789. He first lived at Caen, but in 1787 he removed to St. Servan, adjoining St. Malo.   In 1792 his father's death made him a lackland baronet. In September 1793 he was arrested as an 'English lord' by Carrier, his letters and other effects were seized, and he was sent up to Paris charged with being an emissary of the English Government. The St. Malo municipality vainly pleaded for his release. Among his papers, indeed, was a manuscript copy of the long letter which the Marquis de Bouillé, famous for the Nancy mutiny in 1790, addressed to the Assembly in June 1791 on his retreat to Luxemburg after the King's arrest at Varennes. This letter, filling three closely written quarto pages, was a very compromising document, for it justified the King's flight and threatened Paris with annihilation if a hair of his head were touched. Had it been found on a Frenchman, or had Codrington revealed the name of the copyist, the consequences would certainly have been serious. About a score letters in English addressed to Codrington were harmless

[1] Christopher (an Admiral) on his cousin's death claimed the baronetcy, disputing the son's legitimacy, but his grandson obtained a new baronetcy in 1876.

enough, though some of them contained English political gossip or English impressions of French anarchy. Codrington corresponded with the Lowther family—James Lowther talked of paying him a visit—and also with a Forsyth family, one member of which, the Rev. W. Forsyth, was or had lived at Avignon, and bespoke Codrington's interest for a vacant benefice. There was likewise a letter signed 'B. D.,' dated Stratton Street, London, March 19, 1791, beginning 'Dear William,' and retailing the gossip of the day, how so-and-so was married and so-and-so dead, informing him that Christopher, his cousin and supplanter, had gone to Antigua, that his father wondered at his silence, and thought he should not thus have forgotten his family and country. The writer presumed that France was safer for foreign residents than for natives, which implies that Codrington had scouted the idea of molestation. Codrington's second wife, Eleanor Kirke, the niece of his first wife and thirty-seven years his junior, was evidently of inferior station, for a letter dated London, January 18, 1792, from her brother to his 'loving sister,' betrays an unpractised hand and phonetic spelling. Referring to Codrington's infant son,[1] Kirke said, 'Kiss the pretty fellow for me and his grandmother.' At the foot are a few

---

[1] Who must have died in childhood, for William Raimond who succeeded William was not born till 1806.

lines by Kirke's son Charles to his uncle and aunt, the writing almost as good as his father's and the spelling no worse. 'This is the first time,' said the boy, 'I ever wrote to anybody, so I hope you will excuse me. I hope I shall write better next time. From your dutiful nephew, Charles Kirke.' All these letters, inspected by me in the Paris archives, had probably lain untouched since 1794.

Codrington, though advised by his counsel to remain quiet at the Conciergerie, found the place so crowded and unhealthy that he thought he might as well risk the guillotine as die of jail fever. He accordingly pressed for a trial, and some of the English letters having been translated into French, he appeared on November 4, 1793, before the 'Council Chamber' of the Revolutionary Tribunal, a kind of grand jury, and frequently so styled, but consisting of judges, the notorious Coffinhal being on this occasion president. This was the stage preliminary to a trial, and here is the official record of the examination:

Asked his name, age, profession, country, and residence, the accused replied that his name was William Codrington, his age fifty-six, that he lived on his property, that he was a native of London, and at the time of his arrest was living at St. Servan, district of St. Malo, department of Ille-et-Vilaine.

At what date did you leave England and for what

reason?—I left England and came to France about
twelve years ago on account of my health, and since
then I have remained in France and have been at St.
Servan for six years without interruption.

Have you not since then travelled in states subject
to the Empire, or in the German electorates?—No.

Have you not carried on correspondence with England
and Germany?—Yes, I have corresponded with friends
or relatives, but for more than a year I have had no correspondence with Germany—as far as I can remember.
[These last words are added in the margin.]

Have you not since 1789 corresponded with Englishmen living or travelling in France?—No, I have corresponded only with Schmitt, a Dutch merchant, respecting the hiring of a house at St. Servan.[1]

Have you corresponded with Englishmen belonging
to the enemy's armies in France?—No.

Being shown a copy of a letter addressed to the
Constituent Assembly by the traitor Bouillé, we asked
him, it being found among his papers, whether he
knew the handwriting, and why he had procured and
preserved it.—I know it was in my possession; it
is not in my handwriting. I do not know when or
by whom it was written, or how it came among my
papers.

A note at the foot of the copy was read to him, and
it was pointed out to him that this indicated a design
on the part of the sender, a design in which he appears
to have been a sharer or executor. We invited him to

---

[1] A letter signed not Schmitt but Smith, written in English
and to all appearance by an Englishman, offers Codrington the
remaining four years of the lease of an unfurnished house, 'formerly occupied by the well-known R. Bright'—well-known then,
but quite forgotten now.

recall the facts and explain them.   He persisted in his
previous reply.

Why had you correspondents in England informing
you as to the movements of the English ministry and
parliament ? —It was to satisfy my curiosity.

Are you not related to some members of the English
ministry or parliament ?—I have relatives who ten years
ago were in the English ministry.   Lord Lansdowne,
Lord Shelburne, and Charles Fox are related to me, and
are members, the first of the English House of Lords,
and the other two of the House of Commons, but I do
not correspond with them.

What are your means of subsistence in France ?—
The income I derive from England.   While my father
was living my creditors were unable to touch my income.
He died eighteen months ago and made arrangements
protecting my income from my creditors.   My income
is about 75,000 livres in old French money.

Have you corresponded with the enemies of France ?
—No.

Have you seen counsel ?—M. Tronson Ducoudray,
rue des Enfants Rouges.

After hearing the public prosecutor (Fouquier
Tinville), Coffinhal decided, on January 18, 1794,
that there was no proof of dealings with enemies
of the republic, or of intrigues with the Court of
London, and that there was, accordingly, no case ·
for trial, but that under the law declaring that all
British subjects should be detained, he was to
remain in prison.

Considering Codrington's possession of Bouillé's
letter, and the free comments of his correspon-

dents on both French and English politics, it was
not unnatural that in such an atmosphere of suspicion he appeared at first sight deeply implicated,
and he might consider himself as having had a
lucky escape. Six months later, when the Terror
was at its climax, his chances would have been
much smaller, but Coffinhal apparently compre-
hended that an eccentric Englishman's curiosity
might be harmless, though unaccountable. Codrington remained in captivity [1] till December 2,
1794, when he induced a printer (probably his
countryman, John Hurford Stone) to claim his
services as a compositor. On this pretext he was
released. In 1806 he was living at Rennes, and
his grandson now resides in that neighbourhood.
His son, after Waterloo, received 23,000*l.* compen-
sation out of the sum paid by France for indemni-
ties to British subjects.

Count (or in England the Hon.) Arthur Dillon
had no such fortunate escape, one reason being
that his family had for several generations been as
much French as British. His grandfather was not
only an Irish viscount, but a French peer and
general, and was killed at Philipsburg. His great-
uncle, Arthur, also a French general, distinguished
himself in the defence of the Alpine passes, and his

---

[1] See his own account in my *Englishmen in the French Revolution*, 1889.

name figures on the Arc de Triomphe. His uncle, Arthur the second, was successively Bishop of Evreux, Archbishop of Toulouse, and Archbishop of Narbonne, but had little of the ecclesiastic about him. He was a mighty hunter, and on being asked by Louis XV. how he could reprove his clergy for a passion indulged in by himself he replied, 'Hunting is with them an individual, but with me an ancestral failing.' With equal impertinence, when asked by Louis XVI. whether it was true that he was deeply in debt, he answered, 'Sire, I will inquire of my steward, and shall then have the honour of informing your Majesty.' He spent only a week in the year at Narbonne, but was three weeks at Montpellier as President of the States of Languedoc, one of the few provinces which had preserved its powers of self-government. The remainder of the time was passed by this stately aristocrat at Court or on his estate. In 1787 he presided over the assembly of the French clergy, and as their spokesman he complimented Louis XVI. on his recognition of Protestant marriages. His fellow-prelates were very angry, but etiquette precluded their contradicting this laudable expression of tolerance. Though enjoying 800,000 francs a year, he lived so much beyond his means that in June 1789 he became bankrupt for two millions. 'Every one acquainted with his mode of living and his general character for irregularity in his payments,' the Duke of Dorset, English ambassador, wrote to his Government, ' is only surprised that this event did not take place long ago.' In compounding with his creditors he reserved himself a handsome annuity, but this collapse prevented his sitting in the National Assembly. The Revolution cutting down episcopal emoluments to a small sum, and subjecting bishops to popular election, Dillon quitted France and settled in London. On the Concordat being concluded by Napoleon he refused to obey the Pope's command to resign his see, and remained titular archbishop till his death in 1806.

Count Arthur Dillon, his nephew, was born at Braywick, Berkshire, in 1749. In 1765 he entered Dillon's regiment—the regiment brought over from Ireland by his Jacobite ancestor in 1690—as sub-lieutenant, and in 1767 he became colonel, Louis XV. having kept the colonelcy open till there was a Dillon old enough to fill it. In 1769 he married Lucy Rothes, daughter of a Scotch refugee, by whom he had a daughter, Henriette Lucy, born in 1770. Countess Dillon became the mistress of the Prince de Guêmenée, brother of the Cardinal de Rohan, of pearl-necklace notoriety, and during Dillon's campaigns she and her paramour seem to have lived with Archbishop Dillon, who himself was her mother's lover. This edifying *ménage* was reduced from four persons to three in 1782, when the Countess died.

In 1785 Dillon married Anne Laure Girardin, widow of François Alexandre de la Touche Long-pré. She had a cousin destined to be known as the Empress Josephine. By her Dillon had a daughter, Françoise Henriette Laure, born in 1786.

Dillon served in America, was for a time Governor of St. Kitt's and Tobago, and owned a plantation in Tobago. He does not appear to have been popular at Court, for, like his fellow Jacobites FitzJames and Sheldon, the latter his cousin, he was a satellite of the Duke of Orleans. He had, however, pensions amounting to 160,000 francs a year. On the disbandment of the foreign regiments being first talked of, he asked Louis XVI. to recommend his regiment to the King of Spain, but this idea came to nothing. He sympathised with the Revolution, but did not wish the negroes to reap any benefit from it, and in October 1790 he requested the Jacobin Club, then a highly moderate body, to hear his defence of the planters, but it declined. In 1791 he was elected deputy for Martinique, and repeatedly addressed the Assembly on behalf of the planters. He was not re-elected to the Convention in 1792. In the summer of that year he held the chief command under Lafayette in the army of the Ardennes. On Lafayette's flight he was not entrusted with the vacant post, but served under Dumouriez. The latter describes him as brave, straightforward, and ambitious. He seems to have resembled Dumouriez as a political trimmer, and probably, like him, aspired to being a Cromwell or a Monk. According to the English soldier of fortune, Money—this seems a significant name for a soldier of fortune, yet Money was not mercenary, but simply anxious for activity—he was very indolent, and would lie in bed till noon. He was reproached later on with love for the pleasures of the table, and his papers in the archives show that in August 1792 his fellow Irishman, General Keating, sent him from Boulogne some bottles of cognac. On hearing of the storming of the Tuileries on August 10, 1792, he issued a general order denouncing the act and pledging fidelity to the King and the Constitution, but on finding that royalty had disappeared, he recalled the order as due to misconception. The Assembly, however, meanwhile had declared him unworthy of its confidence, for the treason of Dumouriez naturally drew suspicion upon him, and he was summoned to Paris to account for his conduct. He was six weeks in prison, but succeeded in clearing himself, and the vote against him was rescinded. He pressed for a fresh appointment, and this was promised him in February 1793, but when it proved to be a subordinate command under Custine on the Rhine, he refused it as derogatory. He next applied for a passport for Martinique, but could not obtain it. It was dangerous to be a

general unattached in Paris, and Dillon blindly
aggravated his danger by sumptuous dinners, and
by persuading Camille Desmoulins to extol him as
a military genius.   He pressed, moreover, for a
retiring pension in default of a command.   Had he
gone to the Rhine he might have escaped the guillotine.   As it was, on July 11, 1793, he was rearrested,
charged with heading a conspiracy for the release
and accession of the Dauphin, who by the same
decree was separated from his mother and ordered
to be placed in the best defended room in the
Temple.   Desmoulins, who with his wife had dined
with him the previous day, scouted this charge in
the Convention as fabulous, but a deputy, Levas-
seur, moved that Desmoulins should not be allowed
to disgrace himself, and the discussion was thus
stifled.   Desmoulins had to repudiate Dillon in
order to avoid exclusion from the Jacobin Club,
and on his trial, when taxed with his intimacy
with him, he replied, 'What man is there who has
not had his Dillon?'—that is to say, what man is
there who has not been duped?

Dillon paid 180 francs a month (in assignats)
to the gendarme who guarded him.   He was for a
time in solitary confinement at the Madelonnettes,
in a heated cell without air, as he complained in a
letter to Desmoulins, who published a pamphlet
in his defence.   Solitude, however, would have been
better for him, for on being removed to the Lux-

embourg he fell into perilous company. Not satisfied with backgammon and ample potations—according to Beaulieu, a fellow prisoner, he was almost daily intoxicated—he indulged in indiscreet talk with Amans, ostensibly a fellow·captive, but in reality a spy. That talk formed the groundwork of the pretended prison plot, for which on April 9, 1794, four days after the execution of Danton and his associates, Dillon, with nineteen others, was taken from the Luxembourg to the Conciergerie, and examined by Judge Ardouin. This preliminary stage had now become a mere form, so much so that when Westerman, one of Danton's associates, was put on trial without having undergone it, his objection as to the informality was disposed of by his being taken into another room, and after a question or two being brought back to the dock. Whereas Codrington, as we have seen, was seriously interrogated and allowed to clear himself, only two questions were put to Dillon, ' Have you conspired against the unity and indivisibility of the French Republic?' and 'Have you counsel?' On his replying to both questions in the negative, La Fleutrie was assigned him as counsel. The indictment, ostensibly based on the Chamber interrogatory, but really prepared the day before, was in these terms :

By decree of the 16th Ventôse the public prosecutor is directed to proceed without delay against the author and distributor of manuscript pamphlets, circulated in the markets, and which are contrary to the liberty of the French people and to the National Representation [the Convention], and also to search for the authors and agents of the conspiracy formed against the safety of the people and the authors of the distrust inspired in those who bring food and supplies to Paris. . . . Various intrigues and conspiracies devised by Dillon and his accomplices could not escape the vigilance of the representatives of the people, and must be considered a branch of this vast plot.   It is ascertained that since August 10, 1792, Dillon has constantly been conspiring against the Republic.   It was he who, when the tyrant was overthrown by the people, tried to force citizens to swear allegiance to him, and tried to destroy the victory of liberty over despotism.   It was he who, on the recapture of Verdun by the defenders of the country, as an accomplice of the perfidious treasons of Dumouriez, facilitated the egress of the enemies from French territory, and negotiated with the despots whom he might have vanquished and annihilated on the very soil which they had defiled.   Lastly, it is Dillon who is the soul of all the projects of counter-revolution which have been formed, but have failed, since the establishment of the Republic.   The conspirator Ernest Bucher was especially his agent in this project of counter-revolution formed at the moment of recruiting for Vendée, and the object of which was to excite civil war, to massacre the representatives of the people, and to restore royalty by putting little Capet [the Dauphin] on the throne, a project in which were associated the priest Rameau and other conspirators whom flight has snatched from national vengeance.   It was Dillon, also, whom Pitt indicates in the lists found in the commune of Lille as one of his principal agents.[1] The tribunal has also found in the papers of the conspirator O'Moran proofs of his manœuvres and dealings with the enemies of the Republic. Lastly, he brought to a climax the crimes of which he has been guilty by the conspiracy recently planned by him with Simond, deputy, and accomplice of the traitorous Hérault de Séchelles, the wife of Camille, and the turnkey Lombard [Lambert] their agents in the house of detention where they were confined, and whose object was to rescue from the hands of justice the infamous accomplices of Dillon's conspiracy, to massacre the representatives of the people, and to place on the throne the tyrant's son, thus for ever destroying liberty ; a rising which was so devised that last night there were seditious movements and revolts in the Paris prisons, in which 'Vive le roi!' was shouted. According to the above statement the public prosecutor has drawn up the present charge against Arthur Dillon [here follow the other names] for having, in complicity with the infamous Hébert, Cloots *alias* Anacharsis, Ronsin, Vincent, Marnel, Momoro, Camille Desmoulins, Danton, Lacroix, and others already struck down by the sword of the law, conspired against the liberty and safety of the French people, by striving to disturb the State by civil war, by arming citizens against each other and against the exercise of legitimate authority, in pursuance of which, in the course of last Ventôse and of the present month Germinal, the conspirators were to dissolve the

[1] An Englishman's notebook was said to have been picked up at Lille in July 1793, and one of the entries mentioned a 'letter from Dilon,' which possibly referred to one of Dillon's brothers ; but Barère was then in the full swing of his fabrications, and it is impossible to say whether or not the note-book really showed payments by the English Government to foment insurrections in France.

national representation, assassinate its members and patriots, overturn the republican government, seize on the sovereignty of the people, and give a tyrant to the State.

At ten in the morning of April 10, 1794, the trial opened before François Dumas and three other judges. Dumas, it is said, had always a loaded pistol by his side; he was afterwards executed with Robespierre. The prisoners, according to the printed formula, were 'brought to the bar free and unfettered, and so placed as to be heard by the tribunal and by the spectators.' The President told them to sit down, after which he asked their names, ages, professions, residences, and birthplaces. He warned them to listen to what they were about to hear, and ordered the clerk to read the indictment. Eleven witnesses were then examined. But the minutes simply say after each name 'deposes &c.,' the evidence apparently not being taken down.

Next day eighteen witnesses were examined, and on the third day seven more. The only report of the trial is to be found in the 'Bulletin du Tribunal Révolutionnaire,' but it cannot be implicitly trusted. The informer Laflote, it appears, spoke of Dillon as frequently visiting him in prison, as at first inveighing against the vices and abuses of the old monarchy, but as gradually criticising the authorities, and predicting a general overturn,

because party and private animosities and jealousies
were making everything go wrong. On learning
the prosecution of Danton, Dillon, with a melan-
choly air, expressed his fear that the September
massacres were about to be repeated. (This fear
was not unfounded, for ten weeks later Herman,
one of the judges, reported to the Committee of
Public Safety ' that it might, perhaps, be necessary
to purge the prisons.') The two Committees, he
said, were turning France upside down, conster-
nation was depicted on every face in Paris, and all
honest men desired a new order of things, the
deliverance of the Republic from tyrants. He
spoke of a project for people to go to the Revolutionary Tribunal at night under pretence of asking
a pardon for Danton and his associates, in order
to massacre first the judges and then the two Committees. He had 200 men at his disposal, and 400
others who had served in the army under him,
men of courage who could be depended upon.
Chaumette, moreover, had had signals from his
wife that deliverance was at hand. Laflote remarked that money would be required for all this,
and offered to advance 10,000 crowns. Dillon
replied that funds were provided, but if necessary
he would accept the offer. He urged the importance of secrecy. He knew from Simond that the
people were indignant at so many patriots being
guillotined.

So far the informer's story. Dillon, taxed with having written to Madame Desmoulins, said he was under obligations to her, and wrote to her to this effect:—' Virtuous woman, do not lose heart, your affair and mine are in good train, and the guilty will soon be punished and the innocent triumph.' It appears from the interrogatory of Dillon and of the turnkey Lambert, who was also on trial, that Dillon pressed Lambert to deliver the letter, and, on his refusal, stuffed it into his pocket, but Lambert still refusing, Dillon became sensible of the danger, and either tore off his signature or tore up the whole letter. Lucile Desmoulins denied having received any such letter, or the 3,000 francs which Dillon was alleged to have sent or intended sending her. She stated that though Dillon had rendered her services, he had seldom visited her. Dillon denied Laflote's account of his conversation, maintaining that Laflote on that occasion had brought some lemons, made punch, and drank freely. He had simply repeated to Laflote prison rumours that Danton and his associates had refused to answer the judge, declaring that they would not do so unless confronted with members of the Committee of Public Safety. He had also repeated to Laflote what Simond had told him of a project of massacring members of the Convention and the fantical Jacobins, adding that if the September massacres were to be renewed it was the

duty of a courageous man to defend himself and to
insist on a proper trial. In such a case he should
ask to be tried and then to be led against the
enemy and placed in the front of the battle.
Simond, on being interrogated, said that Chaumette
had told him of his wife's visit having inspired him
with hopes. Dillon had spoken to him of the
patriots being hunted down and liberty destroyed,
and of the prospect of great commotions which
might lead the people to another September
massacre ; but Benoit, the governor of the prison,
told him that Dillon had been lunching too liberally, that his brain was a little turned, and that for
some days he had been very depressed. The
public prosecutor summed up the case thus :—' It
is evident that Dillon confesses all the machinations reproached against him. All his efforts are
confined to toning them down and giving far-fetched
explanations. The jury will distinguish the truth
from the tergiversation and falsehood which seek to
envelop themselves in a thousand subterfuges.'

When the Court met on the fourth day, the
president asked the jury whether they had heard
sufficient evidence. They retired to their room to
deliberate, and on their return replied in the affirma-
tive. There were consequently no witnesses for the
defence nor speeches by the prisoners' counsel. The
jury acquitted seven and convicted nineteen, whereupon the latter were sentenced to death. As they

were about to take their seats in the tumbrils—
Dillon and Lucile were not to go in the same tumbril—Lucile said to Dillon : ' I am sorry to be the
cause of your death.'   Dillon, smiling, replied,
' You were merely the pretext,' and began expressing
sympathy for her.   She rejoined, ' Look at me ; do
I look like a woman needing to be consoled ? '
Nodding to him just as though taking leave in a
saloon, and shortly to return again, she took her
place in the cart.

Dillon's elder daughter had been married in
1786 to the Comte de la Tour-du-Pin.   In 1794, as
royalist exiles, they settled at Albany, U.S., where
she took her own farm produce to market.   She
died at Pisa, in 1853, a second time exiled by the
Revolution of 1830, and her son reduced to wood-
carving for a livelihood.   The younger daughter
Fanny was married against her will to General
Bertrand, for Napoleon had lists of heiresses drawn
up and forced them to marry his generals or functionaries.   Fanny at first refused even to see
her allotted bridegroom, but he won her affection,
and she, according to Stendhal, ' was altogether
English and adored her husband.'   The Bertrands
accompanied Napoleon first to Elba and then to
St. Helena, where the fallen Emperor took much
notice of their children, Arthur—named after his
grandfather Dillon—and Hortense.   He gave the
latter coral earrings, and had her ears bored on the

spot. She began to cry on seeing the gimlet, and
Arthur was indignant at pain being inflicted on
her, but she plucked up courage and was complimented by Napoleon on her nerve. Arthur was on
the expedition sent by Louis Philippe in 1840 to
bring back Napoleon's remains to France. Hortense
married Amédée Thayer, a French Senator, of
American extraction, and she lived till December
1890, being probably the last survivor of the persons
who had known Napoleon. She left no issue, and
Dillon's descendants have thus died out, but the
family continued to be represented in France till
1891, when one of his nephews, Charles Henry, son
of his brother Henry and ex-page to Charles X.,
was run over and killed in the streets of Paris, at
the age of eighty-three.

After an acquittal and a conviction comes a
summary execution. On the night of the 9th
Thermidor, year 2—July 27, 1794—the Convention
decreed the outlawry of Robespierre and his fol-
lowers, then in open insurrection at the Hôtel de
Ville. This decree dispensed with any formalities
on their capture. They were simply identified and
then guillotined,—a just retribution for the condemnation of the Dantonists without their being
even brought into the court. Accordingly, on the
10th Thermidor, Robespierre and ten confederates
were executed, on the 11th sixty-eight members of

the Paris Commune were despatched, and on the 12th twelve more members. This last batch included an Englishman, Jean Jacques Arthur. The Christian name might seem to imply admiration for Rousseau by his father, but he was probably baptised Robert, and assumed the Jean Jacques, for in the list of the Commune he is styled Robert Jean Jacques Arthur. He was born in Paris in 1761. His father was a watchmaker, and was apparently inclined to new ideas, for he had his son inoculated at five years of age by an Irish doctor practising in Paris, Ambrose Hosty. Hosty, eight years afterwards, made a claim for 500 francs for the operation, but the result of the suit is not traceable. Arthur himself, who was termed 'l'Anglais,' but who perhaps had never set foot in England, got into litigation in 1781. He made paperhangings, then lately introduced and used only by the rich. Being a new industry, it was exempt from the tyranny of guilds, which would have made it difficult for a foreigner to carry on business. He also made or dealt in cameo fans and other fancy articles. He supplied the Court, for in 1791 the Assembly paid him 13,000 francs as a Crown debt incurred prior to the Revolution. He bought a house on the Boulevard des Italiens, at the corner of the rue Louis-le-Grand, and was about to make it two stories higher when Marshal Richelieu, the notorious *roué* and grand-nephew of the great Car-

dinal, objected that this would intercept the view
of the boulevard enjoyed by him for twenty years
from his Pavillon du Hanovre, at the opposite
corner of the street. The Marshal had a mansion
standing back from the boulevard, but at the north-
west corner of his grounds the Paris municipality
had allowed him to encroach on the rue Louis-le-
Grand by building a kind of summer-house or
retreat. The populace had named this the Pavillon
du Hanovre, in the belief that the money with
which it was erected was a bribe received by the
Marshal for the Convention of Closterseven in 1757,
by which the Duke of Cumberland and 38,000 Han-
overians were allowed to disperse, and Richelieu
had cynically accepted the name, which the building
bears to this day. He not only objected to Arthur's
extra stories, but claimed Arthur's house, alleging
that the vendor, the Duc d'Antin, had had no title,
and under a privilege enjoyed by the nobility, he
had the case transferred from the ordinary tribunals
to the Intendant, in order to ensure indefinite
delay, if not a favourable decision. Whether,
however, by the threat of lampoons or by humbling
himself, or by both, Arthur induced the Marshal
(who died in 1788, at the age of ninety-two), to
desist.

Arthur, on leaving the court with a judgment in
his favour, exclaimed to his opponent, who was
entering his carriage, 'Two stories more, M. le

Maréchal,' and he lost no time in giving his house
' the air of threatening the clouds.' [1]

Like the brewer Santerre, Arthur must have
lost his best customers by the Revolution, which
drove away the wealthy class; but this is scarcely
a proof of public spirit, as he could not have
foreseen that result. He had grants, indeed, from
the Assembly, that he might continue to employ his
400 men, and he supplied the paper for the assignats. He and his partner, Robert, twenty years
his senior, contributed liberally to the patriotic
fund, and in July 1790, at the head of his men,
he helped to prepare the Champ de Mars for
the Federation festival. He was chairman of the
Section des Piques, named after his street, which
had been styled the rue des Piques. Robespierre
inhabited that section, and Duplay, the joiner with
whom he lodged, was a member of the sectional
committee until appointed a juror of the Revolutionary Tribunal. In Robespierre's notebook
Arthur is in a list of 'patriots having more or less
ability,' and Riouffe describes him as 'more
factious and sanguinary than the Héberts and
Chaumettes.' A member of the usurping municipality of August 1792, he took his turn in
mounting guard over the royal family at the Temple,
and on Christmas Day 1792 he was one of the
thirty nominated for that duty. He was a member

[1] Lescure, *Correspondances Secrètes.*

also of the Jacobin Club, and in December 1793
was one of the committee which 'purged' it of
lukewarm patriots. He accused Lamarche of dis-
honesty in the manufacture of assignats, and of
having, while dining with him, advocated national
bankruptcy. This evidence helped to send Lamarche
to the guillotine in company with Madame Roland.[1]
Arthur was to have given evidence also against
Clavière, who committed suicide on the eve of his
trial, and against Danton, had not that trial been
cut short. The Committee of Public Safety sent
him to the Haute-Marne to buy steel for muskets,
and he had only just returned when the Thermidor
crisis arrived. On the night of the memorable 9th
Arthur was one of the committee of eight—only
two were French—who rallied round Robespierre,
and his second partner, René Grenard, was likewise a member of the rebellious municipality.
Grenard was executed on the 11th, but Arthur was
apparently not discovered till the 12th. Here,
from the archives, is the official minute of his
condemnation :

12th Thermidor, public audience of the Revolutionary
Tribunal. On the requisition of the public prosecutor,
the tribunal introduced, free and unfettered, the conspirators, late members of the Commune of Paris, and
others, and declared them guilty of rebellion and outlawed. The decree of the Convention was read to each of
them, the identity of the said conspirators having been

[1] See p. 21.

previously certified by their own confession and also by the declarations of two witnesses for each of them.
. . . Jean Jacques Arthur, paper maker, aged 33, native of Paris, living there, rue des Piques, whose identity has been certified by Laurent and Garnier.

Michel Laurent, 40, sculptor, rue des Piques, and Henri Laurent Garnier, 37, wheelwright, had previously identified another of the twelve prisoners. Laurent, as will be noticed, was a neighbour of Arthur's, and perhaps felt some compunction at thus virtually signing his death-warrant:

All the said members of the General Council of the Seine, convicted of having taken part in the liberticidal and rebellious deliberations of the Commune of Paris during the 9th of the present month and the night of the 9th–10th, while it harboured the traitors decreed to be under arrest by the National Convention : The public prosecutor having been heard, the tribunal orders that the above-named twelve conspirators be immediately handed over to the executioner of criminal judgments, to undergo this day the punishment of death due to the conspirators and traitors to the country outlawed by the National Convention. . . . Orders that the present judgment be carried out in the Place de la Révolution [now Concorde] of this city, and be, by the diligence of the public prosecutor, printed and placarded throughout the Republic. Declares the property of the said twelve conspirators forfeit to the Republic, under the terms of article 2 of the law of March 10, 1793.

Arthur was apparently unmarried. If the confiscation was carried out, let us hope that his father, who according to Lamarche deplored his son's fanaticism, benefited by the law of May 3, 1795, which ordered the restitution of the property of the condemned to their families. A Philiberte Catherine Arthur, who in October 1794 obtained a divorce from a man named Compain, may have been Arthur's sister.

We have seen the Revolutionary Tribunal at work; let us now see how it was constituted. It was composed of four sections, each having four judges, and of sixty jurors, so selected as to represent all parts of France.[1] Both judges and jurors received 18 francs a day, the amount also awarded to members of the Convention, and though 126 francs a week sound ample, the depreciation of assignats made this barely sufficient for maintenance. The president or chief judge of each section had, however, 8,000 francs a year, or about 22 francs a day, as likewise had the public prosecutor, the infamous Fouquier Tinville, who levied blackmail on wealthy prisoners—Dr. Johnson's old friend Madame de Boufflers for instance—as the price not of liberating them but of not bringing

---

[1] On June 10 a decree, introduced without notice, and adopted at once, Couthon and Robespierre refusing even two days' adjournment for its consideration, reduced the number of jurors to 50; 29 of the old jurors were reappointed; 31 were dismissed—evidently the scrupulous or lukewarm—and 21 new men were nominated. What was still more serious, the preliminary examination and defence by counsel were abolished.

them to trial. The four sections met daily, except on Décadi, two to prepare indictments and two to try prisoners, which was done in courts re-christened with bitter irony Salle de la Liberté and Salle de l'Egalité. The juries were ostensibly drawn by lot from among the sixty, seven being necessary for a conviction, and twelve (or after June 10, nine) being usually empannelled, but Fouquier, at least in important cases, made his selection. Not satisfied with this, he even sounded or 'coached' them before the trial, and went stealthily into their room while they were considering their verdict. It was proved at his own trial that in some instances printed forms had not been filled up, that essential documents had not been even opened, that notice of trial had frequently, towards the end of the Terror, not been served on the prisoners till the same morning, and that condemnations had been passed and executed without proper formalities. He pleaded in excuse the press of business or the negligence of subordinates.

Delahante, who with two other assistant revenue farmers was discharged in the middle of the trial resulting in the condemnation of Lavoisier and his colleagues, states that both judges and jurors ridiculed or wilfully misconstrued the answers given by the prisoners to the interrogatories. He also states that in the twenty minutes' interval following the interrogatories, some of the jurors left the court, while others drank or chatted with the spectators seated behind them. It was also alleged on Fouquier Tinville's trial, that some jurors could not read or write, that some were habitually drunk, and that judges on the bench toyed with their mistresses who had seats behind them ; but these allegations do not appear to have been substantiated. It is true that Riouffe, in his memoirs, speaks of jurors being called in to identify the body of Clavière, who had committed suicide, or to pass sentence posthumously, and that he talks of their ' frightful air, their red caps, which seemed to us (the prisoners) stained with our own blood, their coarse language, their barbarous merriment,' but we find from Beugnot that these fiends were not jurors but the witnesses, some of whom actually struck and kicked the corpse. Although, moreover, two judges were executed with Robespierre and twelve of the remaining fourteen, together with seventeen jurors, were prosecuted along with Fouquier, only three judges and six jurors were condemned.

Among the eleven acquitted jurors were Duplay, the host of Robespierre, who must through him have been habitually posted up in the details of the trials, and Souberbielle, a doctor, who lived till 1848, and was to the last, when questioned by Louis Blanc, an admirer of Robespierre. These eleven and the nine acquitted judges were virtually murderers, but the men who tried them thought it fair to make allowance for heated imagination, universal suspicion, and exasperation consequent on famine and invasion. Forty-three jurors were not even prosecuted, yet though some of these had never or scarcely ever acted—David, the artist, placed his pupil Gérard on the list in order that he might escape military service, and Gérard tried only a single case which resulted in an acquittal—the majority of them must have been responsible for condemnation.

There were, for instance, four—Meyère, Sambat, Presselin and Topino-Lebrun—who had the character of refusing to convict against their consciences, and two of them have left documents which give us an insight into the psychology of comparatively scrupulous jurymen. Meyère, whose letters were published by M. Rouvière in 1884, was, though a thorough Jacobin, evidently an honest man. His wife accompanied him to Paris from Laudun, and he scorned to go to theatres or to indulge in dissipations, for he regarded himself as serving his country. He refused the post of judge of the Revolutionary Tribunal in the Gard, because the Paris authorities wished him to remain. He kept up an active correspondence with his local and political friends and with the clubs; he encouraged and even stimulated them to make arrests and send up prisoners to Paris; but he was really apprehensive of a counter-revolution, and therefore convinced of the necessity of the Terror. He writes on December 7, 1793:

The Revolutionary Tribunal goes well; there are resolute men on it; it could not exist except in Paris; elsewhere it would be rather mischievous than useful. Take, for instance, our own department. Do you not clearly see that if a tribunal was established among us, entrusted with the same functions as ours, all our scoundrels would be acquitted? To condemn them, tangible proofs would be necessary, and you know better than I or anybody how, by their artifices, the wretches have made it impossible for us to adduce such proofs. Frequently, therefore, they cannot be reached except by reading and probing their hearts and their inmost moral nature. This is what we do here, and in this way the thing marches. . . . Terror is not enough to quiet the aristocrats; it is necessary, and this is the only way of taming them, to shorten them by a head, at least I think so, and surely you do not know me for a man of blood, far from it.

'Not a man of blood!' Yet Meyère on June 17, 1794, condemned fifty-four unfortunates, including ten women and two poets, André Chénier and Roucher. This fearful batch was never but once exceeded. With equal complacency Meyère mentions the execution of leading Girondins, sometimes without comment, sometimes with distinct approval, and he styles Barnave 'the greatest of wretches, one of the abominable authors of all the horrors in the colonies, especially in St. Domingo.' There are still Frenchmen, indeed, who imagine that the September massacres caused the retreat of the Prussians, and that the guillotine was a necessary auxiliary to the army in repelling the invader. This opinion, assuredly, was largely held at that time, yet we know that the army looked with loathing on the butcheries in Paris.

Topino-Lebrun was on the jury which condemned Danton, and he took notes which were discovered at the Paris Prefecture of Police and published in 1875. He describes himself in these notes as ' a revolutionary juror, a mixture of justice and rigour, whom ardent patriotism makes impassioned when anyone accused of counter-revolution comes before him, like a man in presence of his private enemy, and he ought then to beware of the spirit of prejudice.' His notes show that Desmoulins challenged one of the jury as being an avowed enemy, but ineffectually. They do not tell us, what is however known from other sources, that on the fourth day, before the court opened, Topino, Sambat, and Trinchard called on the artist David to consult him, as they did not think Danton was guilty. David rated them as cowards and persuaded them to condemn him. Fouquier and Judge Hermann, moreover, went into the jury room to urge them to declare that they had had sufficient evidence.

Topino was himself guillotined for participation in the infernal machine plot against Bonaparte in 1801, but there is no reason to suppose that he had suffered remorse—a feeling quite unknown among the Terrorists. They evidently persuaded themselves that having acted in good faith they had no cause for self-reproach, and Carnot, who, though he had never formally pronounced sentence of death, had signed multitudes of decrees which were virtually death-warrants, even convinced himself that he had had no share in the atrocities, so that only three years afterwards, with the composure of an easy conscience, he could stigmatise the very government of which he had been a member as 'a tyranny which in the name of liberty erected anarchy, debauchery, delation, and ferocity into civic virtues.'

There were, however, jurymen of the most sanguinary stamp, and these were evidently selected by Fouquier whenever the eminence of the accused or the flimsiness of the evidence would otherwise have made conviction uncertain. Thanks to this precaution Fouquier could always overnight, or on the morning of the trial, order the requisite number of tumbrils. The worst of these men were Leroy, Antonelle and Vilate, two of whom, it is consoling to think, met with retribution. Leroy, who had altered his name to 'Dix Août' (the date of the capture of the Tuileries) was notoriously deaf, yet always convicted. Antonelle cut short the defence of Brissot and his associates by indecently exclaiming that he had heard enough. The judge was bound to disregard this exclamation and to direct the jury to withdraw and deliberate. This sanguinary marquis, then aged forty-seven, lived to be a septuagenarian royalist. Vilate, an ex-priest who had dubbed himself Sempronius Gracchus, scarcely ever even withdrew with his fellow jurors, but paced up and down the court. On one occasion, impatient at their tardiness, he said to a bystander, 'I am convinced that the accused are doubly guilty of conspiracy, for I feel that they are conspiring against my stomach.'

> And prisoners hang, that jurymen may dine.

He is also alleged to have said that 'in a revolution all who appear before the tribunal ought to be condemned,' and that were he public prosecutor he would have the prisoners bled before being brought into court, so that they might not show so much firmness.[1] Retribution befell him, for he was executed. It is likewise asserted that some jurymen on entering the court would satirically say that they were going 'to order file-firing.'

It might be imagined that these daily butcheries threw a gloom over Paris, especially when, in the last six weeks of the Terror, 1,361 persons were immolated, whereas in the previous fourteen months

---

[1] If bleeding was suggested on one side, the Princess of Monaco *rouged* her face before going to execution, in order that, if she turned pale, it might not be seen. Bailly shivered, but was anxious to have it known that this was from cold, not from fear.

there had been only 1,256. But all the ordinary amusements of the city went on as usual, and there was even in 1793 the usual exhibition of pictures, the Salon, at the Louvre, though portraits of deputies had supplanted those of aristocrats. People driving to the theatres who met the tumbrils on their way to the cemetery merely lowered the blinds of their carriages. The newspapers, strange as it may seem, did not as a rule give even the names of the condemned; the 'Moniteur,' though the best record of the trials, has many omissions. The list of guillotined was frequently crowded out by what was considered more important news. As for the Jacobin prints, their tone may be judged from the 'Rougyff,' a title which was an anagram of Guffroy, the editor and a member of the Convention. It habitually speaks of prisoners as *gibier de guillotine*, and it contains paragraphs like this :

Dame Guillotine tried her razor yesterday (July 19, 1793) on an *émigré*. After showing the whole length of aristocratic impudence while promenading in Sanson's carriage, on mounting the scaffold he displayed the whole extent of loyalist fanaticism, and defying the nation and justice, he exclaimed five or six times, ' Vive le roi ! ' While being arranged on this shaving dish, he again cried, ' Vive la crac ! ' . . . Quick, quick, let him (General Custine) play blind man's buff with the guillotine.'

Even if the list of the victims is given, there is not a word on the scene in the court or at the

execution.   No newspaper, moreover, could venture to betray the slightest sympathy.   Occasional
glimpses, however, of the temper of the spectators
may be caught from memoirs and from contemporary documents in the archives, viz., the reports of
the twenty-four commissaries or observers employed
from September 1793 to April 1794 in reporting
to the Minister of the Interior on the temper of
the population.   Some of these reports have been
utilised by M. Dauban and by a German investiga-
tor, Adolf Schmidt, while I have extracted others.

First as to the spectators at the trials.   Beugnot
tells us that when he was taken to the Conciergerie
in October 1793, he had to mount a staircase
leading to the tribunal.   It was crowded with
women waiting to see the departure for the guillotine of two men condemned on the previous day.
On Beugnot's appearance they clapped, stamped,
and shouted for joy, as for fresh prey, and loaded
him with insults as he passed.   At five in the
morning, moreover, from his cell he could hear
people pushing and scrambling up a staircase to
get into the court, though the trials did not begin till
nine or ten.   One of the commissaries was present
on December 21, 1793, at the trial of six nuns and
a maidservant charged with sheltering a recusant priest.   He says : ' I perceived that they were
pitied, and that everybody said, " We must wait for
the verdict of the jury."   The people have always

great confidence in the jury and judges.' The priest, the servant, and one nun were condemned, the other five nuns, who were simply lodgers, being acquitted, but ordered to be detained till the peace. On the same day a tailor was sentenced to death, but 'his tears did not move the people, who cried, "No mercy for forestallers!"' Another commissary on the same day reported that working men were disobeying the official injunction not to neglect their work to attend the trials. He suggested that they and the other spectators should be better watched, for language was said to be used by them which manifestly proved that they were posted there by enemies of the Republic. 'One of these persons said the other day, speaking of a woman who was being interrogated: "What is the good of bringing them here? Is it not known that they are all condemned beforehand?"' Again, on September 18, 1793, at the trial of four inhabitants of Rouen for signing in the previous January a petition to the Convention against the trial of Louis XVI., 'there were many coughers, which would require attention if this device was repeated.' Three of the four were acquitted; the fourth was a chimney-sweep; but there had been a former trial for the same affair with numerous convictions. We hear also, on March 22, 1794, of a group of people in the Place de la Révolution discussing the trial of Hébert and his associates. 'They are not allowed,' said some, 'to defend themselves. The president speaks to them very .roughly, constantly saying, "I ask you to answer yes or no ; let us have no phrases ! " The people, while indignant against the conspirators, are vexed to see the tribunal taking a course so contrary to the laws of humanity and justice.' Sans-culottes, however, silenced these murmurs, or the commissary thought it expedient to represent that this was the sequel. Again, on March 28 we read, on a man being condemned, that 'those leaving the hall said the jury had been more severe than the people would have been. Justice, however, was rendered to the integrity of the jurors.' This saving phrase is not to be implicitly trusted. We likewise read of a man talking to a group of women at the foot of the statue of Liberty apostrophised by Madame Roland, near to which the executions then took place, and trying to persuade them that the victims went straight to Paradise.

As to the witnesses of the executions, the commissaries' reports differ, and this argues their fidelity, for they show the conflicting sentiments which prevailed, and the rapid changes of tone. Dutart, on June 19, 1793, was present at the death of twelve Breton conspirators. The Marquis de la Rouerie had obtained commissions and proclamations from the King's brother with a view to a rising in Brittany, simultaneously with a foreign invasion, in order to restore the monarchy and the old institutions. He took shelter under an assumed name with Lamotte de Laguyomarais, near Lamballe, died there, and was buried secretly in a wood. Rumours arose ; the doctor who had attended him was arrested, the body was discovered, and in the garden of a man named Desilles was dug up a bottle containing royalist documents. Laguyomarais and his wife, their two sons, their brother-in-law, gardener, manservant, Desilles' three daughters— Desilles himself had fled—a female cousin of Rouerie, three doctors, and others, twenty-seven in all, were arrested, and twenty were put on trial. Laguyomarais' two sons, two of Desilles' daughters, and two others were acquitted ; two prisoners were sentenced to transportation (they were afterwards guillotined on another charge), and twelve were condemned to death. These included Laguyomarais and his wife, Desilles' third daughter, married and aged twenty-four, and the female cousin aged twenty-five. Dutart describes the victims as comprising an entire family of good position, a woman of fifty or sixty, a young woman of twenty-five, and a girl of fifteen. He evidently mistook the daughter of twenty-four for a girl of fifteen. Twelve, in these early days of the guillotine, was an unusually large batch, and Fouquier wrote to the captain of the escort :—' Considering the large number of the condemned, I call upon the citizen commandant to give orders for having the largest possible number of cavalry and an imposing armed force, especially as they are *des ci-devant* (aristocrats) and great conspirators, who have a following.' Alas, there was no fear of a rescue, for Dutart writes:

The people said nothing, but closely watched the attitudes and gestures of the unfortunates. The latter were made to alight from the cart; presently one mounted the scaffold, turning round to salute the people; three or four men preceded the women; in ten minutes all was over. Among the male prisoners some laughed, while others, as well as the women, were quiet, almost like persons resigned to an inevitable disaster. . . . I think I noticed much indifference [among the spectators] for we must discriminate between curiosity at so striking a spectacle, and actual compassion. As to the latter feeling, fully two-thirds of the spectators would have pardoned the prisoners, particularly the women. . . . Politically, these executions produce the greatest effect, the most noticeable being that they allay the resentment of the people at the evils which they are experiencing. They thus exorcise their vengeance. The wife who has lost her husband, the father who has lost his son, the tradesman whose business has left him or who buys everything so dear that his profits are reduced nearly to nothing, agree only to put up with the evils they endure on seeing persons more unfortunate than themselves, and in whom they fancy they discern enemies.

This is perhaps the best explanation of the apathy with which the executions were in general regarded.[1] There were, however, some instances

[1] Mérimée noted a similar feeling in 1848: 'A great vice of our time and country is envy and hatred of superiorities. This

of commiseration. Thus on February 25, 1794, a batch of seventeen included a man apparently nearly ninety, so feeble that he had to be lifted on to the scaffold. 'The people seemed much touched at this spectacle. What crime, said several, can a man in that state of decrepitude have committed? Why should not old age, which is so much like childhood, share its immunity from punishment? This opinion appeared to be general. The people were indignant at the brutality with which the executioner performed his functions. He seized several of these criminals, it is said, with a roughness which revolted many spectators.' When, again, three army tailors were acquitted by the tribunal, they were crowned with laurel and led in triumph to the Jacobin Club, and on March 12 a man who had been present at the trial of a nun insisted that banishment was the extreme punishment deserved by her. The executioner was censured for pulling the red cap over Hébert's nose when on the scaffold, as though beheading was not sufficient punishment, yet some had demanded a more lingering death for him. On another occasion

is carried so far that the sight of a neighbour's ills is enough to console one for his own. The populace, who are losing everything in Paris, where all fabrication *de luxe* is annihilated for a long time, forget their distress on seeing the discomfiture of the rich. The day when Rothschild is bankrupt will be a grand day for all the small tradesmen, who will be ruined the day after. When a shoemaker fails all the cobblers are delighted.' (*Revue des Deux Mondes*, May 1, 1893.)

(March 24), a condemned man having to wait twenty minutes till the guillotine was ready, there were many murmurs. We likewise hear of murmurs at the condemnation of Frouillé, for publishing a pamphlet glorifying Louis XVI. He had assured a pork butcher present at the execution of his innocence, and the man believed him.

Carrier, on returning from his Nantes butcheries in March 1794, complained at the Cordeliers Club that he found in Paris much pity for the condemned, but he asserted that those who disliked the guillotine showed that they themselves deserved it. One commissary reports that the firmness of the condemned makes no impression on the people, who even complain that a single guillotine is not enough, and that there ought to be four ; but another relates how a girl who had once involuntarily witnessed an execution could never pass the guillotine without fainting. He adds that people would like to have the tumbrils always take the same route, so that sensitive persons could avoid them. This fainting scene, he urges, enables ' aristocrats ' (reactionaries) to direct public attention to the multitude of executions. 'You cannot walk out, they say, without seeing the guillotine or the tumbrils. Children will become cruel, and infants may be born with marks on their necks.' A conversation is narrated in which a man objects to daily executions, maintaining that it would be

better if necessary to have a huge batch of 400
once a quarter. 'From our habit of coming here,'
he said, 'there is not one of us who shudders at
the punishment.' This commissary, Perrière, even
ventures timidly—taking his text from the slaugh-
tering of pigs outside the butchers' shops, which
forced sensitive women to shut themselves up to
avoid hearing the animals' screams—to suggest that
executions should be private.

Up to May 10, 1793, the guillotine had
stood in the Carrousel, but the Convention, on
occupying the Tuileries, did not like its proximity,
and relegated it to the Place de la Concorde. The
inhabitants of the rue St.-Honoré, however, objected
to the passage of the tumbrils, albeit the windows in
that street had been eagerly hired on the day of the
execution of Hébert, and accordingly, on June 13,
1794, the guillotine was removed to the Barrière du
Trône. On the fall of Robespierre it was brought
back to the Place de la Concorde.

It was not a little dangerous to evince commiseration. On February 28, 1794, a number of
men and women expressed pity for two persons,
about to be guillotined. 'When shall we be tired,'
said one, 'of shedding blood ?' 'When there are
no more guilty,' replied a second. 'If there was
guillotining for thoughts,' remarked a third,
'what numbers would perish.' 'Do not talk so
loudly,' rejoined a fourth, 'or we may be overheard

and arrested.' In March a *citoyenne* who, when several persons were being guillotined, exclaimed ' How horrible ! ' was angrily asked by those around her whether she pitied conspirators, and she had to pretend that she meant it was surprising so many executions had not brought people to reason. Fouquier, looking down on July 13 from a Conciergerie window on the departure of the victims, perceived in the crowd two men who seemed to deplore the fate of so many unfortunates. He immediately ordered them to be arrested, and next day they were guillotined. Etienne Delécluze describes how, when he was twelve years old, his mother and he were stopped on April 18, 1794, at the foot of one of the bridges and compelled to wait till seven or eight carts went by, containing twenty-five or thirty persons, including Laborde, the Court banker. His mother covered her eyes and leaned on the parapet, overcome with horror, but an artisan said in a low tone, ' Control yourself; you are surrounded by people who might misconstrue your emotion.' Etienne could not help looking at the fearful procession, and the insults of the mob informed him that one of the prisoners was Laborde, whose daughter was afterwards his fellow art student at the Louvre.

Assuredly sensitive persons avoided the sight of the convoys and the executions, as Madame Delécluze would fain have done. A commissary tells us of a mistress being told by her cook at the end of dinner that seventeen persons were to be executed. She was angry, and told the cook that she wanted no such news to facilitate digestion or amuse her for the rest of the evening. Then, turning to her guests, she quietly said she did not impugn national justice, but she wished to hear or see nothing of the executions. Upon this a young man, seizing her youngest child and drawing his sword, pretended to be about to slaughter it. On the mother shrieking, he told her that such would be the fate of her children if the people pitied by her got the upper hand. The poor woman was silenced, but not, let us hope, convinced. Grelet, tutor to the Noailles family, was pursued, arrested, and detained some hours, because, while the three ladies of that family were being taken from the Luxembourg to the Conciergerie, one of them clasped his hand, and made gestures signifying that she sent her last blessing to her three children. And Carrichon, the priest in lay dress, who by gestures gave absolution to these ladies on the way to the scaffold, was horrified at finding, in spite of a heavy rain, a crowd of people who laughed and were amused at the spectacle.[1] As the Maréchale de Noailles was

---

[1] Carrichon himself was strangely composed, watching the whole operation and committing all the details to writing. He too, had apparently become habituated to these massacres.

jolted along in the cart, tottering on the plank on which she was seated, her hands tied behind her back, the crowd exclaimed: 'Look at the Maréchale; what a grand equipage she used to have, and now she goes in a tumbril like the others.' This is a striking confirmation of the feeling noted by Dutart.

Louis XVI. was executed amid silent apathy, the shops being open as usual all day and the theatres at night; but Charlotte Corday was hooted during the two hours' ride to the scaffold, and when Hébert—who, however, ought not to be mentioned in the same breath with her—was executed, a cloud of hats were waved in the air. Robespierre's last journey was likewise made amid a torrent of imprecations and exultations.

Verninac de St.-Maur was but too true a prophet when, objecting in December 1789 to the adoption of the guillotine, and advocating hanging alike for high and low, he said : 'The habit of seeing blood shed will inflame the eye and harden the heart. The novelty will attract a crowd, people will clap as at a theatre, and may come to desire frequent performances.' Yet it must not be forgotten that the Parisians were suffering from chronic dearth, so that—though this was later on, in 1796—persons fell down in the streets from inanition, and that the scarcity was attributed to the machinations of the royalists.

The resignation or heroism of the victims

helped, moreover, to shut men's eyes to the horror of the spectacle. 'The people who witness the executions,' reports a commissary on January 18, 1794, 'are astonished at the firmness and courage shown on the way to the scaffold. It seems like going to a wedding. People cannot understand this, and some say it is supernatural.' Had many victims struggled like Madame Dubarry, the mob might have been sensible of the barbarity of these daily butcheries, in which in fifteen months 2,625 persons perished. As it was, regard for human life seemed to have disappeared. Allowance, indeed, must be made for the frequency of capital punishments a century ago. In 1794 Robert Wall was executed at Edinburgh for sedition, and in December 1792, at the London Old Bailey Monthly Sessions, nineteen capital sentences were passed, nine of the culprits being hanged, all on one day. Robbery and forgery were then punished with death in England, and even in the new French code of 1791 arson and ship scuttling were capital offences. But after making all allowance for the Draconic laws of the period, the fact remains that not merely Paris but Lyons, Nantes, Bordeaux, and other provincial towns were fast reaching the situation existing in China in the present day, as depicted in a newspaper cutting of May 1893 :

The correspondent of a Shanghai journal, writing from Paoting Fu, the capital of the province in which

Q

Pekin is situated, says that the populations of provincial capitals are quite *blasé* in the matter of punishments and executions. It is exceedingly common to hear the sound of clanking fetters in the street, and presently meet several unwashed, unshorn, haggard, and miserable wretches, looking like victims escaped for a moment from Dante's Inferno. The ghastly processions that pass to and fro from the execution ground scarcely excite remark. A few delighted boys run and caper in advance, the bystanders shout out jesting remarks and witty salutations to the proudly self-conscious executioner and the poor, half-stupefied wretch who peers out from the tattered coverings of the cart. As they reach the execution ground, marked merely by a post erected where the roadway is a few feet wider than is common, the scattered attendants close in hurriedly, the neighbouring cake-sellers and hucksters move up to the centre of attraction, and for perhaps three minutes all business within a radius of a hundred feet or more is suspended. Then the good-natured crowd breaks up laughing, the empty cart with the guard of mounted soldiers returns to the *yamen*, and if one passes the spot half an hour later there will be only the trodden dust by the roadside to mark the tragedy that every dweller in the city holds so lightly.

CHAPTER VII

WOMEN AS VICTIMS

France had shown a light to all men, preached a gospel, all men's good ;
Celtic Demos rose a Demon, shrieked, and slaked the light with blood.
                    TENNYSON, *Locksley Hall, Sixty Years After.*

Equality of the Sexes—Capitulation of Verdun—A Basket of
    Sweetmeats—Imprisonment—Guillotine and Pillory—The
    Compiègne Carmelites—Tribulations—' Veni, Creator.'

WHEN we think of the women who perished by the
guillotine, we are apt to remember only Marie
Antoinette, Princess Elisabeth, Madame Roland,
Charlotte Corday, or Madame Dubarry; yet, after
all, these executions were not the greatest atrocities
of the Terror. There were reasons, howsoever
barbarous, for the slaughter of these celebrated
personages. Marie Antoinette had occupied a
throne, and was believed to have taken an active
part in politics. Elisabeth, though pure and
blameless, was the King's sister, and almost inevitably shared his fate. Madame Roland could not
plead her sex, for she had been (so to speak) a
Girondin statesman, and when she refused pity to

Marie Antoinette she recognised the principle that if women mix in politics they must accept the risks. Charlotte Corday, much as we may admire her motives, was a murderess, and was executed as such. Madame Dubarry, though for twenty years in retirement, had enriched herself at the expense of France; yet she would probably have escaped had it not been for the relentless persecution of an Englishman, Grieve. The most unpardonable crimes of the Revolution were the butchery of harmless and (in many cases) obscure women, for heedless talk, for letters or remittances to *émigré* husbands or sons, for sheltering fugitives, for possessing medals of Louis XVI., for hearing mass celebrated by recusant priests. Family affection and generous instincts were then crimes. Louis Blanc professed to regard the Terror as no worse than the repression of the Indian Mutiny or of the Jamaica rising; yet, for a parallel to the murder of these women, some high-born but others humble, we must go back to the infamous trial by Jeffreys of Alice Lisle for sheltering one of Monmouth's rebels, or to the diabolical execution by Henry VIII. of the aged Countess of Salisbury, whose only offence was that her son, Cardinal Pole, had denounced the King's divorce.

I am not speaking, it will be observed, of Madame de Lamballe and other victims of the September massacres, for those horrors were the work of a band of assassins; nor of the even more fiendish holocausts at Nantes, for those had no semblance of judicial formalities. I confine myself to the condemnations of the Revolutionary Tribunal of Paris, condemnations preceded by the form at least of a trial, with judges and juries, the interrogation of the accused, and usually the calling of witnesses. I select the Paris tribunal because, although all France was dotted over with tribunals, Paris was probably the high-water mark of what may be called judicial ferocity. '

The first capital sentence on a woman was passed on April 12, 1793. Catherine Clère, a domestic servant at Valenciennes, fifty-five years of age, was found drunk at night in the streets of that town, shouting 'Vive le roi' and singing revolutionary songs. Probably it was a case of *in vino veritas*, albeit her master assured the tribunal that during five months in his service she had shown no anti-republican sentiments; and there was no evidence of her having meddled in politics. Next day two members of the Convention, horrified at the infliction of death for so light an offence, urged a respite; but the Convention declined to interfere, and it is said that even while the brief discussion was going on the guillotine had done its work. Two months later three Breton women, aged twenty-four, twenty-five, and twenty-seven, implicated with twenty men in a royalist plot, detected by the digging up of papers in a garden, suffered the same penalty.[1] A few weeks more and it was the turn of Charlotte Corday. By this time the Parisians had become accustomed to the ' equality of sexes ' before the guillotine, and the monthly statistics—I follow the Jacobin calendar—show a terrible *crescendo* of executions :—Vendémiaire, 3 women (including Marie Antoinette) and 7 men; Brumaire, 3 women (including Madame Roland) and 62 men; Frimaire, 10 women (including Madame Dubarry) and 57 men; Nivôse, 10 women, 51 men; Pluviose, 8 women, 60 men; Ventôse, 11 women, 105 men; Germinal, 12 women, 143 men; Floréal, 27 women (including Princess Elisabeth), 327 men; Prairial, 33 women, 476 men; Messidor, 93 women, 703 men; Thermidor, 1st to 9th, 59 women, 283 men. If Robespierre had not been overturned, and if Thermidor had continued as it had begun, the monthly number of women would have risen to 177. As Edgar Quinet remarks, the longer the system lasted the more the Terrorists were doomed to prolong it; an eternity of murders would have been necessary before the favourable moment for clemency was found. It should also be mentioned that the acquittals, which at first considerably outnumbered the convictions, became after Pluviose (January–February 1794) a dwindling minority,

[1] See p. 217.

and that of the 8,000 persons still in prison in Paris when Robespierre fell, we may assume one third to have been women.

Some women threw away their lives rather than survive husband or brother. When Captain Lavergne was arrested for the capitulation of Longwy, his wife (she was only twenty-six) courageously went to the Jacobin Club and read a justification of him, but without effect. When the poor man, fifty years of age, but prematurely old and infirm, was brought into court on a mattress, and was tried and condemned, she exclaimed, ' We want a king. Monsters, executioners, I mean to go to the guillotine with my husband.' She was immediately arrested, the preliminaries were hurried through, and being put in the dock she was convicted. She was placed in the cart with her husband. He was senseless most of the way, but at last revived, and they exchanged expressions of affection and sympathy. A few weeks afterwards a similar scene took place. A bookseller named Gattey being condemned for the sale of anti-revolutionary publications,[1] his sister Marie Gattey, an ex-nun, thirty-nine years of age, cried three times, ' Vive le roi ! ' At once arrested and interrogated, she gave as the reason of her act, ' Because I loved my brother.' In this case the

[1] In 1782 he was imprisoned six months in the Bastille for possessing a prohibited book.

proceedings were not quite so rapid. She was not condemned till the following day. Another woman who deliberately sacrificed herself, though not for the sake of kindred, was a dressmaker of forty-seven, Claude Françoise Loisillier. She wrote and posted on the wall an appeal to the Parisians to put an end to the guillotine. She did it, she told the examining magistrate, out of humanity, as too much blood was being shed. Alas! she only swelled the number of victims. On the same day two women of twenty-one and twenty-five, a hair-dresser and a dressmaker, were sent to the guillotine for having at night offered a policeman, as their certificates of *civisme*, two manuscripts of their own composition in favour of poor little Louis XVII. and against Robespierre. The dressmaker's spelling was faulty, but her heart was in the right place.

How suddenly the blow might fall is shown by the case of Madame Marcandier. Her husband, formerly secretary to Desmoulins, was appalled at the September massacres, and published a reactionary newspaper until the hawkers, afraid for their own safety, refused to sell it. He evaded arrest for a year, then, tired of homelessness and suspense, he sent his wife to deputy Legendre [1] to reveal his whereabouts. Legendre received the wife,

---

[1] The Paris butcher who, with the brewer Santerre, headed the invasion of the Tuileries in June 1792.

took the address from her, then arrested her and gave information which led to the husband's apprehension. Marcandier was tried on July 11, 1794, and his wife, who had been released, was present. During the trial—brief enough such trials were— she was again arrested, placed in the dock on the charge of selling her husband's pamphlets, and condemned with him. A man named Donet happening to say when interrogated that his wife (then a prisoner) might be able to explain some points, she was sent for, tried, and condemned with him. Equally thrilling was the fate of Madame Mayet, a widow forty-eight years of age. She was brought up on the 7th Thermidor by mistake for the Viscountess de Maillé, the pronunciation of the two names being identical. The questions put to her related, of course, to the viscountess, but as the charge was the vague one of royalist conspiracy, this was immaterial; the spelling of the name was altered in the document handed to the jury, and she was condemned. The gaolers, as they led her away, told her she had been tried by mistake, 'but it is so much disposed of, as well to-day as to-morrow.' The belief of the prisoners at St.-Lazare was, that to atone for the blunder Madame de Maillé, carried off the same night while in hysterics, was guillotined without trial, but happily this was wrong. She was brought into court on the 9th Thermidor, but again fell into hysterics.

She was kept in court all day, in order to be tried on her recovery, but happily for her the hysterics continued, and she was sent to the hospital. She thus lived to give evidence against the infamous prosecutor Fouquier Tinville. Her son, however, a lad of seventeen, had been guillotined the day before this blunder was committed. Her husband had apparently emigrated.

If all were victims it cannot be expected that all were heroines. It is true that Madame Dubarry was almost the only sufferer of either sex recorded to have betrayed fear of death, but not a few women pleaded pregnancy for a respite; in some of them the clinging to life being so strong as to induce sham confessions of dishonour. Madame de Kolly, a Breton conspirator, the second woman convicted, thus prolonged her life for six months after the execution of husband and lover. She gave a piercing shriek on the scaffold. The respite in any case was only temporary, the Jacobins became very sceptical as to this plea,[1] and a Madame Quétineau was guillotined eleven hours after a miscarriage. Her offence was having complained, when her husband, a colonel, was awaiting trial, of the decree forbidding all visits to prisoners.

An idea of the Terror, however, is much better formed from the study of one or two cases than

[1] Only eight women respited on this account were in prison on the 9th Thermidor, and their sentences were commuted by the Convention on September 17.

from a general survey, and I select what seem to me the most thrilling tragedies—thrilling, yet comparatively little known. The first is that of the 'Virgins of Verdun.' Verdun was a fortified town. It was so ill equipped and garrisoned that when the Prussians advanced against it in August 1792, they might easily have stormed it; but, not knowing its defenceless condition, they occupied the heights commanding the town, and, after repulsing a sortie, began a bombardment. Four houses were burnt down and eighty much damaged. The inhabitants had to seek refuge in their cellars. Among those who did this were a Madame de Lalance and her three nieces; but the latter, on their neighbour's house taking fire, courageously sallied forth, and amid falling shot and bombs helped to remove the furniture. The humbler inhabitants assembled, forced the wealthier residents to join them and place themselves at their head, and, collecting outside the town-hall, clamoured for a capitulation. The commandant, Beaurepaire, called a council of war, and it pronounced for surrender; but Beaurepaire, unduly sensitive as to his supposed honour, shot himself—thereby earning interment in the Pantheon at Paris. The capitulation was signed on September 2. A Prussian officer, passing through the streets just afterwards, was fired at from a hairdresser's window and killed. All the town was in a panic, fearing that the capitulation

would be annulled and the place given up to pillage.
' I do not know,' says Barbe Henry, a girl of whom
there is more to be said presently, ' who conceived
the idea of a deputation going to the King of
Prussia and offering sweetmeats '—Verdun was
famous for its sweetmeats—' but this idea was
generally adopted. The ladies offered their money,
and young ladies were chosen to present his
majesty with a pretty basket containing the sweetmeats. My aunt, the Baroness de Lalance, had
her horses harnessed to her waggon and took us to
the camp '—which was two miles off. ' All was
done so hurriedly that we had not the least notion
of what we were wanted to do. Our relations
spoke together, but without saying a word to us.'
The deputation consisted of Madame de Lalance,
whose husband was a royalist *émigré*, Madame
Masson, a widow,—these two had bought the
sweetmeats at a confectioner's,—Madame Tabouillot,
her daughter Claire, aged fifteen, and Madame de
Lalance's three nieces, Suzanne, Gabrielle, and
Barbe Henry, aged respectively twenty-four, twenty-
three, and fifteen. According to one account they
were coldly received and the King refused the basket
of sweetmeats offered him by the two girls Claire and
Barbe ; but Goethe, who though with the besiegers
was not present, states that his Majesty, disregarding
the advice not to eat the sweetmeats, lest they should
be poisoned, gallantly accepted and tasted them.

Goethe himself, in lieu of the ornaments which he had confidently expected to purchase in captured Paris, sent off a box of sweetmeats to his mistress or wife, Christiana Vulpius. It is not clear whether flowers were also offered; possibly the basket was decorated with them.

Two days afterwards, the Prussians being about to raise their camp, there was some curiosity to see the cannon which had so terrified the inhabitants. Crowds went to the camp, and the then Crown Prince, afterwards Frederick William III., a young man of twenty-two, who kept a diary of this French campaign, speaks of meeting a party of women and pretty girls. He politely accosted them; they returned his greeting; and, leading his horse by the bridle, he accompanied them a short distance, pleased with their conversation. There can be little doubt that this party included Mademoiselle Lagirouzière, and three sisters, Anne, Henriette, and Hélène Watrin, aged twenty-three, twenty-one, and twenty, or rather two of them. They saw the King, who asked Hélène whether there was a theatre at Verdun, and she replied in the negative.

Be it remembered that the Tuileries had been stormed three weeks previously, that the King and Queen were prisoners in the Temple, that a large, perhaps the larger, portion of Frenchmen welcomed the Prussians who were to put down the Paris mob and restore the monarchy, and that the Prussians throughout the campaign had had constant proofs of the friendliness of the people. Nothing, therefore, could be more natural than these amenities at Verdun—to say nothing of the fact that the first deputation was designed to avert the pillage of the town. The Paris Jacobins, however, denounced the capitulation as due to the intrigues and clamours of the royalist inhabitants; the deputations were magnified into triumphal processions, with girls dressed in white for the occasion—September 2 was a Sunday, and the Sunday dresses may have been white—and a ball was said to have been given to the Prussian officers. When, six weeks afterwards, the invaders had to evacuate Verdun, the French generals refused to admit any stipulations in favour of the inhabitants, many of whom, Goethe says, had voluntarily and joyfully worn white cockades. 'I pity the unfortunate townspeople,' he writes to a correspondent, 'if without a capitulation they are again in the hands of the patriots.' His fears were but too well grounded, for though, when the French troops entered, the trembling inhabitants were 'punished only with contempt,' the Convention speedily issued thundering decrees against the inhabitants, ordering the arrest of the district and municipal authorities. In January 1793 most of these were liberated; but a prosecution was ordered against the members of the council of war and against gendarmes who had continued to serve during the Prussian occupation.

In February the Convention acknowledged that the place had been defenceless, and declared that the inhabitants had not deserved ill of their country; but, with not unusual want of logic, it ordered the prosecution both of the men who had clamoured for capitulation and of the women who had visited the Prussian camp. Women, the report urged, were the chief cause of the emigration of the nobles, and, together with the priests, kept up an anti-revolutionary fanaticism. Moreover, if left unpunished, they would teach their children hatred of liberty. This implied that punishment was to make them love liberty—that is to say, Jacobin rule. Whether in anticipation or in consequence of this decree, the women and girls were one evening summoned to the bishop's palace and interrogated. For a time nothing followed, and the affair seemed at an end; but by-and-by they were arrested and confined in a convent in the town, 'where we passed the winter,' says Barbe Henry—but probably it was the summer—'as agreeably as possible.' The accused, with the exception of the Baroness de Lalance, belonged to the upper-middle class rather than to the aristocracy. Madame Masson was a magistrate's widow; the Henrys were a magistrate's daughters; Mlle. Lagirouzière was a forest official's daughter; the

Watrins' father had been an officer; another prisoner was a captain's widow; and another sold watches. In the spring, Barbe says—but it must have been in November or December 1793—it was decided that they should be tried by the departmental tribunal at St.-Mihiel. After being again interrogated they were accordingly taken thither, about ninety in all, for besides these women and girls there were male inhabitants, charged with intriguing for the capitulation. The soldiers who escorted them were very kind to the prisoners; but at St.-Mihiel they encountered a ferocious mob, and the soldiers had to draw their swords to save them from being massacred. The women and girls were detained four months in a convent. Then orders came from Paris that they should be conducted thither. The local authorities, evidently perceiving that this was tantamount to a death-warrant, remonstrated against the expense of transporting prisoners and witnesses to Paris, and were very dilatory in collecting the evidence. The accused were taken back to Verdun, and again interrogated. Barbe gave her age as fifteen; but the magistrate, who wore the Jacobin emblem, the red cap, told the clerk to write down that she was *fille majeure*—an adult. 'No, citizen,' objected Barbe: 'I am not of age, for I am only fifteen.' 'Hold your tongue,' was the reply. 'You like the Capets, for you offered sweetmeats and flowers to the Prussian tyrant.' Then, turning to the clerk, he repeated, ' Write "*fille majeure.*" ' Barbe, however, again protested, and her correct age was then given. Her life depended upon it.

On March 10 the accused were placed in open carts and started for Paris. There was no straw, and while some of the prisoners sat on their small bundles of clothes, others were forced to stand, or lean against the side of the cart. The gendarmes showed as much humanity as fear of compromising themselves allowed, and sometimes permitted them, when tired of their constrained posture and of the jolting, to get down and walk. At St.-Ménéhould there was an attempted rescue by officers who had overtaken them from Verdun; but it was ineffectual. The journey lasted a fortnight; and on arriving in Paris they were taken at once to the Conciergerie, either because the other prisons were full or because an immediate trial had been resolved upon. Like the other inmates, they found the Conciergerie crowded and fetid, but they prayed fervently. The prisoners were interrogated by Fouquier Tinville. Even that infamous man seems to have had compunctions as to the juniors. He tried to make them cast the whole responsibility on their parents or relations; but, resigned to their fate, they refused to incriminate their elders. With perhaps impolitic reticence, indeed, they revoked their previous frank admissions, Barbe

R

denying that she saw any sweetmeats, though, as we have seen, she actually offered them. One of the Watrins had not been to the camp at all, but had merely sent money to her *émigré* brother. All were alike asked, even the two girls, whether by their intrigues they had not forced the garrison to capitulate. 'I was too frightened for that,' replied Anne Watrin. 'I hid myself in the garden to see the bombs fall.' The fourteen women and girls—the three Henrys were orphans, and the Watrins had no father living—were brought on April 24 before the tribunal, together with twenty-one men, viz., the captain who signed the capitulation, several municipal officers and gendarmes, five ecclesiastics, a druggist, a hairdresser, a chandler, &c. Barbe states that behind the judges sat women toying and jesting with them. The counsel assigned the prisoners was allowed only a quarter of an hour to speak in their defence.

All were convicted and sentenced to death; but the law then, as now, provided that capital sentences on persons under sixteen should be commuted. Barbe and Claire were accordingly condemned to twenty years' imprisonment and to stand six hours on the scaffold. Had they been a few months older they would doubtless have perished, for boys just over sixteen and girls of eighteen were sacrificed on other occasions. Some of the spectators had shown compassion

during the trial; but when sentence was pronounced there were plaudits, in which the witnesses
joined. Thereupon, either from misconception or
from bravado, the Watrins clapped their hands also;
their companions followed suit, ' indulging in I
know not what transports,' says Barbe, who did not
at the moment understand that her life was spared.
Taken out of court, their hair was cut off and their
hands tied behind them. The executioner was
about to prepare Barbe also for the guillotine; but
her sister Suzanne exclaimed against the mistake, and he desisted. Barbe fainted. When she
recovered consciousness she found herself in the
bed of Madame de Boufflers, a fellow-prisoner, who
showed the poor child every kindness. When the
clock struck seven—Barbe says, ' in the morning,'
a very excusable inaccuracy, for it must have been
evening—Madame de Boufflers said, ' It is all
over,' and all *was* over. The twelve had been
guillotined. Next day Barbe and Claire were
placed, not, it is said, beside the guillotine, but on
a platform erected for the purpose, an inscription
stating that the girls had furnished money, food,
and munitions to the enemy; but passers-by
shrugged their shoulders and not a single insult
was uttered. How long the girls were imprisoned
is not known; but it is probable that they were
liberated in 1795.

Three-and-thirty years after this tragedy Barbe

Henry,[1] then the wife of a Colonel Meslier, wrote, for her daughter's perusal on the eve of confirmation, the narrative from which I have quoted. It was not written for publication, and has never yet been printed in its entirety; but the sculptor David d'Angers having with his revolutionary fanaticism justified the executions, Cuvillier Fleury, in a volume entitled ' Portraits Politiques et Révolutionnaires,' was allowed in 1851 to give extracts from it. The narrative bears the stamp of truth, though of course after thirty years the writer may have fallen into slight inaccuracies. Her statement, moreover, as to the Prussian officer having been shot, which seems to have been studiously suppressed at the trial, is confirmed by the Prussian Crown Prince's diary, published in 1846.

On July 17, 1794—another eleven days and Robespierre's fall would have saved them—sixteen Carmelite nuns from Compiègne were butchered on even flimsier pretexts. Their troubles had begun with domiciliary visits. They were repeatedly invited to re-enter the world, but unanimously refused. Some were even pressed by their families

---

[1] In 1815, according to information furnished in 1847 by a Prussian diplomatic attaché to M. Mérat for his *Verdun en 1792*, she was offered a pension of 1,200 francs by her old acquaintance the Crown Prince, then Frederic William III., and refused it. Five years later, however, her residence near Metz having been burnt down, and having four children to bring up on small means, she applied for the pension; and she received it from 1821 till her death in 1836.

thus to study their own safety, and the brother of a novice of sixteen (Marie Jeanne Meunier) went so far as to threaten force; but the novice, while thanking her family for their solicitude, declared that death alone should part her from the community. In September 1792, however, all were compelled to quit their convent and assume secular dress. The prioress was one day in Paris on business, accompanied by Sister Philippe, and as they were passing along the rue St.-Antoine, the tumbrils containing victims on their way to the guillotine overtook them. They could not make their way out of the crowd, and could almost have touched the tumbrils. 'Look at those two men,' said Sister Philippe; 'their eyes are fixed on us and they seem to say " You will soon follow us." ' 'Ah, what a blessing,' replied the prioress, ' if God should deign us that favour.' The nuns were quartered in four houses in Compiègne, scanty pensions being assigned them out of their confiscated property; but even these pensions became conditional on taking an oath to be faithful to the nation and to maintain liberty and equality. They were entrapped into signing a blank paper as being merely a promise not to disturb public tranquillity; but this turned out to be the oath. They corresponded with their ex-chaplain and with relatives who did not conceal their sadness at the state of affairs, and one of their correspondents warned them to be more discreet in their letters and conversation. In June 1794 their lodgings were searched, and letters were seized, as also a portrait of Louis XVI. sent to Sister Brard by a cousin, Mulot de la Ménardière. A Voltairean bookseller, and an incorrigible rhymester, he had written under the portrait a quatrain extolling the King, It was imprudent to have preserved their letters, for one condemned the King's execution, and another expressed satisfaction at a repulse of the 'French patriots' in Belgium. There were also verses sighing for the end of crimes and of devouring vultures. Sister Brard having been prevented by the cold from working in the garden, Mulot again in verse wished the cold would destroy not only insects but Jacobin deputies. After being three days confined to their lodgings the sixteen nuns were lodged as prisoners in the Visitation Convent.

Thanks to Sister Philippe, who happened to be away in Paris, and survived in a convent at Sens till 1856, we have some particulars of these unfortunate ladies.[1] The prioress was Marie Charlotte Ledoine, forty-two years of age. In girlhood she felt a vocation for the cloister; but her parents were too poor to pay a dowry. Princess Louise, daughter of Louis XV., who had joined the Carmelites at St.-Denis, heard of and sent for her, and induced Marie

---

[1] Another nun was on a visit of comfort to a bereaved family, and she also escaped.

Antoinette (not yet Queen, but Dauphine) to pay the money. In eleven years Marie Ledoine became prioress, and she composed hymns for use in the convent. Two of the nuns were in 1794 in their eightieth year. Another, Sister Croissy, was grand-niece of Louis XIV.'s able minister, Colbert; the then Queen was present at her taking the veil, and she was for eight years prioress. Then there was a widow, Rosalie Chrétien de Neuville. Married at eighteen and a widow at twenty-three, she was for eighteen months inconsolable, refusing to see anybody, and had her rooms hung with crape. She was at length persuaded to resume her music and drawing, and after some reflection entered the convent. For a time rather unsettled, she gradually became composed. Sister Brard, now fifty-eight, had known Louis XV.'s queen, who styled her 'my amiable philosopher-nun.' She was no doubt fond of talking to the juniors of her royal friend. Sister Petras, aged thirty-four, had been for five years nurse in the hospital at Nevers. The others were mostly between forty and fifty. There were four 'converse' sisters or servants. Two of them had not taken the veil— Térèse Soiron, forty-two years of age, formerly so beautiful that the Princess de Lamballe, on a visit to the convent, tried hard to persuade her to enter her service; and Jeanne Vézotal, only thirty, who had come as recently as 1787, and though warned that troubles were approaching, was not to be deterred.

Louise Soiron, another 'converse,' was probably Térèse's elder sister.

At the Visitation Convent the prisoners found twenty-one English Benedictine nuns from Cambray, and would gladly have embraced 'these venerable sisters, whom Anglican intolerance had formerly forced to take refuge in France, and whom a still crueller proscription was to cast back into the arms of their first persecutors;' but windows and doors had been walled up to prevent communication. For three weeks the Carmelites remained in the convent, singing hymns and repeating prayers. They were refused change of linen, and when at last they obtained permission for a wash they were, in the midst of the washing, hurried off in their wet garments to Paris. They left amid the insults of the mob, and even women who had formerly benefited by their bounty clapped their hands, saying it was well to get rid of useless mouths. Possibly they would have escaped the fatal journey if, on hearing that their bishop, safe across the frontier, had condemned the oath, they had not sent for the mayor, and, despite his remonstrances and warnings, repudiated their blank paper signatures.

They reached Paris on Sunday, July 13. What a Sunday for them! Taken from prison to prison, all too full to receive them, they were at last lodged in the Conciergerie. Poor Marie Thouret, seventy-nine years of age, and handcuffed like the rest, was too infirm and stiff, after a three-days' journey, to get out of the cart, whereupon a gendarme brutally dragged her out and threw her on the pavement. She was picked up with bleeding face. At the Conciergerie the nuns sang their hymns and exhorted their fellow-prisoners. July 16 being a great Carmelite festival, Sister de Neuville composed a hymn, and wrote it down with a piece of coal. On the 17th they were tried. They were accused of holding nocturnal meetings, of corresponding with *émigrés*, and of concealing royal robes—simply robes which at Christmas they threw round wax figures of the Magi, to ornament their Bethlehem. Mulot was included in the prosecution, and they had found him already at the Conciergerie, where the persuasions of the prioress induced him to abjure his sceptical opinions. Though a bookseller and a married man, his wife being then in prison at Chantilly, he was described as a recusant priest. Seeing a fellow-townsman on the jury, Mulot appealed to him to confirm his protest on this point; but the juror replied, 'Hold thy tongue, wretch! Thou hast no right to speak; do not add to the number of thy crimes.' The nuns were asked whether they had not concealed arms for the *émigrés*. 'Behold,' said the prioress, producing a crucifix, 'the only arms we have ever possessed.' The prisoners acknowledged, however, that they were sincerely attached to the monarchy. As to corresponding (on religious subjects only) with their ex-chaplain, the prioress urged that she alone was responsible, for no one else could write a single letter without her permission, and that the servant-sisters who posted the letters knew nothing of the contents, and were bound to do what they were ordered. 'Hold your tongue!' interposed the judge; 'their duty was to give information to the nation.'

On sentence of death being passed, the nuns thanked their judges—all but Térèse Soiron, who, poor soul, fainted, but quickly recovered on water being sent for, and excused herself to her companions for her weakness. Brought into court without breakfast, and refused even the slightest 'bite' before going to the scaffold, they would have been famished had not the sub-prioress, by offering her mantle to the prison keeper, procured some morsels of chocolate, which were divided among them. After an affectionate parting with their fellow prisoners, they started for the Barrière du Trône. During the three-mile ride they sang the 'Miserere,' 'Salve, Regina,' and the 'Te Deum.' The spectators, touched by their white robes and their fortitude, were silent. At the foot of the scaffold the nuns sang 'Veni, Creator,' the executioner, with unusual indulgence, allowing them to sing it through; the prioress, at her own request, was guillotined last. Sister Meunier, only eighteen, was the first to mount the steps, and, refusing the executioner's assistance, laid her head on the block. Each, as her turn came, knelt before the prioress and besought her blessing. The spectators preserved unwonted silence.

For most of these details we are indebted to Sister Philippe, who assiduously collected information respecting her unfortunate comrades ; but I may add an interesting, though not entirely accurate, passage from the narrative of the English Benedictines of Cambray, first published in my ' Englishmen in the French Revolution.'

About the middle of June 1794, sixteen Carmelite nuns were brought to Compiègne and lodged in a room which faced ours ; they had not been long there before they were hurried off to Paris, without any previous notice, for no other crime than that an emigrant priest, who had been their chaplain, had written to them and made mention of a bishop, who was also an emigrant, desiring compliments to an elderly gentleman who was cousin to one of the community. This person unfortunately possessed considerable property, a crime not easily overlooked in those days. This venerable man was also conducted to Paris with the nuns. A servant who attended him seemed ready to die with grief, and the good old gentleman shed tears at parting. The above religious quitted the Compiègne prison in the most saint-like manner. We saw them embrace each other before they set off, and they took an affectionate leave of us by the motion of their hands and other friendly gestures. On their way to the scaffold itself (as we were informed by an eye-witness of respectability and credit), they behaved with a firm and cheerful composure which nothing but a spotless conscience could inspire, resulting from a joyful hope and confidence in the blessed recompense that attended their sufferings in the cause of virtue. They repeated aloud on the scaffold the Litanies of the Blessed Virgin, until the fatal axe interrupted the voice of the last of this holy company. . . . Being repeatedly assured we had not money to purchase [secular] clothes he [the mayor] went himself to the apartment which those respectable ladies had occupied, and brought us some of the poor clothing they had left there; these he desired we should put on without delay. The next day the news became confirmed that the poor Carmelites had been put to death by the guillotine. The old clothes, which before appeared of small value, were now so much esteemed that we deemed ourselves unworthy to wear them; still, forced by necessity, we put them on, and these constituted the greater part of our mean apparel on our return to England. We yet keep them, a few excepted, which we have disposed of to particular friends.

On the 9th Thermidor, the day of Robespierre's fall, twenty-four persons were condemned in one court and twenty-two in the other, each batch numbering two women. In one of the lists prepared for the 11th the fifteen prisoners included one woman; we know nothing of the composition of the second list of forty. After two months' interval, on September 29, a woman was guillotined for anti-revolutionary talk, and another on the 30th.

After this five months elapse, and on February 21, 1795, a woman was executed, not strictly speaking for a political offence, but for passing forged notes. Aspasie Carlemigelli was executed, as we have seen,[1] on June 7, 1796, but she had been one of the murderers of Féraud, trampling him to death with her clogs. Five women were put on trial in 1796 as accomplices of Babeuf, but they were acquitted. Practically, therefore, the infliction of capital punishment on women for political offences ceased, as it had commenced, with the Terror.

[1] See p. 155.

CHAPTER VIII

THE PRISONS

Bring the old Dark Ages back, without the faith, without the hope ;
Break the State, the Church, the Throne, and roll their ruins down the slope.
TENNYSON, *Locksley Hall, Sixty Years After.*

' Suspects '—Prisons, old and new—Non-resistance—Keepers and
Turnkeys—Hotel Charges—Diet — Studies — Frivolities —
Religion—Sham Guillotining—English Hostages—Girondin
Deputies—Chantilly—Lyons—Mortality—If Robespierre had
triumphed.

THE wholesale arrests in Paris in August 1792, the
stepping-stone to the massacres of September, were
the illegal acts of a usurping municipality ; but on
September 17, 1793, the Convention gave a semblance of legality and a vast extension to such
measures by a decree ordering the apprehension of
all ' suspects.'   Suspects were thus defined :

1. Those who, by their conduct, relations, conversation, or writings have shown themselves partisans of
federalism and tyranny, and enemies of liberty.

2. Those who cannot in the manner prescribed by
the law of March 24 last prove their means of existence
and the performance of their civic duties.

3. Those to whom certificates of civism have been refused.

4. Public functionaries suspended from their functions by the National Convention or its commissaries and not reinstated, especially those who have been or are to be dismissed by virtue of the law of August 12 last.

5. Those ex-nobles, husbands, wives, fathers, mothers, sons or daughters, brothers or sisters, and agents of *émigrés* who have not constantly manifested their attachment to the Revolution.

6. Those who have emigrated between July 1, 1789, and the publication of the law of April 8, 1792, whether they returned to France within the time fixed by that law or previously.

As though these provisions were not sufficiently elastic, the Paris municipality, on October 10, 1793, declared suspects those who pitied greedy farmers and tradesmen punished for violating the maximum, those who associated with nobles and moderates, and interested themselves in their fate, those who absented themselves on the plea of business or incapacity for public speaking from the sections, and lastly ' those who, having done nothing against Liberty, have also done nothing for it.'   In December 1793 Barère, in a report to the Convention, went even further, for he classed as suspects nobles, priests, courtiers, barristers, bankers, foreigners, stockjobbers, grumblers, and men afflicted at military successes.

The arrests were entrusted concurrently to the municipalities and to Revolutionary Committees, but in one half of France no such committees were or could be formed. 'Village ruffians' either did not exist or were too few to attempt to overawe their neighbours. It may also be assumed that in half the parishes where committees were formed, they did as little as possible. It must not, however, be inferred that arbitrary arrests were therefore confined to one-fourth of France. A peaceable village was exposed to the fanaticism and resentment of agitators in the nearest town, and even if the town did not interfere there was the department, and above all these the Paris Committee of Public Safety, not to speak of deputies on mission, the Carriers and Lebons, by whom indescribable atrocities were committed. A landowner might be beloved by his neighbours and yet be haled against their will to the adjacent town or to the capital. Thus Count Dufort de Cheverny was incarcerated at Blois, the inhabitants of the two villages through which he was taken closing their doors and windows and shutting themselves up in their cottages, in token of grief, and on his liberation he had to dissuade them from mustering in force to give him a noisy welcome.

Considering the powers of mischief possessed by a single man tempted by fanaticism or spite to anonymous or other secret denunciation or to open violence, it is not surprising that in the height of the Terror the prisons contained nearly 300,000 suspects, while another 100,000 were under custody more or less strict in their own houses. And even this number does not represent the aggregate number of arrests, which, owing to the deliberate or accidental destruction of documents, cannot be ascertained with any pretence to accuracy; it is only the number simultaneously in detention. If as many persons had altogether been liberated as remained in prison in Thermidor, the apprehensions numbered 600,000; nor must it be urged as an objection that France could not have contained 600,000 'aristocrats.' Multitudes of peasants were thrown into prison, especially in the spring of 1794, some because, though originally zealous for the Revolution, they had incurred suspicion or resentment, but most because they had been so harassed by requisitions and regulations that they preferred imprisonment to obedience.[1] Paris alone had in Thermidor nearly 8,000 suspects, and, allowing for the greater frequency of liberations there than in the provinces, it may safely be concluded that, irrespective of the 2,600 victims of the guillotine, 15,000 or 20,000 persons suffered incarceration in the capital. The difficulty of accommodating 8,000 captives

---

[1] These men acutely suffered from want of air and exercise, and in the Doubs we hear of their obtaining leave to tan leather for soldiers' shoes or to go out under escort and cut down a wood. Many of them, both in Paris and the provinces, were released on the approach of harvest, not for the sake of their own, but of the national interest.

was extreme.   The Bastille, which might have held
some hundreds, had been destroyed.   The Conciergerie, so overcrowded that putrid fever committed
great havoc, contained 650.   Ste.-Pélagie held 350,
St.-Lazare 780, La Force 480, the Madelonnettes
270, Bicêtre 720, the Salpêtrière 435, Vincennes
291.   The prison attached to the Abbey of St.
Germain des Prés, commonly styled the Abbaye,
one of the scenes of the September massacres, contained 41.   All these regular prisons or peniten-
tiaries erected by the old monarchy could not contain more than 2,000 inmates, even if the beds
were 'placed so near together that one was obliged
to get in at the feet.'[1]   Hence the municipality
was obliged to utilise the Luxembourg, at first only
the annex, which Monsieur (the future Louis XVIII.)
had occupied, but eventually the entire palace,
which, 'full up to the attics,' lodged nearly a thousand persons.   The monastic buildings, mostly
vacated, were next appropriated.   The Carmelite
monastery, reeking with the blood of the September
massacres, was a tolerably spacious building,
and held 182 suspects.   There was also Port Royal,
associated with the Jansenists, though less closely
than their suburban house, razed to the ground by
Louis XIV.   With grim irony re-christened Port
Libre, it eventually contained 600 prisoners.   Picpus

[1] Sir W. Codrington's letter in *Englishmen in the French
Revolution*, 1889.

Convent accommodated 91. The seven or eight British monasteries and colleges were all utilised. The Benedictine monks were the involuntary hosts or rather fellow captives of 300 suspects. The Scotch College, where St.-Just was taken on the 9th Thermidor, accommodated 166, the English and Irish seminaries had also their quota. The Benedictine and Conceptionist nuns were eventually transferred to the Austin Convent, which had likewise 177 female prisoners, so that their buildings might be available respectively for 120 and 60 suspects. The Plessis College had 400 inmates, and other French colleges and seminaries were also appropriated.

But even yet there was not room, and prisoners from the country, reaching Paris at night, were sometimes refused admission at prison after prison, were driven from pillar to post, and with difficulty obtained shelter. The Hôtel des Fermes, where under the old monarchy the contractors who farmed the taxes had their quarters, became a prison, containing at one time its old proprietors who had been required to produce their accounts, until most of them, Lavoisier, the great chemist, included, were sent to the scaffold. Private houses had to be hired or requisitioned. The Hôtel Talaru accommodated 200 persons, among them its owner Talaru, until the guillotine called him away. A large house in the rue de Sèvres held 160. Lastly there were guard-houses or lock-ups, whither a person was usually first taken on being arrested. These were often so packed and unhealthy that it was a relief to get transferred to a regular prison, and Helen Maria Williams was grateful for the favour of being conducted direct from the section to the Luxembourg. The Collège Mazarin (now the Institute) was about to be fitted up for 2,000 inmates when Thermidor arrived. Altogether there were in Paris thirty-six houses of detention and ninety-six lock-ups.[1]

These prisons, until June 22, 1794, bore the inscription 'Liberty, Equality, Unity, Indivisibility,' but the motto was then removed as too great an honour to buildings and inmates considered extra-territorial or non-French. They were of various degrees of discomfort. The Conciergerie was the worst. It was part of the Palace of Justice, was deprived of all view of the outer world, and had damp, sunless cells, in which the prisoners were under lock and key from five P.M. till ten A.M. At the Carmelites the very corridors were crowded with beds. Dampness prevailed, and the windows were blocked up three-fourths of their height. At Plessis College there was a large court for exercise, but the sun in summer made it intolerable till the very hour (eight o'clock) when the inmates were relegated to their cells. The English Benedictines had a spacious

[1] Carlyle mistakenly speaks of twelve prisons and twelve thousand prisoners. A thousand persons could not have been packed into any one of the prisons, except perhaps the Luxembourg, much less could this have been the average number.

garden commanding an agreeable view. The Conceptionists had also a garden, and when the Englishwomen were removed thither from the Luxembourg in October 1793, visitors were allowed to advance up to a grating. At the Luxembourg Miss Williams had to mount on a table to see the garden from the upper and unblocked part of her window, but the common room window, entirely unblocked, had an unobstructed view, so that signals could be exchanged with friends in the garden, unless the sentry happened to be in a surly humour. A child held up in its mother's arms could stretch out its hands towards its captive father. Lucile Desmoulins was in the garden all the time her husband was in the Luxembourg, and Hérault de Séchelles's mother sat there all day in view of her son's window ; but the heedless man, instead of being on the watch for her, was playing quoits with a child in the court, and when Danton, with whom he was soon to perish, arrived, he was playing *bouchon*, a kind of Aunt Sally. Latterly, however, a rope—a feeble but sufficient barrier—prevented promenaders from approaching within sight of the prisoners. At Plessis College the windows of neighbouring houses were visible, and gestures from persons stationed at these conveyed the first hint of the fall of Robespierre. At the Austin Convent, however, the prisoners were forbidden, on pain of being fired upon by the sentry, to look out of the front windows.

At St.-Lazare passers-by could approach so near that heartless wretches amused themselves by drawing their hands across their throats, to signify to the inmates that the guillotine awaited them. The Madelonnettes had street windows from which friends could be greeted. At the rue de Sèvres house, where a separate room could be hired at prices ranging up to twelve francs per day, a female newsvendor with stentorian voice daily shouted the names of the guillotined, and when there were not more than twenty she expressed a savage hope that next day there would be a larger batch. Or was this an artifice for communicating intelligence without incurring suspicion ? At the Hôtel des Fermes, in like manner, the inmates could hear the number of condemnations cried by a newspaper hawker.

It seems strange at first sight that there was no resistance to arrest, no attempt to break open or out of the prisons. Danton, one would have thought, might have had all his fellow-townsmen at Arcis at his back, yet he quietly allowed himself to be taken to Paris. Possibly he counted on an acquittal, for he had been urged to fly, and had refused. The truth is that the decrees of the Convention were submitted to as law even by those who knew that that body was coerced by the Paris mob. Robespierre himself was helpless when at last the Convention threw off his yoke. 'In the name of what ?' he is said to have objected, when pressed to sign a manifesto of insurrection; and, still hesitating, he had affixed only the first two letters of his name to an appeal to the Section of Pikes when, most of the sections declining to raise a hand against the Convention, he was overpowered. As to flight or revolt, the fate of the Girondins was not encouraging. Barbaroux, mistaking pleasure-makers for pursuers, killed himself. The bodies of Buzot and Pétion were found in a cornfield, half devoured by dogs. Roland shot himself. Condorcet took poison on being captured, a few hours after he had quitted his concealment. Louvet had hair-breadth escapes. In this severe ordeal, moreover, friends often refused to shelter fugitives, lest on detection they should share their fate,[1] for domiciliary visits were practised to an extent never before known. Miss Williams, it is true, concealed Rabaut St.-Etienne, but her courage was not common. So cowed were the Parisians, that detectives (whether real or sham seems uncertain) levied blackmail by calling mysteriously at night and promising, for twenty, thirty, or fifty thousand francs to save a man from what they represented as imminent arrest. 'What was worst under Robespierre,' an old man remarked to a Dutch traveller in 1795, 'was that in the morning you were never sure of sleeping in

---

[1] This was bad enough, but there were dastards like a Mademoiselle Mignot, employed by Madame Roland as music teacher to her little girl, who had the infamy to report the conversations at the Rolands' dinner table.

your own bed at night.' Flight, moreover, even if successful, involved the confiscation of property and the arrest of wife and children. The same reasons —not to speak of the spies, sham prisoners, who, not satisfied with mere delation, showed their zeal by concocting stories which cost many lives—explain the absence of any prison mutiny. It would assuredly have been easy to overpower the few warders, especially if numerous visitors were allowed, and it would have been equally easy for eighty prisoners conveyed in carts across Paris before daybreak, as, for instance, from Ste.-Pélagie to St.-Lazare, to give their small escort the slip; yet nothing of the kind was attempted, for escape would have been merely the beginning of difficulties and dangers. Hence it is not surprising to hear that at Blois the prisoners actually called the keeper's attention to an unbarred back door. Was not France one huge prison? Even, therefore, when large parties were marched long distances on foot, attempts at escape were very rare.

The keepers or concierges and their subordinates were of every variety of character. Benoit, keeper of the Luxembourg, was one of the best specimens. He was a native of Neufchâtel, and greeted Helèn Williams as a fellow worshipper at the Dutch Embassy chapel. He was dismissed in the spring of 1794 for having taken charge of seventy-five gold louis, entrusted to him by a man about to be condemned for delivery to his wife. According to the regulations, the money was forfeit to the government. He was put on trial, moreover, as an accomplice in the pretended prison plot, having, it was alleged, suppressed a document drawn up by a spy inmate giving warning of the conspiracy, but he insisted that he had sent a copy to the authorities, and he was acquitted but not reinstated. His successor, Guyard, an ex-butcher, had been a keeper at Lyons during the wholesale executions, and armed with sabres and pistols, had dogs following at his heels. On a gouty prisoner tottering towards the dinner table he angrily exclaimed 'Get along, scoundrel! I have not time to wait for you.' The next was Bertrand, who was still more brutal. Naudet, keeper at St.-Lazare, was likewise put on trial as responsible or accessory in the escape of a prisoner, and was likewise acquitted. He was succeeded by Semé, a brutal and rapacious man, whose wife presided at the common table, but Verney, chief warder at the Luxembourg, was latterly placed over him. At the Abbaye, Charlotte Corday speaks well of the jailors, but another prisoner says the keeper was rude and his wife extortionate, yet consequently laxer. Four dogs assisted him in his duties. At the Conciergerie, Richard was a real tyrant, and if any petty favour was to be asked, his occasional moments of good humour had to be awaited. Though the prisoners were locked up at five P.M., he went the round of the cells with two turnkeys and two mastiffs at midnight to see that all was right, by thumping with staves against the ceiling and with a hammer against the iron window-bars. His wife, however, is generally well spoken of. Charlotte Corday, who, it is true, had only three days' acquaintance with Richard and his wife, would have taken her last meal with them had not her trial been rather more protracted than she expected, and she cut off for Madame Richard a lock of her hair. Haly, who was first at Port Royal, then at St.-Lazare, and afterwards at Plessis, was an unbearable tyrant, stretching his authority to the utmost, deaf to any complaint of diet or accommodation, habitually threatening prisoners with the guillotine, and sometimes even terrifying them with false alarms or wantonly disturbing their slumbers by noisy nocturnal rounds. It was believed that he had formerly kept a menagerie, which was not unlikely, for in November 1793 the authorities had seized on all the menageries in Paris to stock the Jardin des Plantes, compensating the owners and finding them other employment. At the Madelonnettes, Vaubertrand and his wife were extremely kind, and their little boy was petted by the inmates. At Ste.-Pélagie the keeper was eventually dismissed, as also the keeper of La Force, because they refused to concoct prison plots. The Ste.-Pélagie keeper's wife allowed Madame Roland the use of her sitting-room, her cell being small and close, and Madame Roland had her piano fetched, and had several visitors, Helen Williams among them. She was afterwards provided with the best room in the prison, and a female criminal was permitted to fetch water and act as her servant, till a surly inspector insisted on her being treated exactly like the other inmates, with whom she was thus brought more in contact. The municipal inspectors, indeed, were frequently more brutal than the keepers, and their visits the signal for fresh rigour and annoyances. One of them at the Luxembourg in October 1793 was the notorious Henriot who was slaughtered with Robespierre. Bertrand, at the Austin Convent, was morose. Schmidt, a German, at the Hôtel Talaru, was very mild, and was accompanied, not like others by a dog, but by a pet lamb. His subordinates, too, were easily 'humanised' by a bottle of wine or an assignat. The warders, indeed, were mostly open to bribes, but even venality was a lesser evil than surly incorruptibility. Commissary Perrière reported in March 1794 that the warders at Ste.-Pélagie, the Scotch College, and the Austin Nunnery were scarcely ever sober. At the Conciergerie a turnkey would give a prisoner notice that he would be tried on the morrow by thrusting the indictment into his hand, with the words 'Look, here is thy death register.' The doomed man was sometimes without a candle, and could not even read the indictment—the 'evening paper' was a slang term for it—till daylight. At Plessis a warder kicked a poor woman, who, cramped and exhausted by a long ride from the country, was unable to mount several flights of stairs. At the Luxembourg the Duchess de Noailles, eighty-three years of age, forced to support herself by sidling along the wall, to avoid being knocked down in the rush to the dinner table, was roughly pushed by a warder into the only empty seat. Some turnkeys not merely levied blackmail, but stole everything they could lay their hands on. A few were as indulgent as they could safely be, and at the Conciergerie we hear of some who, their nightly round being the signal for the cessation of games, chatted a few minutes and were treated with wine by the inmates.

The prisons, except that they had gratuitous guests, were really hotels, for many prisoners paid largely not merely for food and attendance, but for rooms. Even Charlotte Corday, during her three days and a half imprisonment, ran up a bill of thirty-six francs, which she archly bequeathed as a kind of legacy to her counsel, Chauveau Lagarde, in token of gratitude for the few sentences uttered by him. The poor slept at the Conciergerie on straw in the cells or corridors, which were closed during the day, the occupants having then to keep in the courtyard, no matter what the weather.

New-comers had to be warned of the danger of being robbed by their fellow-captives. Even the furnished cells were often stifling and filthy, and all sanitary measures were lacking. Candles and fires were not always obtainable even for money. Rats and mice ran about the cells in the Conciergerie. Of smaller pests the less said the better. At Plessis, though this was one of the most aristocratic prisons, pigs roamed about the room during dinner. The medical attendants were mostly ignorant or negligent. 'Ah, he is better already,' said one at the Conciergerie, on stopping before a patient's bed. ' Yes, citizen doctor,' replied the attendant, ' but yesterday's patient is dead and this man has taken his place.' 'Oh, well,' was the rejoinder, 'go on with the potion.' Yet Thomas Paine speaks gratefully of a Polish doctor, Markoski, at the Luxembourg, who, moreover, kindly conveyed friendly messages between different prisons, and a Doctor Bayard, at the Hôtel Dieu and the Bishop's palace annexed to that hospital, refused to give up for trial patients manifestly too ill to defend themselves ; but he was soon superseded. In no case could the prisoners, if taken ill at night, get assistance till next morning.

As for diet, the municipality allowed the keepers two francs a day per head for maintenance. Roland, when Minister of the Interior, had reduced the allowance from five francs to two, little imagining that it would ever apply to political prisoners, or that the depreciation of the currency would render it very inadequate. Until towards the close of the Terror, however, prisoners could board themselves or pay for extras. One of the best cooks in Paris catered for La Force. Beugnot, thanks to a good turn formerly rendered to Danton, was assigned a share of the best room there, and once invited his wife to dinner, the wife of his fellow-deputy and fellow-prisoner Duquesnoy also joining the party. Both ladies had taken up their quarters in a small hotel opposite the prison. Whist followed the dinner. But such indulgence was not repeated, and visits were soon limited to one a week. At Port Royal the rich paid for the poor, an elected treasurer collecting the funds and ordering the viands. At the English Benedictines, Pauline de Tourzel cooked for her mother and sister, and was allowed to send out for butter, milk, and vegetables. The Jacobins, however, spread rumours of sybarite fare in the prisons, and of nocturnal supplies being secretly laid in, whereupon in June 1794 the common mess was introduced, and was enforced by the prisoners being deprived of all their money exceeding fifty francs, the food being paid for with the two francs a day. The complaints of this system were loud and almost universal, the purveyors in many cases supplying dishes almost or altogether uneatable. There was watery soup, stale herrings, bad bread, medicated wine. It was even believed in some prisons that the flesh of the guillotined was served up. At the Carmelites, however, the fare was tolerably good, for though there was only one meal a day, the supply of bread was unlimited and a small bottle of wine was provided. But at Ste.-Pélagie there was only a pound and a half of bread and a plate of beans. Here and there the soup was tolerable and three courses were served. At La Force the guests sat down in alphabetical order to wretched fare. At the Conciergerie there were three relays, the dinner hours being eleven, twelve, and one, and each inmate had to bring a plate and a bottle of wine. At the Carmelites the twenty women—the future Empress Josephine was one of them—dined apart after the men. At the Concier-gerie a café was till latterly open all day for the men, and though a grating separated the male and female corridors, dinner was often served in these, so that conversation could be carried on then as at other times between the two companies. It was there that Madame Roland charmed every listener. The railings were not so close together that a slim man could not slip through unobserved at night.

The degree of freedom inside the prison depended partly on the disposition of the buildings, partly on the caprice of the keepers; but as a rule prison-ers had their choice of solitude or society, and all the lightheartedness of the French character was displayed. 'Most of us,' says Sir W. Codrington, 'thought we had but a short time allotted to us, and that it was better to enjoy that little as much as we could. . . . Never have I since seen so many cheerful people.' Here and there, indeed, serious studies were carried on. Madame Roland, at the Abbaye and at Ste.-Pélagie, wrote her memoirs, and at the Conciergerie she taught English from Thomson's 'Seasons' to Pétion's son, who had accompanied his mother thither. Beugnot studied English, and had taken with him Epictetus, Marcus Aurelius, and Thomas à Kempis, but had not been allowed to take Tasso, for anything connected with Jerusalem, as was remarked by the commissary who arrested him, had an ill odour. Camille Desmoulins, who knew English, had provided himself with Young's 'Night Thoughts' and Hervey's 'Meditations,' whereupon Réal, who indulged in the violin and singing, said, 'Do you want to die twice over ? Look at my book ; it is Voltaire's "Pucelle."' Roucher, the poet, translated Smith's 'Wealth of Nations' and Thomson's 'Seasons,' besides giving lessons to his son, eight years old, who was allowed to be with him. Duquesnoy, the deputy already mentioned, resumed his study of German. Dupont de Nemours, at La Force, discoursed, lectured as it were, on political economy. Dannou, another deputy and an ex-Oratorian, grudged any time diverted from Cicero and Tacitus. Florian, the fabulist second to Lafontaine,

composed at Port Royal his ' William Tell,' one of his
poorest poems. Cassini, an hereditary astronomer,
formed a drawing class at the English Benedictines ;
his conversation also was very entertaining. Sillery,
Madame de Genlis's husband, painted water-colour
landscapes at the Luxembourg. Mademoiselle de
Girardin, daughter of Rousseau's host, translated
at Plessis one of Bolingbroke's essays. But these
occupations were the exception. Amusements were
the order of the day. Cards, backgammon, chess,
draughts, battledore, ball, quoits, and Aunt Sally
whiled away the time. At the Abbaye Delahante
found his four room-mates absorbed in eating,
drinking, and gambling. One of them tried to
entrap him, on playing backgammon at fifteen sous
a game, by acting the novice, but Delahante was
too wary, and speedily made way at the board for
an Orleans priest, whose snoring disturbed his
night's rest. But the commonest diversion was
bouts rimés, which had for 150 years been a
favourite diversion in aristocratic circles, and which
a generation ago still lingered in England. Words
were given to end verses, and the lines had to be
filled up. Versifying of other kinds, charades, and
acrostics, were highly popular. The verses were
mostly for or upon women, for gallantry was supreme.
Marron, ex-chaplain to the Dutch Embassy and
afterwards French pastor at Paris, an easy-going
man who accepted and extolled successive dynasties,

T

was a versifier, and he excuses the grossness of some of his companions' rhymes, as pardonable on the part of prisoners. André Chénier alone wrote serious verses, in some of which he reprobated the frivolity of his comrades. Vigée, brother of the artist, Madame Vigée Lebrun, versified freely at Port Royal. At Plessis republican songs were sung in chorus, and patriotic verses on Toulon and other victories were composed at the Conciergerie. In many prisons, indeed, the reports of victories were hailed with enthusiasm, though there must have been a royalist minority who did not share that feeling. At Port Royal Baron Witersbach, an accomplished violinist, entertained the company by his performances, and there in the evening the women knitted or embroidered and the men read or wrote, a supper winding up the day and all retiring at nine to their dormitories, unless indeed the warders allowed a quarter of an hour's grace. It was like a family party, especially as this improvised prison lacked bolts and gratings. At a patriotic festival a woman speechified, and music and dancing followed. Yet there was a serpent in this Eden, for a lady's watch was stolen. The culprit, an apparently respectable young man, was detected by his sending it to his mistress to dispose of; but a second theft, that of a considerable sum of money, could not be detected. At the Carmelites the inmates for a time were shut up in their rooms, but finding that by shouting they could make each other hear, conversations were carried on, limited, however, to persons admitted to the so-called club, forgers of assignats and other non-political delinquents being excluded ; but eventually the corridors were open to all for four hours a day. The best room at La Force, with its whist and conversation, was so agreeable that Louis XV.'s foster-brother, a man of eighty-six, declared that if offered liberty he should decline it, for nowhere else could he expect to find better society or more attentions. Nobody could be admitted to the room except by ballot, and the twelve inmates included an ex-judge and an actor, as also the pamphleteer Linguet, ex-prisoner and historian of the Bastille, who was so quarrelsome that he had to betake himself to other quarters pending the stroke of the guillotine. At the Madelonnettes ex-ministers and ex-judges exchanged ceremonious visits. At the Luxembourg in Helen Williams's time, each room had its self-imposed regulations, such as the cessation of music at ten or eleven at night. An English housemaid there amused herself and others with her dog, which she had been allowed to bring, and which barked furiously when she exclaimed 'Charlotte,' the name of her daughter, at school in England. At the Benedictines Pauline de Tourzel amused herself with a swing in the garden, and the aristocratic prisoners exchanged formal visits, just as though at liberty.

Beugnot, at the Conciergerie, witnessed a clairvoyant performance, got up by an officer in order that General La Marlière might know his destiny. A boy was sent for, and after some hesitation he said he saw in the magic mirror a national guard knocking down an officer and cutting off his head. La Marlière, though assured that this was absurd, was quite unnerved, and three days afterwards the forecast was realised, for he was guillotined by an executioner dressed as a national guard. Beugnot, though convinced that there was trickery, could not discover it.

At the Conciergerie the menial work devolved on criminals, and in some prisons charwomen were allowed, but at the Luxembourg the inmates of a room took turns in cooking and cleaning, and the aged Marshal de Mouchy and his wife were not latterly permitted to keep their maidservant. At the Hôtel Talaru there was a hired bedmaker, but the prisoners in rotation washed up the crockery till the bedmaker recognised Pastor Marron engaged in this duty, and relieved him and his roommates from such functions. Although the Terror did not last long enough for new clothes to be necessary, and although shoes did not quickly wear out by short promenades in a court or garden, tailors and cobblers plied their trade in prison, hairdressers were in request, watchmakers found employment, and, at the Conciergerie, a young man with a talent for painting prepared medallions or portraits, with a lock of hair, perhaps, attached, to be transmitted by bribed warders to surviving relatives. Artists of note, like Suvée, Le Roy, Robert, and Boze, made portraits or sketches which they distributed among their fellow captives.

The diversions at Port Royal and elsewhere were sometimes saddened by the evening paper, which brought information of the guillotining of a friend or relative ; yet the ultimate prohibition of newspapers was a severe privation. Their contents too were sometimes mercifully concealed. Madame de Lafayette, alarmed at the ominous silence of her companions at Plessis, questioned the Duchess de Duras, whose torrent of tears revealed the terrible fact that her mother, sister, and grandmother had all perished. Mademoiselle de Pons in like manner conjectured from the demeanour of her fellow-captives that her father had been executed—a fearful blow for her ; not so fearful for her mother, whom he had for years neglected in favour of the notorious Madame Ste.-Amaranthe, who, curiously enough, was executed with him. Yet newspapers were scarcely necessary as a *memento mori*, for latterly drafts were made by the guillotine even on the prisons which had long enjoyed immunity, so that at the Benedictines the female captives sought explanations of the *modus operandi*, and made low dresses in readiness, in order that the executioner might not need to bare their necks. As for ordinary dress, except at the Carmelites, where it was disregarded, toilette asserted its claims. At the Conciergerie the men hurried into their corridor as soon as the cells were opened, while the women were a little later in appearing in the parallel corridor. The ladies' morning *négligé* was so graceful that nobody could have believed it followed a night spent on a rude mattress or on straw. At noon this was changed for full dress, company dress, the hair, too, being duly powdered, and in the evening there was *déshabillé*. The afternoon gathering reminded Beugnot of a flower garden, so bright and varied were the costumes, but a garden bordered by iron bars.

All the good and all the bad instincts of mankind luxuriated in the hothouse of prison life. On the one hand we hear of pathetic partings between the victims of the guillotine and their fellow captives, or of a collection being made for an acquitted prisoner, that he might return to his native village. On the other we hear of savage execrations over the condemnation of the Hébertists; and of the Duplay family, Robespierre's hosts, being received at the Conciergerie with mock-regal honours, a cruel hoax moreover being practised, for Duplay and his son were informed that the wife and mother—' the Princess ' as she had been ironically dubbed—had committed suicide. The prison was no school of virtue, and Ferrières, justifying himself at the Jacobin Club on February 14, 1794, for releasing some English children under twelve years of age, could fairly urge that he was rescuing them from vice as well as providing employment for sans-culotte teachers.

Friendships are said to have been formed and flirtations, nay even intrigues, carried on in these crowded and often noisome receptacles where comedy and tragedy elbowed each other. Clavière, an ex-minister, committed suicide in his cell, in the presence of the other inmates, on the eve of the day fixed for his trial. At the Luxembourg a man did the same on hearing that his wife had been also arrested, leaving their four little children helpless. At Plessis a doctor's wife, addicted to drink, threw herself from the only unboarded upper window and was killed. Many prisoners, in view of an easier death, had provided themselves with lau-danum drops prepared by Doctor Guillotin, whose advocacy had led to the adoption of a mode of execution new in France but old enough in Scot-land and elsewhere. Latterly no prison was safe from a morning summons. A bell at ten o'clock would collect all the inmates, and an usher would call out the names of those who were to be trans-ferred to the Conciergerie to await trial or to be tried that very day at half-past eleven. The cart was waiting outside, and there was barely time to address letters or souvenirs to wife or children. Décadi, the Jacobin Sabbath, was the only day when these Job's messengers did not appear, for the tribunal and the guillotine rested every tenth day. Yet the ushers were sometimes scoffingly asked on entering, ' How many heads do you want to-day ? '

Strange to say, many prisoners deluded themselves with the hope that they would not be tried or would be acquitted. Even Marie Antoinette is said to have been thus buoyed up, yet this appears incredible. Some, again, were lighthearted to the very last. Gossenay, an ex-soldier, twenty-seven years of age, made a good breakfast before going to the tribunal, and at starting said to his companions, ' We have breakfasted well, but that is not enough, supper must be thought of, and you should give me the address of a good *restaurateur* in the other world that I may order a good meal for this evening.' After being condemned he ate and drank with a relish, and on mounting the tumbril asked a warder with whom he had been familiar for a glass of cherry brandy.

Of religious consolations we hear extremely little. It is true that seven out of the twenty-one Girondin deputies received absolution. The priest Fauchet confessed to Lothringer, Bishop Gobel's vicar-general, who refused to follow the bishop in his apostasy, and who, at the earliest opportunity, retracted his oath to the civil constitution of the

clergy; Sillery then confessed to Fauchet; Du-
perret, Gardien, Beauvais, Lehardy, Vigier, and
Gorsas also confessed to Lothringer or Fauchet;
but, as both were then under excommunication by
the Pope on account of their oath, the validity of
the absolution seems open to question. Brissot,
though he did not confess, expressed his belief in a
future state of rewards and punishments. Orleans-
Egalité also sent for Lothringer, and made a general
confession. ' I have deserved death,' he said, ' as
expiation for my sins. I contributed to the death
of an innocent man [Louis XVI.], but he was too
good not to forgive me. God will join us both with
St. Louis.' Egalité received a second and last
absolution at the foot of the scaffold. Custine also
died a Catholic. Even Gobel sent to a priest a
written confession, and asked for absolution as the
cart passed.[1] The three Noailles ladies, already mentioned, died as Christians, and Madame de Duras,
who at Plessis heard of the execution of her parents,
Marshal and Madame de Mouchy, regularly said
prayers in expectation of death. Helen Williams,
with her mother and sisters, during their fortnight
at the Luxembourg, had evening prayers, in which
they were secretly joined by Lasource, deputy and
pastor, and Sillery, the inmates of an adjoining

---

[1] Lothringer is the sole authority for all these episodes, related
by him in the *Annales Catholiques*, iv. 167, and embellishment,
if not pious fraud, may be suspected.

room, but forbidden communication with other prisoners. Lasource and Sillery jointly composed a hymn which was sung before prayers in an undertone, so as not to be overheard by the warders.

But all these episodes were exceptional. Assuredly there were nuns and pious women of the laity who felt the privation of religious rites, especially absolution *in articulo mortis*, but the upper and middle class prisoners were mostly of the religion of Rousseau's Savoyard vicar. They were simply theists, some scarcely that. Charlotte Corday civilly declined the services of Abbé Lothringer. In the poet Roucher's letters to his wife and daughter we hear much of botany and literature, but the word God does not occur. If the festival of the Supreme Being was celebrated at Port Royal by singing and dancing, it was because it was mistakenly hailed as betokening a brighter era. At the Conciergerie, Ducorneau, a young man from Bordeaux, a destined prey to the guillotine, diverted his companions by teasing a Benedictine monk, abstracting his breviary and blowing out his candle, and actually getting up a parody of the Mass. The pious monk would pretend to be asleep, but at length, unable to tolerate such blasphemy, he would try to shout it down with a *De profundis*, and would attempt to knock down the sham altar. He had hopes of converting the Spaniard Marchena, who was apparently dying, but the latter, collecting all his strength, exclaimed, 'Vive Ibrascha,' the name of the God of Reason whose worship had been set up. Even the guillotine, moreover, was parodied. At the Conciergerie, a new-comer was shown, by a contrivance with chairs, how the axe fell, and some of the versifying made light of the guillotine, which Bishop Lamourette—he was doomed to try it—described as 'merely a chuck of the chin.' Sometimes a mock trial was held, an inmate personating Robespierre or Fouquier Tinville, and a sham execution following the sham condemnation. When Alfred de Vigny in 'Stello' had represented the prisoners at St.-Lazare as 'acting' executions, Molé, in receiving him at the Academy in 1846, rebuked him as imputing to them derogatory conduct; but a passage from the memoirs of H. M. Fleury, a prisoner there, recently published by M. Kerviler, says:

In order to inculcate courage, the sanhedrim, actuated by folly, devised the following punishment as a guillotine experiment. Two mattresses were placed on the table; the culprit was laid on them on his face. If he grasped in time the edge of the table, the mattress alone went to the other end of the room; otherwise, man and mattress went there together. This was great fun for us, without a thought that the next day we might make a more serious experiment.

This gaiety has been compared to the 'Decameron,' where fugitives from the plague amuse themselves at a safe distance, but here the guillotine was constantly demanding victims.

The pretended prison plots, too, were everywhere made a pretext for increased rigour. The money, knives, and other articles, of which the captives were deprived were ostensibly to be returned to them on their liberation, but many were guillotined, and probably those released after Thermidor were too eager for liberty to stay to claim their property. At Port Royal some of the men took to their beds on the arrival of the commissaries, in order to escape the indignity of minute personal search. At Plessis knives were henceforth prohibited, even at dinner. The inmates had to use their fingers, and when they borrowed scissors to trim their nails, the warder waited during the operation to have the scissors returned. All sorts of devices, however, were naturally resorted to for the concealment of money and souvenirs in the floor and ceiling. In one room at Port Royal the inmates escaped the search by smoking so vigorously that the commissaries, for fear of suffocation, passed on. Even General O'Hara, a prisoner of war captured at Toulon, underwent the search, to which he submitted with equanimity, but when it was over he sarcastically said to the warder, ' I have one favour to ask ; it is that no Frenchman should enter my room.' Visitors and correspondence being likewise almost or altogether prohibited, letters were secretly written with coal dust and water, or even with blood, an iron nail serving as a pen, and they were smuggled in or out in the laundress's bundles, or in asparagus, chickens, or other viands, if these could still be sent for. Mercier, the author, learned at Port Royal the fall of Robespierre by a note enclosed by his wife in a loaf of bread. At Port Royal a dog long carried letters under his collar.

At the Hôtel Talaru, where wives, children, and mistresses had for a time been allowed to visit the prisoners, it became a great favour to see a friend through a grating. Newspapers were also excluded, but an inmate being still employed at the Treasury, where he spent the day at accounts, he at night ' by oversight ' frequently brought a newspaper in his pocket. At St.-Lazare police permits for visitors were negotiable, like bills of exchange.

Two classes of prisoners, the English and the Girondin deputies, were treated with comparative lenity. On August 1, 1793, the Convention decreed that foreigners of all countries at war with France, unless domiciled in France before July 14, 1789, should be arrested, and this, after some hesitation and modification, was enforced against the English in the following October. Tradesmen, artisans, and children under twelve years of age were exempted, but parents were allowed to have their children with them. St.-Just's assurance, on behalf of the Committee of General Safety, that the detention should be as mild as possible, seems, on the whole, to have been fulfilled. The uniform dietary does not appear to have been enforced on persons able to board themselves. During the first few weeks, indeed, before the Luxembourg was assigned them, they underwent discomforts. Sir Robert Smith, baronet and banker, and ladies of position, were incarcerated in a single room at a guardhouse in company with grooms and maidservants. At the section du Roule, men and women had to lie on straw, and even this was scanty. But afterwards, according to Sampson Perry, the outlawed editor of the London 'Argus,' many who could have claimed exemption preferred detention, because in revolutionary Paris they would have had difficulty in earning a livelihood. The women, transferred to the English Conceptionist Convent, were ultimately relegated to the Austin Convent. That building was crowded, for Frenchwomen of all ranks were also sent thither, but there was the advantage of a spacious garden. The men were shifted from prison to prison for reasons which do not appear, but latterly, according to Perry, the rigour relaxed and the discomforts lessened at every remove. The animosity at first felt against the English on the capture of Toulon and the false rumour of deputy Beauvais having been put to death there, had disappeared. The English were at first under serious uneasiness of prison massacres, but the Paris municipality now 'felt some compunction,' says Perry, 'for the hardship it had made them endure by laying them under all the restrictions of the most confirmed conspirators . . . and the transfer, though only from one prison to another, was nevertheless like a transition from Purgatory to Paradise.'

The seventy-three Girondin deputies, whom Robespierre refused to bring to trial, though the Hébertists clamoured for their blood, had also at first some privations to undergo, but were ultimately treated with consideration. At La Force they amused themselves with ball, draughts, backgammon, chess, and Aunt Sally, even the elderly Dussieux taking the lead in this last pastime. They slept the first night on sacks, but the keeper did his best for them. Removed to the Madelonnettes, they were mixed with criminals and had wretched accommodation, till they managed to smuggle a petition to the Committee of Public Safety, two of whose members went to see them and were struck with pity. They were accordingly transferred by night to the English Benedictines, which was clean and spacious, and had a good garden and a pleasant view. Locks and bars, moreover, were absent. Each had a separate room—many female prisoners had had to be crowded up to make way for them—and they dined and spent the day together. Yet visitors and correspondence were not allowed. On Robespierre's fall they were removed to the Hôtel des Fermes, where locks re-appeared, while the promenade was very limited and the air bad ; but visits were permitted, so that after ten months they had tidings of their friends. The warders, at first surly, soon became civil when they saw which way the wind was blowing. Dispersed over several prisons, however, the deputies had to wait till October 24, 1794, for release, and till December 8 for readmission to the Convention.

The mixture with criminals was not peculiar to the Madelonnettes. Barnave compared the mingling of philosophers, politicians, and criminals at the Conciergerie to the company on the banks of the Styx. At St.-Lazare criminals were introduced from Bicêtre, but the very first night they made such an uproar, stealing the money of the suspects, smashing and setting fire to the furniture, and breaking open the wine-cellar, some, moreover, escaping into the bargain, that they were sent back to Bicêtre. Madame Roland in her first room at Ste.-Pélagie, was shut off only by a thin plaster partition from assassins and prostitutes whose talk she could not help hearing.

In the provinces the keepers and warders seem at least in some cases to have been more brutal and tyrannical than in Paris. Just as there had been greater subserviency on the part of the lower classes prior to the Revolution, so the reaction brought greater barbarity. The tables were turned,

and as an ex-slave was commonly the hardest of
taskmasters, so an ex-dependent was the most vin-
dictive of tyrants. Of Chantilly palace as a prison
we have full descriptions by the Duchess de Duras,
Mademoiselle de Girardin (afterwards Countess
Bohm), and Mademoiselle de Pons, who afterwards
married the Marquis de Tourzel, son of the gover-
ness to the Royal Family who took part in the
flight to Varennes. Madame de Duras had from
the first to wait on herself, and commenced her
lessons in housekeeping by learning to make her
own cocoa. Madame de Pons and her daughter
were for a few weeks allowed the services of their
maidservant. Finding that the imprisonment was
likely to be protracted, they sent for their books and
piano. Prisoners were allowed to bring their
children, and boys of fourteen or fifteen played
ball in the court. One of these lads, a year afterwards, at the age of fifteen, was guillotined along
with his father. Cards, chess, and proverbs were
played. There was music and dancing in the
largest room, but several of the inmates objecting,
this was given up. A few, however, assembled for
prayers and religious reading. Some of the ladies
continued to wear flowers, feathers, and ribbons,
and had their hair curled and powdered as regularly as if at liberty. For a time they could order
what viands they pleased of purveyors in the
palace, and there were then picnic dinners and

teas, but a common dietary was afterwards enforced. The aged and infirm were still permitted to have meals in their own rooms, but all the other 600 dined and supped in three relays, 200 at a time—families at twelve and six, the unmarried at two and seven, and priests and nuns at three and nine. Each inmate had to bring knives, glasses, &c. The fare was so poor and scanty that the company rose with an appetite. Revolutionary committeemen in red caps marched round the table to see whether any of the prisoners observed fast days. A balcony on the third floor was the only promenade, but this commanded a picturesque view. The larger dormitories contained twenty-five persons, and rich and poor were mixed together, the latter being strictly forbidden to render any menial services, but they had sufficient delicacy to retire to bed as late and to get up as early as possible. There was even a mixture of sexes. One room contained a republican general and his wife, a priest, several boys, and two women with their five or six daughters, aged from fourteen to twenty. Another contained a soldier and two or three nuns. This, says Madame de Duras, 'was a calamity peculiar to our prison.' Rare, no doubt, but not altogether peculiar. We do not hear of it in Paris, where the women had either separate prisons or separate wards, as at Plessis, Ste.-Pélagie, and the Madelonnettes, but at Versailles the octogenarian Dr. Gem, ex-physician to the

English Embassy at Paris, shared a room with Mrs. Grace Dalrymple Elliott, ex-mistress of the Prince of Wales (George IV.) and of the Duke of Orleans. The lady, who had a lively imagination, asserts in her memoirs that Gem used to wake her up at four A.M. to argue materialism with her. Chantilly was not free from jealousy and intrigue, and as in Paris, prisoners sought to obtain release by talebearing which might lead others to the guillotine.

Let us pass on to Lyons. M. des Echerolles, who had helped to defend the town against the Jacobins, had hairbreadth escapes, from which he emerged safe but ruined, while his sister, for refusing to divulge his hiding-place, was thrown into the penitentiary, in company with fishwives, peasant women, and prostitutes. Most of the inmates had to lie on straw, and the supply even of this was scanty; it was changed once a fortnight. The warders had to be bribed to allow the admission of a mattress and chairs, and the appearance of a table was hailed as a godsend, for the prisoners could now take turns in having their meals at it, instead of having to eat out of their laps. Two hundred women would daily assemble outside with baskets of provisions, but there was often much delay in these supplies being admitted. At noon the warders (sent for from Paris so as to be subject to no local influences) went away for two hours for dinner and the admissions were suspended; but warders or their wives would go among the crowd, offering for high pay immediate acceptance of the baskets. These, however, on passing the gate were sometimes opened, the contents spread out, and portions openly abstracted. Permission to walk in the courtyard was capriciously granted or refused; if granted, the inmates had to mix with criminals. Yet even amid these surroundings, a sculptor, Chinard, who had studied at Rome, modelled busts of the keeper and several of his fellow prisoners. There was much versifying, singing, and gaiety among the 1,200 inmates, groups of whom made their provisions a common stock. Removed to a convent, Mademoiselle des Echerolles was one of fifteen inmates of a large damp lumber-room, in which spiders had for a century been so industrious that their webs formed quite a canopy extending half-way to the floor, and the warders made it a favour to allow these to be swept away, at a heavy expense to the suspects, by the criminals confined in another part of the building. There was no window, the only light coming from a grating in the door, and in an adjoining room the inmates, locked up as usual for the night, were once on the point of being suffocated by the fumes of their stove. Their screams at last brought assistance just in time. Among the prisoners was an English girl four years old, with her nurse, both ignorant of French. In the daytime the court was open to all, including the

criminals, and Mademoiselle des Echerolles' purse
was stolen there. Yet in this squalid room three
nuns, resigned to death, daily recited prayers
and sang hymns. As for Mademoiselle, who had
been accustomed to luxury and to good society, she
never uttered a word of complaint of privations
which aggravated a chronic rheumatism. Her sole
anxiety was for the safety of her fugitive brother and
of his child, her adopted daughter, a girl of twelve,
whose youth and diminutive stature facilitated
her almost daily visits to the prison, yet who had
to undergo many rebuffs and to display all the
activity, perseverance, and tact of a grown-up
woman. Even the ferocious Marino, a commissary
from Paris, of sorry reputation, relented at the
sight and at the entreaties of a child, and gave her
permissions which he brutally refused to others.
The poor girl was herself under surveillance at home,
being probably allowed to remain there in the
expectation that her father would visit her and
could thus be arrested. Her watcher was inoffen-
sive, but his wife never missed an execution, a habit
she had formed before the Revolution, and on her
evening visits to her husband she gloated in the poor
child's presence over the horrors she had witnessed.
In February 1794 Mademoiselle des Echerolles
was guillotined. Her only crime was that her
brother had assisted the besieged.

It would be unfair to represent these horrors as

universal in the provinces. There, as in Paris, were instances of mildness. Thus at Blois we hear of whist, backgammon, fencing, and versifying. A kind of musical and scientific class was formed, and a microscope afforded much entertainment. Newspapers were admitted, containing, however, too often the names of relations and friends guillotined at Paris. The order sent down from the capital for a common dietary was quietly ignored. Yet these eighty favoured suspects at Blois were accustomed to the arrival of convoys of weary prisoners, who on their way on foot to Paris spent a night under their roof.

Who can estimate the number of persons who succumbed in these toilsome marches, in which they occasionally met with compassion, but more frequently with insults and menaces, or of those who fell victims in prison to jail-fever, anxiety, bad fare, and lack of medical treatment? The mortality from all these causes probably equalled the ravages of the guillotine and of the fusillade, which in sixteen months, without allowing for lists which have disappeared, counted 17,000 victims.

What would have been the fate of these 300,000 suspects had Robespierre triumphed, who can say? Could he himself have said? His apologists of course assert that he would speedily have emptied the prisons, and that if he guillotined Desmoulins it was because Desmoulins was premature in advocating liberation. His enemies allege that he would have allowed his partisans to empty the prison as they had been emptied in September 1792, by massacre. The latter was assuredly the belief of the suspects themselves. That pits were being dug ready for the corpses of the massacred is a legend; that the guillotine not only at Paris but at Bordeaux [1] was about to have four blades, in order to despatch four persons at one blow, is a fact. It is also a fact that Dumas proposed trying 160 Luxembourg prisoners in one batch, and constructed an immense dock for that purpose, but had to be checked by the Committee of Public Safety, which insisted on having only sixty at a time. The Convention moreover on the 4th Thermidor resolved on creating four additional divisions of the Revolutionary Tribunal, to operate in the provinces and to make circuits from town to town. All this manifestly did not foreshadow an era of lenity. Undoubtedly the Thermidorians were not actuated by humanity. They simply meant to save their own heads. They had, however, undertaken, in order to gain the co-operation of the 'Plain' or Right in overturning Robespierre, that the holocausts should be diminished. Events proved too strong for them. The fifty-five persons marked out for trial on the 11th Thermidor could not be tried on that day because the tribunal was engaged in identifying and ordering the execution of Robespierre's municipal councillors. On the 12th that

---

[1] Where there had been forty-four executions in nine months.

task had to be continued. On the 14th the Convention unanimously repealed the law of June 10, thus restoring the right of preliminary examination and of defence by counsel. Meanwhile one of the judges, Dumas, had been guillotined, and another, Coffinhal, outlawed, and several jurors were under arrest. The tribunal was thus disorganised, and, pending its reconstitution, its sittings were suspended from the 18th when Coffinhal was executed. Even a few days had sufficed to disaccustom the Parisians to the sight of blood, and any attempt to continue these sanguinary assizes would certainly have evoked demonstrations of horror in the court itself or in the streets. The Faubourg St.-Antoine, after its respite from the revolting processions—for the Robespierrists were executed at the Place de la Concorde, not at the Place du Trône—would probably have risen up in protest. Thermidor, however little its authors intended it, brought deliverance to the captives. Not that all were immediately released, for many had weary months of waiting, but the relaxation of rigour was prompt, and the waiting was not aggravated by fear of the guillotine.[1]

---

[1] The chief authorities for this chapter are contemporary pamphlets, most of them reprinted in Dauban's *Prisons de Paris*, 1870; Nougaret's *Histoire des Prisons*, 1794; the Comtesse de Bearn's *Souvenirs de Quarante Ans*, 1868; Delahante's *Famille de Finance*, 1881; and Alexandrine des Echerolles' *Famille Noble dans la Terreur*, 1843.

INDEX OF NAMES

signifies guillotine or other violent death ; and † imprisonment.

PRINTED BY
SPOTTISWOODE AND CO., NEW-STREET SQUARE
LONDON